Lecture Notes in Computer Science 14152

Founding Editors

Gerhard Goos
Juris Hartmanis

The series Lecture Notes in Computer Science (LNCS), including its subseries Lecture Notes in Artificial Intelligence (LNAI) and Lecture Notes in Bioinformatics (LNBI), has established itself as a medium for the publication of new developments in computer science and information technology research, teaching, and education.

LNCS enjoys close cooperation with the computer science R & D community, the series counts many renowned academics among its volume editors and paper authors, and collaborates with prestigious societies. Its mission is to serve this international community by providing an invaluable service, mainly focused on the publication of conference and workshop proceedings and postproceedings. LNCS commenced publication in 1973.

Luca Manzoni · Luca Mariot ·
Dipanwita Roy Chowdhury
Editors

Cellular Automata and Discrete Complex Systems

29th IFIP WG 1.5 International Workshop, AUTOMATA 2023
Trieste, Italy, August 30 – September 1, 2023
Proceedings

 Springer

Editors
Luca Manzoni 🔟
University of Trieste
Trieste, Italy

Luca Mariot 🔟
University of Twente
Enschede, The Netherlands

Dipanwita Roy Chowdhury
Indian Institute of Technology Kharagpur
Kharagpur, India

ISSN 0302-9743   ISSN 1611-3349 (electronic)
Lecture Notes in Computer Science
ISBN 978-3-031-42249-2   ISBN 978-3-031-42250-8 (eBook)
https://doi.org/10.1007/978-3-031-42250-8

This Springer imprint is published by the registered company Springer Nature Switzerland AG
The registered company address is: Gewerbestrasse 11, 6330 Cham, Switzerland

Preface

This volume contains the papers accepted and presented at the 29th International Workshop on Cellular Automata and Discrete Complex Systems, AUTOMATA 2023, which was held in Trieste, Italy, on August 30 – September 1, 2023. The workshop was organized by the Department of Mathematics and Geosciences of the University of Trieste, and it hosted the annual meeting of the IFIP working group 1.5.

The AUTOMATA workshops began in 1995 as an established annual series of events whose main objective is to bring together researchers in the fields of cellular automata and discrete complex systems, in order to foster collaboration and sharing of recent findings on such themes. Throughout the years, the range of topics covered has steadily expanded. In this edition, the scope of discussion further broadened to include fresh areas of interest, particularly focusing on correlated models of automata and their applications to machine learning.

The current focus of AUTOMATA encompasses a wide range of aspects and features pertaining to these systems. While not exhaustive, the current topics include dynamics, topology, ergodicity, algebraic properties, algorithmic considerations, complexity analysis, emergence of properties, formal languages, symbolic dynamics, tilings, models of parallelism and distributed systems, timing schemes, synchronous and asynchronous models, phenomenological descriptions, scientific modeling, and practical applications.

AUTOMATA 2023 featured two invited talks, given respectively by Dora Giammarresi and Kévin Perrot, to whom we extend our thanks for accepting the invitation and for their very interesting presentations. The invited contributions are included in this volume.

In total, AUTOMATA 2023 received 11 full paper submissions. Each paper was reviewed in single-blind mode by at least three program committee members or external reviewers. Following the review and discussion phases, the committee decided to accept 7 papers to be included in the proceedings and presented at the workshop. One of these papers went through an additional shepherding phase, managed by a member of the program committee. We would like to thank all authors for their submissions, which contributed to a substantial part of the AUTOMATA 2023 scientific program. The workshop also featured short presentations of exploratory papers and extended abstracts, which are not included in these proceedings. We wish to thank all authors of the exploratory track as well.

This volume also includes the proceedings of the previous edition of the workshop, namely the 28th International Workshop on Cellular Automata and Discrete Complex Systems, AUTOMATA 2022. This workshop took place online on October 11–12, 2022, and it was organized by the Indian Institute of Technology Kharagpur, India. AUTOMATA 2022 received 18 submissions for the full track, out of which 3 papers were finally accepted. Each paper was reviewed in double-blind mode by at least two members of the program committee.

We are indebted to the program committees of AUTOMATA 2023 and 2022, and to the external referees for their precious help in reviewing and selecting the submitted papers. We further thank the members of the local organizing committees, namely Giulia Bernardini, Giuliamaria Menara and Gloria Pietropolli for AUTOMATA 2023, and Palash Dey and Ayan Chaudhury for AUTOMATA 2022. We are also grateful for the support by the Department of Mathematics and Geosciences and the University of Trieste. Finally, we thank the LNCS team of Springer for their help in producing this volume in time for the conference.

August 2023

Luca Manzoni
Luca Mariot
Dipanwita Roy Chowdhury

Organization – AUTOMATA 2023

Steering Committee

Pedro Paulo Balbi	Universidade Presbiteriana Mackenzie, Brazil
Nazim Fatès	Inria Nancy, France
Pierre Guillon	Université d'Aix-Marseille, France
Dipanwita Roy Chowdhury	IIT Kharagpur, India
Hector Zenil	University of Cambridge, UK

Program Committee

Jan Baetens	Ghent University, Belgium
Pedro Paulo Balbi	Universidade Presbiteriana Mackenzie, Brazil
Alonso Castillo-Ramirez	University of Guadalajara, Mexico
Sukanta Das	IIEST Shibpur, India
Alberto Dennunzio	University of Milano-Bicocca, Italy
Andreas Deutsch	TU Dresden, Germany
Nazim Fatès	Inria Nancy, France
Enrico Formenti	Université Côte d'Azur, France
Maximilien Gadouleau	Durham University, UK
Anahí Gajardo	Universidad de Concepción, Chile
Pierre Guillon	Université d'Aix-Marseille, France
Tomasz Gwizdałła	University of Lodz, Poland
Rolf Hoffmann	TU Darmstadt, Germany
Jarkko Kari	University of Turku, Finland
Martin Kutrib	University of Giessen, Germany
Andreas Malcher	University of Giessen, Germany
Luca Manzoni (Co-chair)	University of Trieste, Italy
Luca Mariot (Co-chair)	University of Twente, The Netherlands
Kenichi Morita	Hiroshima University, Japan
Kévin Perrot	Université d'Aix-Marseille, France
Dipanwita Roy Chowdhury	IIT Kharagpur, India
Ville Salo	University of Turku, Finland
Biplab K. Sikdar	IIEST Shibpur, India
Georgios Ch. Sirakoulis	Democritus University of Thrace, Greece
Siamak Taati	American University of Beirut, Lebanon
Guillaume Theyssier	Université d'Aix-Marseille, France

Ilkka Törmä   University of Turku, Finland
Hiroshi Umeo   Osaka Electro-Communication University, Japan

Organizing Committee

Giulia Bernardini   University of Trieste, Italy
Luca Manzoni (Co-chair)   University of Trieste, Italy
Luca Mariot (Co-chair)   University of Twente, The Netherlands
Giuliamaria Menara   University of Trieste, Italy
Gloria Pietropolli   University of Trieste, Italy

Additional Reviewers

Niloy Ganguly
Souvik Roy

Organization – AUTOMATA 2022

Steering Committee

Pedro Paulo Balbi	Universidade Presbiteriana Mackenzie, Brazil
Alonso Castillo-Ramirez	University of Guadalajara, Mexico
Nazim Fatès	Inria Nancy, France
Pierre Guillon	Université d'Aix-Marseille, France
Hector Zenil	Cambridge University, UK

Program Committee

Jan Baetens	University of Gent, Belgium
Jaydeb Bhowmik	Jadavpur University, India
Alonso Castillo-Ramirez	University of Guadalajara, Mexico
Sukanta Das	IIEST Shibpur, India
Abhijit Das	IIT Kharagpur, India
Alberto Dennunzio	Università di Milano-Bicocca, Italy
Andreas Deutsch	TU Dresden, Germany
Nazim Fatès	Inria Nancy, France
Paola Flocchini	University of Ottawa, Canada
Enrico Formenti	University Côte d'Azur, France
Anahí Gajardo	University of Concepción, Chile
Niloy Ganguly	IIT Kharagpur, India
Pierre Guillon	Université d'Aix-Marseille, France
Tomasz Gwizdałła	University of Lodz, Poland
Raju Hazari	NIT Calicut, India
Rolf Hoffmann	TU Darmstadt, Germany
Katsunobu Imai	Hiroshima University, Japan
Jimmy Jose	NIT Calicut, India
Jarkko Kari	University of Turku, Finland
Biplab K. Sikdar	IIEST Shibpur, India
Swapan Maiti	JIS University, India
Luca Manzoni	University of Trieste, Italy
Luca Mariot	Radboud University, The Netherlands
Giancarlo Mauri	University of Milano-Bicocca, Italy
Kenichi Morita	Hiroshima University, Japan
Kolin Paul	IIT Delhi, India
Pedro Paulo Balbi	Mackenzie Presbyterian University, Brazil

Kévin Perrot	Université d'Aix-Marseille, France
Dipanwita Roy Chowdhury (Chair)	IIT Kharagpur, India
Ville Salo	University of Turku, Finland
Georgios Ch. Sirakoulis	Democritus University of Thrace, Greece
Indranil Sengupta	IIT Kharagpur, India
Siamak Taati	American University of Beirut, Lebanon
Hiroshi Umeo	Osaka Electro-Communication University, Japan
Hector Zenil	Cambridge University, UK

Organizing Committee

Dipanwita Roy Chowdhury (Chair)	IIT Kharagpur, India
Palash Dey	IIT Kharagpur, India
Ayan Chaudhury	IIT Kharagpur, India

Additional Reviewers

Tapadyoti Banerjee
Sumita Basu
Bidesh Chakraborty
Raju Hazari
Supreeti Kamilya
Pacôme Perrotin
Souvik Roy

Sandpile Models and P-completeness
(Abstracts of Invited Talk)

Kevin Perrot

LIS, Aix Marseille University, 163 avenue de Luminy, 13009 Marseille, France
kevin.perrot@lis-lab.fr

Sandpile models are number conserving cellular automata, where grains move from cell to cell according to local rules. On finite grids it has a beautiful algebraic structure with a mysterious identity element. The "complexity" of such models can be studied through the algorithmic hardness of predicting the dynamics, which is feasible in polynomial time simply by simulating the whole stabilization process of grains move. From a theoretical point of view, whether it is possible or not to do better, i.e. predict sandpiles in logarithmic time on parallel machines (PRAM), is still open. This corresponds to the complexity class NC (Nick's Class), which is not known to be equal or differ from P (neither to be equal or differ from NP), hence there is a notion of P-completeness. We will discuss the circuit value problem (CVP, the canonical P-complete problem), its variants and connections with sandpiles. All this will be presented while playing with a sandpile simulator.

Contents

Regular Papers – AUTOMATA 2022

Invited Paper

Isometric Words and Edit Distance: Main Notions and New Variations

Giuseppa Castiglione[1], Manuela Flores[1], and Dora Giammarresi[2(✉)]

[1] Dipartimento di Matematica e Informatica, Università di Palermo, Palermo, Italy
{giuseppa.castiglione,manuela.flores}@unipa.it
[2] Dipartimento di Matematica, Università Roma "Tor Vergata", Rome, Italy
giammarr@mat.uniroma2.it

Abstract. Isometric words combine the notion of edit distance together with properties of words not appearing as factors in other words. An edit distance is a metric between words that quantifies how two words differ by counting the number of edit operations needed to transform one word into the other one. A word f is said isometric with respect to an edit distance if, for any pair of f-free words u and v, there exists a transformation of minimal length from u into v via the related edit operations such that all the intermediate words are also f-free. The adjective "isometric" comes from the fact that, if the Hamming distance is considered (i.e., only replacement operations are used), then isometric words are connected with the definitions of isometric subgraphs of hypercubes. We discuss known results and some interesting generalizations and open problems.

Keywords: Isometric words · Edit distance · Generalized Fibonacci cubes

1 Introduction

Isometric words inherit their name from their strict connection with the problem of finding isometric subgraphs of the hypercube.

The *hypercube* Q_n, is the graph with 2^n vertices, each one associated to a binary word of length n. Two vertices in Q_n are adjacent when their associated words differ in exactly 1 position, i.e. when their Hamming distance is 1. As a consequence, the distance of two vertices in the hypercube (as the length of the shortest path connecting them) coincides with the Hamming distance between the two words associated to the vertices. The *Fibonacci cube* F_n is the subgraph of Q_n whose vertices correspond to words avoiding the factor 11. It was introduced by Hsu in [17] that also showed that the number of vertices of

Partially supported by INdAM-GNCS Project 2023, PNRR MUR Project ITSERR CUP B53C22001770006 and FFR fund University of Palermo, MUR Excellence Department Project MatMod@TOV, CUP E83C23000330006, awarded to the Department of Mathematics, University of Rome Tor Vergata.

L. Manzoni et al. (Eds.): AUTOMATA 2023, LNCS 14152, pp. 3–16, 2023.
https://doi.org/10.1007/978-3-031-42250-8_1

F_n is a Fibonacci number. As important fact, F_n is an isometric subgraph of Q_n, that is, the distances of two vertices in F_n is the same as they were in Q_n (i.e. it is still the Hamming distance between the corresponding words).

In [19], starting from a word f, *generalized Fibonacci cubes* $Q_n(f)$ are defined as the subgraphs of Q_n obtained by selecting the vertices corresponding to words that do not contain f as factor. Then, the word f is called *isometric*[1] if $Q_n(f)$ is an isometric subgraph of Q_n.

During the same time, in [18], isometric words were introduced and studied in a language combinatorics setting by combining the important notions of avoiding factor in words, overlaps, and edit distance. As a result, isometric words are also connected with problems on similarity on strings (also DNA sequences) and find applications in pattern matching with errors [11–13,15]. The definition in [18] refers to binary strings to which the operation of replacement of a symbol can be applied at each position. The distance of two strings u and v is the minimal number of replacement operations needed to transform u in v. This corresponds to the classical Hamming distance between words; we indicate it as $dist_H(u, v)$. Given a word f, a word u is f-free if it does not contain f as factor. A word f is *isometric* if for any pair of f-free words u and v, there exists a sequence of length $dist_H(u, v)$ of symbol replacement operations that transform u into v where all the intermediate words are also f-free. In [18,19,21–23] the structure of non-isometric words is completely characterized and related to special property of their overlaps.

The notion of isometric words can be extended and generalized in several different ways, for example by enlarging the alphabet or using other edit distances. In [4], k-ary alphabets are considered together with Lee distance. It turns out that, for the isometricity, special interest deserves the case $k = 4$. Note that the quaternary alphabet is relevant for the applications to biological sequences that are defined on the nucleotide alphabet. Moreover, in some applications coming from computational biology, it seems natural to consider the *swap* operation that exchanges two adjacent different symbols in a word. An edit distance based on swap and mismatch errors seems worth to be considered [1,16]. In [2,3] this distance is referred to as *tilde-distance* and tilde-isometric words have been defined and studied from a combinatorial point of view.

Furthermore, a generalization of isometric word to two dimensions is given in [9] where isometric pictures are defined on the binary alphabet and with Hamming distance. As usual, in two dimensions all the notions become more involved but still the property of being isometric can be related to special kinds of picture overlaps.

In this paper we start by surveying the original notion of isometric word on binary alphabet and Hamming distance together with its characterization and then report the above-mentioned generalizations. In the last section we propose a new variation for the notion of isometric word by considering *isometric sets of words*. Besides the theoretical motivation of going from single elements to sets,

---

[1]   In the literature, these *isometric* words are sometimes called *good* words while the non-isometric are called *bad* words.

this could be a solution to the following problems related to isometric subgraphs of the hypercube and its applications. We are given a generalized Fibonacci cube $Q_n(f)$. If f is non-isometric then $Q_n(f)$ is not an isometric subgraph of the original hypercube. Can we delete some more vertices in $Q_n(f)$ to make it isometric to Q_n? Translating this question on strings, this is equivalent to look for an "isometric set of words" that includes the non-isometric word f. On the other hand, suppose that f was isometric and therefore $Q_n(f)$ is an isometric subgraph of the original hypercube. Can we delete some more vertices in $Q_n(f)$ by maintaining the property? Again we need to look for an "isometric set of words" that includes the isometric word f.

Another motivation for studying the concept of isometric set comes from the observation that not all the isometric subgraphs of the hypercube can be seen as $Q_n(f)$ for some isometric word f. Then, we were inspired by the example in [14] where the authors study the special case of $Q_n^{(11)} \cap Q_n^{(101)} \cap \cdots \cap Q_n^{(10^{h-1}1)}$ where $Q_n^{(f)} \cap Q_n^{(g)}$ denotes the subgraphs obtained from the hypercube by deleting the vertices that contains either f or g as factor. Actually, the authors there propose this as a generalization of the Fibonacci cube.

The final aim for the last section is to characterize the isometric sets but the research is still in a germinal state. We only provide some interesting examples that make evident the difficulties of the problem and show that isometry is, also in this case, strictly linked to overlaps with errors.

2   Basic Notation on Words

Let Σ be a finite alphabet. A word (or string) w of length $|w| = n$, is $w = a_1 a_2 \cdots a_n$, where $a_1, a_2, \ldots, a_n$ are symbols in Σ. The set of all words over Σ is denoted Σ^* and the set of all words over Σ of length n is denoted Σ^n. For any word $w = a_1 a_2 \cdots a_n$, the *reverse* of w is the word $w^{rev} = a_n a_{n-1} \cdots a_1$. If $x \in \{0, 1\}$, we denote by $\bar{x}$ the opposite of x, i.e. $\bar{x} = 1$ if $x = 0$ and viceversa. Then we define *complement* of w the word $\bar{w} = \bar{a}_1 \bar{a}_2 \cdots \bar{a}_n$. Let $w[i]$ denote the symbol of w in position i, i.e. $w[i] = a_i$. If $f = w[i..j] = a_i \cdots a_j$, for $1 \le i \le j \le n$, we say that f is a *factor* of w that occurs in the interval $[i..j]$. Given a word f, a word w is said f-*free* if f does not occur in w.

The *prefix* and *suffix* of w of length k, with $1 \le k \le n$ are the special factors that occur at the two ends of the words: $\mathrm{pre}_k(w) = w[1..k]$ and $\mathrm{suf}_k(w) = w[n - k + 1..n]$. When for some $1 \le k < n$ we have $\mathrm{pre}_k(w) = \mathrm{suf}_k(w) = u$ then u is here referred to as an *overlap* of w of length k; it is also called border, or bifix.

An *edit operation* is a function $O : \Sigma^* \to \Sigma^*$ that transforms a word into another one. Among the most common edit operations there are the insertion, the deletion or the replacement of a character and the swap of two adjacent characters.

The *edit distance* of two words $u, v \in \Sigma^*$, with respect to a set OP of edit operations, is the minimum number d of operations in OP needed to transform u into v. We will write $dist(u, v) = d$ for a generic edit distance. Note that, since the edit distances are often related to pattern matching algorithms, the fact that $dist(u, v) = d$ is also indicated as v has d *errors* with respect to u. A notion that will be crucial in the next sections is given by the following definition.

Definition 1. *A word f has a d-error overlap of length k if* $\text{dist}(\text{pre}_k(f), \text{suf}_k(f)) = d$.

The case $d = 2$ implies that $\text{pre}_k(f)$ and $\text{suf}_k(f)$ have two errors, in positions i and j, with $i < j$, to which we will refer to as *error positions*. Note that, by definition of edit distance, if we consider a word u and we apply an edit operation at some position i, we get a word v such that $dist(u, v) = 1$. We give the following definition.

Definition 2. *Let $u, v \in \Sigma^*$ such that $dist(u, v) = d$. A transformation from u into v is an ordered sequence $\tau = (O_1, O_2, \ldots O_d)$ of edit operations to be applied starting from u to get v. The sequence of associated words $w_0, w_1, \ldots, w_d$ such that $w_0 = u$, $w_d = v$, are obtained by $w_i = O_i(w_{i-1})$ and $\text{dist}(w_{i-1}, w_i) = 1$, for any $i = 1, \ldots, d$.*

Moreover, let f be another string of Σ^*, the transformation from u into v is f-free if each word w_i, for $i = 0, 1, \ldots, d$, is f-free.

Several edit distances, obtained by selecting the operations for the set OP, were investigated in the literature. The operations of insertion, deletion and replacement of a character in the string characterize the Levenshtein distance which is probably the most widely known; the most basic one is the Hamming distance that uses only replacements.

In this paper we consider the notion of isometric word with respect to different edit distances. The f-free transformations play an important role in the definition of isometric words while the notion of 2-error overlap will be crucial in their characterization.

3   Hamming Distance and Isometric Words

In this section we consider the classic notion of *isometric* words that were introduced in [18, 19] by using a binary alphabet and the Hamming distance.

Given two equal-length words $u = a_1 \cdots a_n$ and $v = b_1 \cdots b_n$, they have a *mismatch error* (or simply a *mismatch*) at position i if $a_i = \overline{b_i}$.

Definition 3. *Let $u, v \in \{0, 1\}^n$, the* Hamming distance $\text{dist}_H(u, v)$ *between u and v is the number of positions where a mismatch occurs.*

In the case of the Hamming distance, Definition 2 of transformation refers to replacement operations. We denote by $R_i(u)$ the replacement of the i-th position of the string u. More formally, given $u = a_1 \cdots a_i \cdots a_n$, the *Replacement operation* at position i gives the word $R_i(u) = a_1 \cdots \overline{a_i} \cdots a_n$. It is worth to point out that the replacement operations that compose a transformation can commute and each symbol of the first string is replaced at most once. The following definition was introduced in [18].

Definition 4. *Let $f \in \{0,1\}^*$. The word f is isometric if, for any pair of f-free words u and v of length $m \geq |f|$ there exists an f-free transformation from u to v.*

Example 5. Let $f = 010$, $u = 0000$, $v = 0110$, $dist_H(u,v) = 2$, since u and v differ in positions 2 and 3. The only two possible transformations from u into v are τ: $w_0 = 0000, w_1 = 0100, w_2 = 0110$, and τ': $w'_0 = 0000, w'_1 = 0010, w'_2 = 0110$. Neither of the two transformations is f-free, then f is not isometric.

On the other hand, a word f is non-isometric if there exists a pair (u,v) of f-free words of length $m \geq |f|$ and $dist_H(u,v) \geq 2$, named pair of *witnesses*, such that there does not exist a f-free transformation from u into v. The minimal length of all possible witnesses is called *index* of f.

Binary isometric words are characterized in [19,21,22] as the words having no 2-error overlap. Starting from Definition 1 and using Hamming distance, we can say that a word f has a 2-error overlap if there exists an overlap of length k and shift $r = |f| - k$ such that $dist_H(\text{pre}_k(f), \text{suf}_k(f)) = 2$.

Example 6. The word $f = 0011010$ has two 2-error overlaps (see Fig. 1). The first one has length $k = 4$, shift $r = 3$ and error positions $i = 1$, $j = 4$. The second one has length $k' = 3$, shift $r' = 4$ and error positions $i = 2$, $j = 3$.

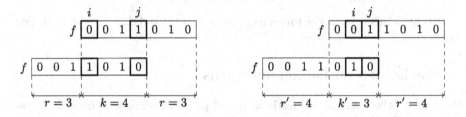

Fig. 1. The word $f = 0011010$ and its 2-error overlaps in Example 6

The two directions of the following statement are separately proved in [19] and [21].

Proposition 7. *Let $f \in \{0,1\}^*$. Then f is non-isometric iff f has a 2-error overlap.*

The most important step in the proof provides the construction of the pairs of witnesses in relation to the 2-error overlaps of the non-isometric word. If $f \in \{0,1\}^n$ has a 2-error overlap of length k, shift $r = n - k$ and error positions i, j, with $1 \leq i < j \leq k$, then $(\alpha_r(f), \beta_r(f))$, where $\alpha_r(f) = \text{pre}_r(f)R_i(f)$ and $\beta_r(f) = \text{pre}_r(f)R_j(f)$, does not admit an f-free transformation. Furthermore, it can be shown that $\alpha_r(f)$ is always f-free (see Lemma 2.2 Claim 1 of [21]). Instead, there are some special cases, in which f has a particular periodicity, where $\beta_r(f)$ is not f-free. These cases are handled either by constructing different witnesses or by considering another 2-error overlap (see Lemma 2.2 Claim 2,3,4 of [21]).

Example 8. The word $f = 111000$ has a 2-error overlap of length $k = 2$, shift $r = 4$ and error positions $i = 1$, $j = 2$. One can verify that the pair $(\alpha_r(f), \beta_r(f))$ with $\alpha_r(f) = 1110011000$ and $\beta_r(f) = 1110101000$, is a pair of witnesses.

Many combinatorial properties can be proved for isometric words. A word is isometric if and only if its reverse, its complement and any its finite powers is isometric. In [19] the density of isometric words with respect to all the words of the same length is given. In [10] a linear time and space algorithm to check whether a word has a 2-error overlap is given. Instead, [5] provides a linear time and space algorithm to compute the index of a non-isometric word.

We conclude by remarking that, in the literature, isometric words have been given in two equivalent ways, either by transformations of words or by hypercubes avoiding a word. The aim was to provide a class of subgraphs of the hypercube Q_n, having a smaller size, but still isometric to Q_n. The following definition and proposition that bring the two concepts together can be found in [19].

Definition 9. *Let $f \in \{0,1\}^*$, with $|f| \leq n$. The n-generalized Fibonacci cube avoiding a word f, denoted $Q_n(f)$, is the subgraph of Q_n obtained by removing those vertices where f occurs as factor.*

Proposition 10. *[19] Let $f \in \{0,1\}^*$. The word f is isometric if and only if, for all $n \geq |f|$, $Q_n(f)$ is an isometric subgraph of Q_n.*

Note that in this context the Fibonacci cube is $Q_n(11)$ and that 11 is an isometric word.

4   Variations on Isometric Words

We refer to the classical isometric words of previous section as *Hamming Isometric words*. We here introduce and survey some natural variations and generalizations that were recently studied and state new open problems. First, we consider two different edit distances, the first one is the Lee-distance over a generic alphabet and the second is the swap and mismatch distance over the binary alphabet. Then, we propose two "pure" generalizations by introducing bidimensional isometric words and set of isometric words, both with Hamming distance.

4.1   Lee-Isometric Words

Let us consider general alphabets, say k-ary alphabets, for $k \geq 2$. In this setting, the Hamming distance can still be considered, but in most cases it is not satisfactory. Thus, the Lee distance is usually used (note that Hamming and Lee distances coincide for $k = 2, 3$).

Definition 11. *Let $u, v \in \mathbb{Z}_k^n$, $u = a_1 \cdots a_n$ and $v = b_1 \cdots b_n$. The Lee distance between u and v is $\mathrm{dist}_L(u, v) = \sum_{i=1}^{n} \min(|a_i - b_i|, k - |a_i - b_i|)$.*

By relating Definitions 1 and 2 to Lee distance, we get the definitions of 2-Lee-error overlaps and Lee-transformations. Thus Lee-isometric k-ary words can be introduced, but it happens that no k-ary word is Lee-isometric when $k > 4$. In [6] it can be found the following formal definition for Lee-isometric words together with a complete characterization in terms of their error overlaps.

Definition 12. *Let Σ be a 4-ary alphabet. A word $f \in \Sigma^*$ is Lee-isometric if for any pair of f-free words u, v of length $m \geq |f|$ and $\mathrm{dist}_L(u, v) \geq 2$ there is an f-free Lee-transformation from u into v. A word is Lee-non-isometric if it is not Lee-isometric.*

Theorem 13. *Let Σ be a 4-ary alphabet and $f \in \Sigma^n$. A word f is Lee-isometric if and only if it has no 2-Lee-error overlap.*

Moreover, in [5], it is given a linear algorithm to compute the Lee-index of a Lee-non-isometric 4-ary word.

The cube structure associated to a k-ary alphabet is called k-ary n-cube. For $k = 2, 3$ the distance between two vertices of a k-ary n-cube is still the Hamming distance. Instead, for $k \geq 4$ it corresponds to Lee distance. The following statements are the equivalent of Definition 9 and Proposition 10, in this scenario. More details can be found in [4].

Definition 14. *Let Σ be a 4-ary alphabet. A 4-ary n-cube, denoted by Q_n^4, is a graph with 4^n vertices associated to all different 4-ary words of length n. Two vertices are adjacent if their associated words differ in exactly one position and the mismatch is given by two symbols a and b, with $a = (b \pm 1) \bmod 4$.*

Proposition 15. *Σ be a 4-ary alphabet and $f \in \Sigma^*$. The word f is Lee-isometric if and only if, for all $n \geq |f|$, $Q_n^4(f)$ is an isometric subgraph of Q_n^4.*

We conclude with an example that shows that the notions of Lee-isometric and Ham-isometric word on quaternary alphabet are not comparable.

Example 16. Let $\Sigma = \{0, 1, 2, 3\}$ be a 4-ary alphabet. Let $f = 0301$, $f' = 021$ and $f'' = 001$, with $f, f', f'' \in \Sigma^*$. The word f has a 2-Lee-error overlap of length $k = 2$. In fact, even if the prefix and suffix of length 2 differ only in one position, $\mathrm{dist}_L(01, 03) = 2$ because symbols 1 and 3 have Lee distance 2. Thus f is Lee-non-isometric, while f has no 2-error overlap with the 4-ary Hamming distance, therefore it is Ham-isometric. The word f' has no 2-Lee-error overlap, thus f' is Lee-isometric. Instead, f' has a 2-error overlap of length $k' = 2$ with the 4-ary Hamming distance, so it is not Ham-isometric. The word f'' has no 2-Lee-error overlap and no 2-Ham-error overlap, therefore it is both Lee-isometric and Ham-isometric.

4.2   Tilde-Isometric Words

We now consider an edit distance based on swap and mismatch errors. It was defined in 70's by Wagner and Fischer [20] who proved that it can be efficiently computed.

Formally, given $u = a_1 \cdots a_i a_{i+1} \cdots a_n$, the *swap operation* at position i, with $1 \leq i < n$ and $a_i \neq a_{i+1}$, gives the word $S_i(u) = a_1 \cdots a_{i+1} a_i \cdots a_n$. In [2] the distance that uses Replacement and Swap operations is referred to as *tilde-distance*, since the $\sim$ symbol somehow evokes the swap operation. The tilde-distance between two equal length words u and v is denoted by $\text{dist}_\sim(u, v)$ and will refer to the number of replacement (R) and swap (S) operations to be applied starting from u to get v. Moreover, using Definitions 1 and 2 we get the notions of tilde-transformations and tilde-error-overlaps. Note that the tilde-errors are now of type R and of type S depending on the associated edit operation. It is worth to point out that the replacement and swap operations that compose a transformation do not commute since one could apply R_i first and then S_i getting something different from the vice versa.

The definition of tilde-isometric words was given in [2] by extending Definition 4 to tilde-distance and tilde-transformations in which each symbol is changed at most once. As result, we get a very interesting notion that deserves to be investigated. It turns out that the 2-tilde-error overlaps have a main role also in the characterization of tilde-isometric words. Interestingly, not only them; we need to consider also 1-tilde-error overlaps when they correspond to a swap operation (type S); this is coherent with the fact that a swap operation changes two positions in the string.

Proposition 17. *If $f \in \{0, 1\}^*$ is tilde-non-isometric then*

1. *either f has a 1-tilde-error overlap of type S*
2. *or f has a 2-tilde-error overlap.*

For the reverse of Proposition 17, the construction of tilde-witnesses for a word is given starting from its error overlaps. This has to be handled with care by distinguishing among all types of overlaps. The authors differentiate non-adjacent and adjacent errors. Non-adjacent errors can be dealt with techniques as in the Hamming case, while the case of adjacent ones shows new issues. All the details can be found in [2].

We conclude by pointing out that, although the tilde-distance is more general than the Hamming distance, the corresponding notions of isometric words are incomparable. In fact, by referring to [2] and to Proposition 7, respectively, we have that the word $f = 111000$ is tilde-isometric but Ham-non-isometric because it has a 2-error overlap. Conversely, $f' = 1010$ is tilde-non-isometric but it is Ham-isometric.

In [3] the tilde-hypercube $\tilde{Q}_n$ of order n and the tilde-Fibonacci cube are defined and recursively constructed.

4.3   Isometric Two-Dimensional Words

In this section we come back to the Hamming distance and consider two-dimensional words known also as *pictures* that are considered as the natural generalization of strings. Pictures and picture languages are extensively studied also from a combinatorial point of view since they occur in many applications. We briefly and informally state some notions and results on isometric pictures. The interested reader can refer to [9].

A *picture* p of size (m, n) is a rectangular array with m rows an n columns of symbols from a finite alphabet Σ. The (top-left) *tl-corner* of the picture is assumed to have coordinate $(1, 1)$. The role of a factor in string w is taken by a *sub-picture* of p that is a picture f of smaller size which occurs inside p at some position (r, s) (i.e. f can be found with its tl-corner at position (r, s) in p).

We restrict to the binary alphabet and the Hamming distance $dist_{2H}$ between two pictures p and q is again the number of positions where p and q differ. Then, Definition 2 can be naturally exported in this 2-dim context to get the notion of f-free transformation from p into q with Hamming distance. This gives immediately the following definition.

Definition 18. *A picture f of size (m, n) is* isometric *if for any pair of f-free pictures p and q of the same size (h, k) bigger then (m, n), with distance $dist_{2H}(p, q) \geq 2$, there exists a f-free transformation from p into q.*

Example 19. The binary picture $f = \begin{array}{|c|c|c|}\hline 1 & 0 & 1 \\ \hline 0 & 1 & 0 \\ \hline\end{array}$ is not isometric. In fact, in Fig. 2 p and q are f-free and they have distance 4; the bits in which p and q differ are written in bold. Replacing each of the bold written bit of p, an occurrence of f is generated. So any transformation from p into q is not f-free.

In a picture we have four corners hence the notion of prefix and suffix do not make sense while the definition of overlap can still be given without referring to a scanning direction.

We distinguish between the *tl-overlap* and the *bl-overlap* that involve the top-left and the bottom-left portion of the picture, respectively. We say also *overlap* without specifying the type. Figure 3 shows some pictures together with their overlaps.

$$p = \begin{array}{|c|c|c|c|c|c|c|}\hline 1 & 1 & 1 & 0 & 1 & 1 & 1 \\ \hline 1 & 0 & \mathbf{1} & 1 & \mathbf{0} & 0 & 1 \\ \hline 0 & 1 & \mathbf{1} & 0 & \mathbf{0} & 1 & 0 \\ \hline 1 & 1 & 0 & 1 & 0 & 1 & 0 \\ \hline\end{array} \qquad q = \begin{array}{|c|c|c|c|c|c|c|}\hline 1 & 1 & 1 & 0 & 1 & 1 & 1 \\ \hline 1 & 0 & \mathbf{0} & 1 & \mathbf{1} & 0 & 1 \\ \hline 0 & 1 & \mathbf{0} & 0 & \mathbf{1} & 1 & 0 \\ \hline 1 & 1 & 0 & 1 & 0 & 1 & 0 \\ \hline\end{array}$$

Fig. 2. Two f-free pictures with f of Example 19

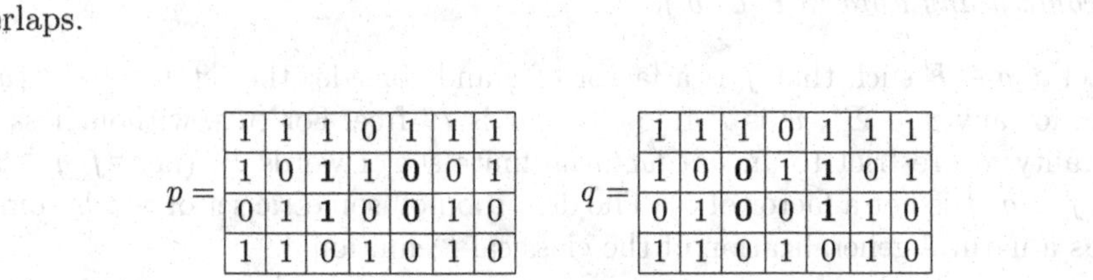

Fig. 3. Some examples of overlaps: p has a tl-overlap, q and r have a bl-overlap while s has a vertical overlap (both tl- and bl-)

Definition and properties of picture overlaps were recently studied in [7,8]. Generalizing Definition 1, we say that a picture p has an *r-error overlap* if p has an overlap as above where the two subpictures in the corners have distance r. It turns out that, also in two dimensions, the notion of 2-error overlap is related to the property of not being isometric. Despite the techniques are quite different and the details are much more involved, in [9] the following proposition is proved.

Proposition 20. *Let f be a picture. If f has a 2-error overlap then f is not isometric.*

Unfortunately, differently from the string case, the vice versa of Proposition 20 is not true and then the presence of a 2-error overlap does not characterize non isometric pictures. The counterexample is given by the Example 19 presented above. Interestingly, a variant of the vice versa holds; the 2-error in the overlaps may be split in two 1-error overlaps of a different kind.

Proposition 21. *Let f be a picture. If f is not isometric then either f has a 2-error overlap or f has a 1-error tl-overlap and a 1-error bl-overlap.*

5   Isometric Sets of Words

In this section we propose a new variation for the notion of isometric words by considering *isometric sets of words*. The motivations for this have been discussed in the introduction. The words are on a binary alphabet and the distance considered is the Hamming distance. We formalize the context by giving the main definitions together with some examples. Furthermore, we prove some preliminary properties.

Definition 22. *Let F be a finite set of words. A word w is said F-free if w does not contain any word in F as a factor.*

Let $f, g \in F$ such that f is a factor of g and consider the set $F' = F \setminus \{g\}$. Then, for any $w \in \Sigma^*$, w is F-free $\iff$ w is F'-free. For this, without loss of generality, we restrict to an *antifactorial* finite set of words F, (i.e. $\forall f, g \in F$, with $f \neq g$, f is not a factor of g). The definition of isometric set of words comes out as a natural generalization of the classical Definition 4.

Definition 23. *Let F be an antifactorial finite set of words in $\{0,1\}^*$. Then F is an isometric set iff for any pair u and v of F-free words of the same length, there exists a transformation from u into v such that all the intermediate words are F-free.*

Conversely, a set F is *non-isometric* if there exist two F-free words u and v of the same length and with distance at least 2 such that *each* transformation from u into v contains an intermediate word having a word of F as a factor. As before, the words (u, v) with this property will be referred to as the *witnesses* for F.

Starting from Definition 9, denote by $Q_n(F)$ the subgraph obtained from an n-hypercube by deleting all the vertices that contains some words of F as a factor. It holds the following proposition that generalizes Proposition 10 to isometric sets; it is a major motivation for investigating a characterization of isometric sets.

Proposition 24. $Q_n(F)$ *is an isometric subgraph of* Q_n *iff* F *is an isometric set of words.*

The following example shows an isometric set that contains an isometric word and a non-isometric word.

Example 25. The set $F = \{11, 101\}$ is isometric. By contradiction, let (u, v) be witnesses with minimal distance d and let τ be a transformation from u into v. The minimality of d implies that, for each $R_i \in \tau$, $w = R_i(u)$ contains either 11 or 101. In the first case, it is $u[i] = 0$, $w[i]w[i + 1] = 11$ and $u[i]u[i + 1] = 01$. It means that $R_{i+1} \in \tau$, since 11 must disappear in v. Then the transformation τ' that applies R_{i+1} before than R_i is F-free. In the second case, it is $u[i] = 0$, $w[i]w[i + 1]w[i + 2] = 101$ and $u[i]u[i + 1]u[i + 2] = 001$. It means that $R_{i+2} \in \tau$. If $i > 1$ then $u[i - 1] = w[i - 1] = 0$. Then the transformation τ' that applies R_{i+2} before R_i is F-free.

The next example shows a set composed by two isometric words and that is not isometric. Therefore, the isometricity of a set does not rely on the isometricity of the words in the set.

Example 26. The set $F = \{111, 100\}$ is non-isometric since (u, v) with $u = 1011$ and $v = 1101$ is a pair of witnesses. Indeed, u and v are F-free, $dist_H(u, v) = 2$. The only two transformations from u into v are $\tau = (R_2, R_3)$ and $\tau' = (R_3, R_2)$, $R_2(u)$ contains 111 and $R_3(u)$ contains 100.

In all the variations of isometric words presented in the paper the presence of some 2-error overlap is crucial. We now show that also for sets of words the 2-error overlap can be defined and connected to non-isometric sets.

Definition 27. *Let* $f, g \in \{0, 1\}^n$, f *has a 2-error overlap with* g *of length* k *and shift* $r = n - k$, *with* $0 < k \leq n$, *if* $dist_H(\operatorname{pre}_k(f), \operatorname{suf}_k(g)) = 2$. *The positions* i, j *in* f *where* $\operatorname{pre}_k(f)$ *and* $\operatorname{suf}_k(g)$ *differs are called the* error positions.

If $g = f$ then the above definition coincides with Definition 1. Note also that it can happen that f has a 2-error overlap with g but g has not any 2-error overlap with f.

Proposition 28. *Let* F *be a set of finite set of words in* $\{0, 1\}^n$. *If* F *is non-isometric then there exist* $f, g \in F$ *(possibly equal) such that* f *has a 2-error overlap with* g.

Proof. Let $F \subseteq \{0,1\}^n$ be a non-isometric set, and (u, v), with $u, v \in \Sigma^m$, with $m \geq n$, be a pair of witnesses for F, with minimal distance $d = \text{dist}_H(u, v)$ among all pairs of tilde-witnesses of minimal length m. Let V be the set of all mismatch positions. The minimality of the distance d implies that, when applying to u a replacement in any position of V, then a word of F appears as a factor. Such an occurrence must disappear in the transformation from u into v, because v is F-free. More precisely, for any $s \in V$, $R_s(u)$ has an occurrence of a word $f_s \in F$ in the interval $[k_s..k_s + |f_s| - 1]$, which contains s and another position of mismatch modified by another replacement operation. The minimality of the length of u implies that the intervals of the occurrences of all the f_s in $R_s(u)$ for all $s \in V$ cover entirely the interval $[1..m]$. Then, there exist $s, t \in V$ such that $[k_s..k_s + |f_s| - 1]$ contains both s and t and $[k_t..k_t + |f_t| - 1]$ contains both t and s. Suppose that $s < t$, then the intersection of $[k_s..k_s + |f_s| - 1]$ and $[k_t..k_t + |f_t| - 1]$ contains a prefix of f_s in $R_s(u)$ and a suffix of f_t in $R_t(u)$ of some length k. Then, f_s has a 2-error overlap with f_t.   □

Example 29. Set $F = \{00101, 11010\}$ is composed of two isometric words but F is non-isometric, indeed (u, v) with $u = 1101101$ and $v = 1100001$ is a pair of witnesses. We observe that f has a 2-error overlap with g with shift $r = 2$.

Note that the reverse of Proposition 28 is not true since Example 25 shows an isometric set that contains a non-isometric word (i.e. with a 2-error overlap). Moreover, observe that if two (equal length) words have Hamming distance equal to two, then they have a 2-error overlap of shift $r = 0$. In this case we have the following.

Proposition 30. *Let $F = \{f, g\} \subseteq \{0,1\}^n$, $dist_H(f, g) = 2$, then F is non-isometric.*

Proof. Let i, j be the two mismatch positions. Then, it is easy to verify that the pair $(u, v) = (R_i(f), R_i(g))$ gives the witnesses.   □

Note that when a set contains a non-isometric word, by Proposition 7, we can construct a potential pair (u, v) of witnesses starting from the 2-error overlap of f. However it can happen that one between u and v contains some words of F as factor. In this case the witnesses 'retract'. The same can occur if F has two words at distance 2. The witnesses defined as in Proposition 30 can retract. The last example shows this situation.

Example 31. Let $F = \{0^n, 0^{n-1}1, 0^{n-2}10, \cdots, 10^{n-1}\}$. For $p > 0$, denote by f_p the words of F such that $f_p[p] = 1$. We have that $dist_H(f_0, f_p) = 1$ for each $p > 0$ and $dist_H(f_p, f_q) = 2$ for each $p \neq q$, with $p, q \neq 0$ with mismatches in positions p and q. The pair $(u, v) = (R_p(f_p), R_p(f_q))$ is a potential pair of witnesses but $R_p(f_p) = f_0$ then the pair of witnesses retracts. Furthermore, each f_p with $p \neq 0$, $p \neq 1$ and $p \neq n$ is non-isometric with a 2-error overlap of shift $r = 1$ and error positions $i = p - 1$ and $j = p$. The pair of classical witnesses $(\alpha_r(f_p), \beta_r(f_p)) = (0^{p-1}110, 0^{n+1})$ retracts because 0^{n+1} contains f_0.

The challenge is to characterize those sets for which this happens for all pairs of witnesses, characterize isometric sets and pair of witnesses.

References

1. Amir, A., Eisenberg, E., Porat, E.: Swap and mismatch edit distance. Algorithmica **45**(1), 109–120 (2006)
2. Anselmo, M., Castiglione, G., Flores, M., Giammarresi, D., Madonia, M., Mantaci, S.: Isometric words based on swap and mismatch distance. In: Drewes, F., Volkov, M. (eds.) DLT 2023. LNCS, vol. 13911, pp. 23–35. Springer, Cham (2023). https://doi.org/10.1007/978-3-031-33264-7_3
3. Anselmo, M., Castiglione, G., Flores, M., Giammarresi, D., Madonia, M., Mantaci, S.: Hypercubes and isometric words based on swap and mismatch distance. In: Drewes, F., Volkov, M. (eds.) DCFS 2023. LNCS, vol. 13911, pp. 21–35. Springer, Cham (2023). https://doi.org/10.1007/978-3-031-33264-7_3
4. Anselmo, M., Flores, M., Madonia, M.: Quaternary n-cubes and isometric words. In: Lecroq, T., Puzynina, S. (eds.) WORDS 2021. LNCS, vol. 12847, pp. 27–39. Springer, Cham (2021). https://doi.org/10.1007/978-3-030-85088-3_3
5. Anselmo, M., Flores, M., Madonia, M.: Fun slot machines and transformations of words avoiding factors. In: Fun with Algorithms. LIPIcs, vol. 226, pp. 4:1–4:15 (2022)
6. Anselmo, M., Flores, M., Madonia, M.: On k-ary n-cubes and isometric words. Theor. Comput. Sci. **938**, 50–64 (2022)
7. Anselmo, M., Giammarresi, D., Madonia, M.: Non-expandable non-overlapping sets of pictures. Theoret. Comput. Sci. **657**, 127–136 (2017)
8. Anselmo, M., Giammarresi, D., Madonia, M.: Sets of pictures avoiding overlaps. Int. J. Found. Comput. Sci. **30**(6–7), 875–898 (2019)
9. Anselmo, M., Giammarresi, D., Madonia, M., Selmi, C.: Bad pictures: some structural properties related to overlaps. In: Jirásková, G., Pighizzini, G. (eds.) DCFS 2020. LNCS, vol. 12442, pp. 13–25. Springer, Cham (2020). https://doi.org/10.1007/978-3-030-62536-8_2
10. Béal, M., Crochemore, M.: Checking whether a word is Hamming-isometric in linear time. Theor. Comput. Sci. **933**, 55–59 (2022)
11. Béal, M.-P., Mignosi, F., Restivo, A.: Minimal forbidden words and symbolic dynamics. In: Puech, C., Reischuk, R. (eds.) STACS 1996. LNCS, vol. 1046, pp. 555–566. Springer, Heidelberg (1996). https://doi.org/10.1007/3-540-60922-9_45
12. Castiglione, G., Mantaci, S., Restivo, A.: Some investigations on similarity measures based on absent words. Fundam. Informaticae **171**(1–4), 97–112 (2020)
13. Charalampopoulos, P., Crochemore, M., Fici, G., Mercas, R., Pissis, S.P.: Alignment-free sequence comparison using absent words. Inf. Comput. **262**, 57–68 (2018)
14. Codara, P., D'Antona, O.M.: Generalized Fibonacci and Lucas cubes arising from powers of paths and cycles. Discret. Math. **339**(1), 270–282 (2016)
15. Epifanio, C., Forlizzi, L., Marzi, F., Mignosi, F., Placidi, G., Spezialetti, M.: On the k-hamming and k-edit distances. CORR arXiv:abs/2303.09144 (2023)
16. Faro, S., Pavone, A.: An efficient skip-search approach to swap matching. Comput. J. **61**(9), 1351–1360 (2018)
17. Hsu, W.J.: Fibonacci cubes-a new interconnection topology. IEEE Trans. Parallel Distrib. Syst. **4**(1), 3–12 (1993)
18. Ilić, A., Klavžar, S., Rho, Y.: The index of a binary word. Theor. Comput. Sci. **452**, 100–106 (2012)
19. Klavžar, S., Shpectorov, S.V.: Asymptotic number of isometric generalized Fibonacci cubes. Eur. J. Comb. **33**(2), 220–226 (2012)

20. Wagner, R.A., Fischer, M.J.: The string-to-string correction problem. J. ACM **21**(1), 168–173 (1974)
21. Wei, J.: The structures of bad words. Eur. J. Comb. **59**, 204–214 (2017)
22. Wei, J., Yang, Y., Zhu, X.: A characterization of non-isometric binary words. Eur. J. Comb. **78**, 121–133 (2019)
23. Wei, J., Zhang, H.: Proofs of two conjectures on generalized Fibonacci cubes. Eur. J. Comb. **51**, 419–432 (2016)

Regular Papers – AUTOMATA 2023

On the Surjunctivity and the Garden of Eden Theorem for Non-uniform Cellular Automata

Pyry Paturi[✉] [iD]

University of Turku, Turku, Finland
pypepa@utu.fi

Abstract. Non-uniform cellular automata are an extension of cellular automata with multiple local rules in different cells. We show that if the distribution of local rules is uniformly recurrent, or recurrent in the one-dimensional case, the Garden of Eden theorem holds. We also present two surjunctive distributions that are counter-examples to both directions of the Garden of Eden theorem respectively. Finally, we present a distribution which is not surjunctive.

Keywords: Non-uniform cellular automata · Garden of Eden theorem · Surjunctivity

1 Introduction

The notion of surjunctivity was introduced by Gottschalk in 1973. A group is said to be surjunctive if all cellular automata (CA for short) over the group have the property that they are surjective if they are injective. It is known that all sofic groups are surjunctive, but it remains an open problem whether all groups are surjunctive [1,2].

A stronger condition than surjunctivity is the Garden of Eden theorem, which states that a cellular automaton is surjective if and only if it is injective on finite configurations. Since an injective CA is obviously also injective on finite configurations, this implies surjunctivity. One direction of the Garden of Eden theorem for CA over integer grids was introduced by Moore in 1962 and its converse by Myhill in 1963. It is known that there are groups that don't satisfy the Garden of Eden theorem. Specifically, the theorem is satisfied by amenable groups [2–4].

Finally, non-uniform cellular automata are a generalization of regular CA which operate with different local rules in different cells. It can easily be seen that the Garden of Eden theorem does not hold in general for non-uniform CA over integer grids. More recently, conditions for the surjunctivity of non-uniform CA have been researched [5–7].

In this paper we further examine the surjunctivity of non-uniform cellular automata over integer grids. We show that in the 1-dimensional case, non-uniform CA with recurrent rule distributions satisfy the Garden of Eden theorem, and in general non-uniform CA with uniformly recurrent rule distributions

ⓒ IFIP International Federation for Information Processing 2023
Published by Springer Nature Switzerland AG 2023
L. Manzoni et al. (Eds.): AUTOMATA 2023, LNCS 14152, pp. 19–32, 2023.
https://doi.org/10.1007/978-3-031-42250-8_2

do as well. We also show that 1-dimensional non-uniform CA defined by distributions that have one cell with a different local rule may not satisfy either direction of the Garden of Eden theorem but are always surjunctive. Finally we present a rule distribution where surjunctivity does not hold.

Research relating to the Garden of Eden theorem has also been conducted on cellular automata restricted to subshifts. For example, it has been shown that CA restricted to irreducible subshifts of finite type satisfy that theorem [8]. This differs from the topic of this paper, because non-uniform CA cannot be characterized as CA restricted to subshifts.

2 Definitions

Definition 1. *Let Σ be a finite set called a* state set *and its elements* states. *Let $d \in \mathbb{N}$. A* configuration *is a function $c : \mathbb{Z}^d \to \Sigma$ and d is the* dimension *of the configuration. An element $\overline{x} \in \mathbb{Z}^d$ is called a* cell *and $c(\overline{x})$ is the* state *of cell $\overline{x}$.*

The configuration space $\Sigma^{\mathbb{Z}^d}$ is equipped with Cantor's topology and is known to be compact [2].

Definition 2. *Let Σ be a state-set and $d \in \mathbb{N}$. A finite set $D \subseteq \mathbb{Z}^d$ is called a* finite domain. *A* finite pattern *is a function $p : D \to \Sigma$.*

Notation 1. *Let $c \in \Sigma^{\mathbb{Z}^d}$ and $D \subseteq \mathbb{Z}^d$. The pattern $c_{|D} \in \Sigma^D$ is the unique pattern for which it holds that $c_{|D}(\overline{x}) = c(\overline{x})$ for all $\overline{x} \in D$.*

Definition 3. *Let $c, e \in \Sigma^{\mathbb{Z}^d}$. If there are finitely many cells $\overline{x} \in \mathbb{Z}^d$ such that $c(\overline{x}) \neq e(\overline{x})$, c and e are called* asymptotic.

Definition 4. *A* cellular automaton *or* CA *for short is a tuple $A = (\Sigma, d, N, f)$, where Σ is a state-set, $d \in \mathbb{N}$ is a dimension, $N = (\overline{n}_1, \overline{n}_2, \ldots, \overline{n}_m)$ is a tuple of cells $\overline{n}_1, \overline{n}_2, \ldots, \overline{n}_m \in \mathbb{Z}^d$ and $f : \Sigma^m \to \Sigma$ is a function. The tuple N is called the* neighbourhood *of A and f is called the* local update rule *of A.*

Definition 5. *Let $A = (\Sigma, d, N, f)$ be a CA and $N = (\overline{n}_1, \overline{n}_2, \ldots, \overline{n}_m)$. The* global update rule *of A is the function $G : \Sigma^{\mathbb{Z}^d} \to \Sigma^{\mathbb{Z}^d}$ which maps any configuration $c \in \Sigma^{\mathbb{Z}^d}$ to the configuration $G(c)$ such that*

$$G(c)(\overline{x}) = f(c(\overline{x} + \overline{n}_1), c(\overline{x} + \overline{n}_2), \ldots, c(\overline{x} + \overline{n}_m))$$

for all $\overline{x} \in \mathbb{Z}^d$.

Remark 1. If the CA A is clear from context, it is referred to by its global update rule G.

Notation 2. *Let* $N = (\overline{n}_1, \overline{n}_2, \ldots, \overline{n}_m)$ *be a neighbourhood,* $\overline{x} \in \mathbb{Z}^d$ *and* $D \subseteq \mathbb{Z}^d$. *The neighbourhood of a cell is denoted as*

$$N(\overline{x}) = \{\overline{x} + \overline{n} \mid \overline{n} \in N\}$$

and the neighbourhood of a domain is denoted as

$$N(D) = \{\overline{x} + \overline{n} \mid \overline{x} \in D, \overline{n} \in N\}.$$

Definition 6. *Let* $r \in \mathbb{Z}_+$. *A radius* r *neighbourhood* N *is a tuple of all vectors* $\overline{n} = (n_1, n_2, \ldots, n_d) \in \mathbb{Z}^d$ *such that* $|n_i| \leq r$, *where* $1 \leq i \leq d$.

Definition 7. *Let* $A = (\Sigma, d, N, f)$ *be a CA with* $N = (\overline{n}_1, \overline{n}_2, \ldots, \overline{n}_m)$ *and* $D \subseteq \mathbb{Z}^d$ *a finite domain. An* update rule *over the domain* D *is the function* $G_{|D} : \Sigma^{N(D)} \to \Sigma^D$ *which maps any pattern* $p \in \Sigma^{N(D)}$ *to the pattern* $G_{|D}(p)$ *with*

$$G_{|D}(p)(x) = f(p(\overline{x} + \overline{n}_1), p(\overline{x} + \overline{n}_2), \ldots, p(\overline{x} + \overline{n}_m))$$

for all $\overline{x} \in D$.

Definition 8. *Let* Σ *be a state set,* $\overline{r} \in \mathbb{Z}^d$ *and* $N = (-\overline{r})$. *The* $\overline{r}$-shift *or* translation *by* $\overline{r}$ *is the CA* $A = (\Sigma, d, N, f)$ *where* f *maps* $f(a) = a$ *for all* $a \in \Sigma$. *The global update function of the* $\overline{r}$-shift *is denoted as* $\sigma_{\overline{r}}$.

Definition 9. *Let* $D \subset \mathbb{Z}^d$ *be a finite domain,* $p_1 \in \Sigma^D$ *and* $\overline{r} \in \mathbb{Z}^d$. *Let* $D' = \{\overline{x} + \overline{r} \mid \overline{x} \in D\}$ *and* $p_2 \in \Sigma^{D'}$. *The pattern* p_2 *is a* translated copy *of* p_1 *if* $p_1(\overline{x}) = p_2(\overline{x} + \overline{r})$ *for all* $\overline{x} \in D$.

Remark 2. Let $c \in \Sigma^{\mathbb{Z}^d}$, $D \subset \mathbb{Z}^d$ a finite domain and $\overline{r} \in \mathbb{Z}^d$. Let D' be as in Definition 9. Clearly $\sigma_{\overline{r}}(c)_{|D'}$ is a translated copy of $c_{|D}$.

Definition 10. *Let* $w \in \mathbb{Z}_+$. *A* hypercube of width w *is a subset* $C \subseteq \mathbb{Z}^d$ *such that for some* $\overline{x} = (x_1, \ldots, x_d) \in \mathbb{Z}^d$,

$$C = \{(y_1, \ldots, y_d) \in \mathbb{Z}^d \mid \forall i \in \mathbb{Z}_+, i \leq d : 0 \leq y_i - x_i < w\}$$

Let $\overline{x} \in \mathbb{Z}^d$, $r \in \mathbb{Z}_+$. *A* radius r hypercube centred on the cell $\overline{x}$ *is the set*

$$C_r(\overline{x}) = \{(y_1, \ldots, y_d) \in \mathbb{Z}^d \mid \forall i \in \mathbb{Z}_+, i \leq d : |y_i - x_i| \leq r\}.$$

It is easy to see that a hypercube of radius r *is a hypercube of width* $2r + 1$. *A 1-dimensional hypercube is called a* segment.

Definition 11. *A configuration* $c \in \Sigma^{\mathbb{Z}^d}$ *is* recurrent *if for all finite domains* $D \subseteq \mathbb{Z}^d$, *there are infinitely many* $\overline{r} \in \mathbb{Z}^d$ *such that* $c_{|D} = \sigma_{\overline{r}}(c)_{|D}$. *In other words, a configuration is recurrent if every finite pattern that appears in the configurations, appears infinitely many times.*

The configuration c *is* uniformly recurrent *if for every finite domain* $D \subseteq \mathbb{Z}^d$ *and finite pattern* $c_{|D}$, *there exists* $w \in \mathbb{Z}_+$ *such that for any hypercube of width* w, *the hypercube contains a translated copy of* $c_{|D}$.

3   Non-uniform Cellular Automata

Non-uniform cellular automata are a generalization of cellular automata with the possibility of having multiple different local rules.

Definition 12. [10] *Let $\mathcal{R}$ be a finite set of local rules with state set Σ and neighbourhood N. A configuration $\theta \in \mathcal{R}^{\mathbb{Z}^d}$ is called a* local rule distribution. *A non-uniform cellular automaton or* ν-CA *for short is the tuple $A = (\Sigma, d, N, \mathcal{R}, \theta)$.*

Definition 13. *Let $A = (\Sigma, d, N, \mathcal{R}, \theta)$ be a ν-CA where $N = (\overline{n}_1, \ldots, \overline{n}_m)$. The* global update rule *of A is the function $H_\theta : \Sigma^{\mathbb{Z}^d} \to \Sigma^{\mathbb{Z}^d}$ that maps any configuration $c \in \Sigma^{\mathbb{Z}^d}$ to the configuration $H_\theta(c)$ such that*

$$H_\theta(c)(\overline{x}) = \theta(\overline{x})(\overline{x} + \overline{n}_1, \ldots, \overline{x} + \overline{n}_m)$$

for all $\overline{x} \in \mathbb{Z}^d$.

Remark 3. Like with regular CA, if the ν-CA is clear from context, it is usually referred to by its global update rule H_θ.

Definition 14. *Let $A = (\Sigma, d, N, \mathcal{R}, \theta)$ be a ν-CA where $N = (\overline{n}_1, \ldots, \overline{n}_m)$. Let $D \subset \mathbb{Z}^d$ be a finite domain. A* update rule over domain D *is the function $H_{\theta|D} : \Sigma^{N(D)} \to \Sigma^D$ that maps any finite pattern $p \in \Sigma^{N(D)}$ to the pattern*

$$H_{\theta|D}(p)(\overline{x}) = \theta(\overline{x})(p(\overline{x} + \overline{n}_1), \ldots p(\overline{x} + \overline{n}_m))$$

for all $\overline{x} \in D$.

Lemma 1. [6] *Let $\theta \in \mathcal{R}^{\mathbb{Z}^d}$ be a rule distribution, $A = (\Sigma, d, N, \mathcal{R}, \theta)$ a ν-CA. The global update rule $H_\theta : \Sigma^{\mathbb{Z}^d} \to \Sigma^{\mathbb{Z}^d}$ is continuous.*

The following lemma is a simple generalization of a lemma in [10].

Lemma 2. *Let $\theta \in \mathcal{R}^{\mathbb{Z}^d}$. The d-dimensional global update rule H_θ is surjective if and only if the partial update rule $H_{\theta|C}$ is surjective for all hypercubes $C \subseteq \mathbb{Z}^d$*

Proof. Let N be the neighbourhood of H_θ. First assume H_θ is surjective. Let $C \subseteq \mathbb{Z}^d$ be a hypercube and $p \in \Sigma^C$. Clearly there is a configuration $c \in \Sigma^{\mathbb{Z}^d}$ such that $c_{|C} = p$. Because H_θ is surjective, there is a configuration $e \in \Sigma^{\mathbb{Z}^d}$ such that $H_\theta(e) = c$. Then $H_{\theta|C}(e_{|N(C)}) = c_{|C} = p$ and therefore $H_{\theta|C}$ is surjective.

Assume then that $H_{\theta|C}$ is surjective for all hypercubes $C \subseteq \mathbb{Z}^d$. Let $C_i = C_i(\overline{0})$ for all $i \in \mathbb{Z}_+$. Let $c \in \Sigma^{\mathbb{Z}^d}$ and $(e_i)_{i=1}^\infty$ a sequence of configurations $e_i \in \Sigma^{\mathbb{Z}^d}$ such that $H_{\theta|C_i}(e_{i|N(C_i)}) = c_{|C_i}$ for all $i \in \mathbb{Z}_+$. Because $H_{\theta|C_i}$ is surjective, such a sequence exists.

Let $c_i = H_\theta(e_i)$. Clearly the sequence $(c_i)_{i=1}^\infty$ converges with limit $\lim_{i \to \infty} c_i = c$. By compactness of the Cantor space, the sequence $(e_i)_{i=1}^\infty$ has a converging subsequence $(e_{i_j})_{j=1}^\infty$. Let $e = \lim_{j \to \infty} e_{i_j}$. Then by Lemma 1,

$$c = \lim_{i \to \infty} c_i = \lim_{j \to \infty} c_{i_j} = \lim_{j \to \infty} H_\theta(e_{i_j}) = H_\theta(e).$$

Therefore H_θ is surjective. $\square$

We introduce the concept of local rule templates to characterize rule distributions. A local rule distribution template is a configuration of symbols which function as templates for local rules. Each symbol can then be assigned a local rule, which yields a local rule distribution. This allows for making general statements about distributions which are obtained from different assignments to the same template.

Definition 15. *Let $\mathcal{R}$ be a finite set of local rules, $d \in \mathbb{Z}_+$ a dimension and T a finite set whose elements are called* rule templates. *A configuration $\tau \in T^{\mathbb{Z}^d}$ is called a* local rule distribution template *and a function $\alpha : T \to \mathcal{R}$ is called an* assignment of local rules. *The rule distribution $\tau_\alpha \in \mathcal{R}^{\mathbb{Z}^d}$ such that $\tau_\alpha(x) = \alpha(\tau(x))$ is called τ with assignment α.*

4 Garden of Eden Theorem

For regular CA, the Garden of Eden theorem states that a CA is surjective if and only if it is injective on finite configurations. This can be stated more generally with the notion of pre-injectivity.

Definition 16. *Let H_θ be the update rule of a ν-CA. H_θ is* pre-injective *if for all asymptotic configurations $c, e \in \Sigma^{\mathbb{Z}^d}$ such that $c \neq e$, it holds that $H_\theta(c) \neq H_\theta(e)$.*

The Garden of Eden theorem is known to hold for regular CA over integer grids. However, it is easy to see that it does not hold over integer grids for ν-CA [11]. In the special case that the rule distribution of the ν-CA is uniformly recurrent, the theorem does hold. The proof is a modification of the proof for regular CA found in [3,4].

Lemma 3. *[3] Let $d, s, n, r \in \mathbb{Z}_+$. For all sufficiently large $k \in \mathbb{Z}_+$, it holds that*

$$(s^{n^d} - 1)^{k^d} < s^{(kn-2r)^d}.$$

Definition 17. *Let $q \in \Sigma$ be a state. The* q-support *of a configuration $c \in \Sigma^{\mathbb{Z}^d}$ is the set*

$$\mathrm{supp}_q(c) = \{\bar{x} \in \mathbb{Z}^d \mid c(\bar{x}) \neq q\}.$$

Lemma 4. *Let $\theta \in \mathcal{R}^{\mathbb{Z}^d}$ be a uniformly recurrent rule distribution. If H_θ is not surjective, then it is not pre-injective.*

Proof. Let $r \in \mathbb{Z}_+$ be large enough that H_θ can be defined with radius-r local rules. Let $s = |\Sigma|$. Suppose that H_θ is not surjective. Then by Lemma 2 there's a domain $D \subseteq \mathbb{Z}^d$ such that $H_{\theta|D}$ is not surjective. Because θ is uniformly recurrent, there is $n \in \mathbb{Z}_+$ such that any n-wide hypercube in θ contains a translated copy of $\theta_{|D}$.

Let $q \in \Sigma$ and $k \in \mathbb{Z}_+$. Let $C \subseteq \mathbb{Z}^d$ be a hypercube of width kn and C' a hypercube of width $kn - 2r$ centred on C. Let

$$K = \{c \in \Sigma^{\mathbb{Z}^d} \mid \mathrm{supp}_q(c) \subseteq C'\}.$$

Now $|K| = s^{|C'|} = s^{(kn-2r)^d}$.

Hypercube C can be partitioned into k^d hypercubes of width n, each of which must contain a copy of $\theta_{|D}$ in θ. Consider then the set $H_\theta(K)$. Because $H_{\theta|D}$ is not surjective, there is a finite pattern $p \in \Sigma^D$ with no $H_{\theta|D}$ pre-image. Then for each of the k^d hypercubes in C, there is at least one finite pattern with no pre-image. Because they are identical outside of C, there are at most $(s^{n^d} - 1)^{k^d}$ configurations in $H_\theta(K)$. Now by Lemma 3,

$$|H_\theta(K)| \le (s^{n^d} - 1)^{k^d} < s^{(kn-2r)^d} = |K|$$

for sufficiently large k. Therefore there must be configurations $c_1, c_2 \in K$ such that $c_1 = c_2$ and $H_\theta(c_1) = H_\theta(c_2)$. Hence H_θ is not pre-injective. $\square$

Definition 18. *Let $c, e \in \Sigma^{\mathbb{Z}^d}$. The difference set of c and e is the set*

$$\mathrm{diff}(c, e) = \{\overline{x} \in \mathbb{Z}^d \mid c(\overline{x}) \ne e(\overline{x})\}.$$

Lemma 5. *Let $\theta \in \mathcal{R}^{\mathbb{Z}^d}$ be a uniformly recurrent rule distribution. If H_θ is not pre-injective, then it is not surjective.*

Proof. Let $r \in \mathbb{Z}_+$ be large enough that H_θ can be defined with radius-$\frac{r}{2}$ local rules. Let $s = |\Sigma|$. Suppose that H_θ is not pre-injective. Let $c_1, c_2 \in \Sigma^{\mathbb{Z}^d}$ be asymptotic configurations such that $c_1 \ne c_2$ and $H_\theta(c_1) = H_\theta(c_2)$.

Because c_1 and c_2 are asymptotic, there is a hypercube $D' \subseteq \mathbb{Z}^d$ such that $\mathrm{diff}(c_1, c_2) \subseteq D'$. Let $n \in \mathbb{Z}_+$ be large enough that every hypercube of width $n - 2r$ in θ must contain a translated copy of $\theta_{|D'}$.

Consider any hypercube $D \subseteq \mathbb{Z}^d$ of width n. There is $\overline{y} \in \mathbb{Z}^d$ such that $D'' = \{\overline{x} + \overline{y} \mid \overline{x} \in D'\} \subseteq D$ and $\theta_{|D''}$ is a copy of $\theta_{|D'}$. Let $p_1 = \sigma_{\overline{y}}(c_1)_{|D}$ and $p_2 = \sigma_{\overline{y}}(c_2)_{|D}$. Let then $e_1, e_2 \in \Sigma^{\mathbb{Z}^d}$ be configurations containing the patterns p_1 and p_2 respectively. Consider any cell $\overline{x} \in \mathbb{Z}^d$. If $N(\overline{x}) \cap \mathrm{diff}(e_1, e_2) = \emptyset$, then clearly $H_\theta(e_1)(\overline{x}) = H_\theta(e_2)(\overline{x})$. If $N(\overline{x}) \cap \mathrm{diff}(e_1, e_2) \ne \emptyset$ then $\overline{x}$ is within $\frac{r}{2}$ cells from a differing cell, and

$$H_\theta(e_1)(\overline{x}) = H_\theta(c_1)(\overline{x} - \overline{y}) = H_\theta(c_2)(\overline{x} - \overline{y}) = H_\theta(e_2)(\overline{x}).$$

Therefore $H_\theta(e_1) = H_\theta(e_2)$, meaning for any hypercube of width n, there are two patterns p_1 and p_2 which can be replaced with each other without affecting the image.

Let C be a hypercube of width kn for some $k \in \mathbb{Z}_+$, and C' a hypercube of width $kn - 2r$ centred on C. If H_θ is surjective, then $H_{\theta|C'}$ is surjective, meaning every pattern in the domain C' has a pre-image in the domain C.

There are $s^{(kn-2r)^d}$ possible patterns in the domain C'. The hypercube C can be partitioned into k^d hypercubes of width n, each of which must contain two patterns p_1 and p_2 such that p_1 can be replaced by p_2 without affecting the image of C. If for each of these hypercubes we fix one of these two patterns to be p_1, then every pattern in the domain C' has a pre-image with no p_2 pattern in any hypercube. There are at most $(s^{n^d} - 1)^{k^d}$ such patterns.

By Lemma 3, for sufficiently large k, it holds that $(s^{n^d} - 1)^{k^d} < s^{(kn-2r)^d}$ and therefore some pattern in the domain C' has no pre-image. Therefore $H_{\theta|C'}$ is not surjective and hence H_θ is not surjective. $\qquad\square$

Theorem 1. *Let $\theta \in \mathcal{R}^{\mathbb{Z}^d}$ be a uniformly recurrent rule distribution. The ν-CA H_θ is surjective if and only if it is pre-injective.*

Proof. The statement follows from Lemmas 4 and 5. $\qquad\square$

In the case that $d = 1$, the theorem holds for all recurrent rule distributions. The proof is a modification of the original proof for regular CA found in [3,4].

Lemma 6. *Let $s, n, r, k \in \mathbb{Z}_+$. For all sufficiently large $m \in \mathbb{Z}_+$, it holds that*

$$(s^n - 1)^m s^{n(k-m)} < s^{kn-2r}.$$

Proof. By Lemma 3, for all sufficiently large $m \in \mathbb{Z}_+$ it holds that

$$(s^n - 1)^m < s^{mn-2r}.$$

Then

$$(s^n - 1)^m s^{n(k-m)} < s^{mn-2r} s^{n(k-m)}$$
$$= s^{kn-mn+mn-2r}$$
$$= s^{kn-2r}.$$

$\qquad\square$

Lemma 7. *Let $\theta \in \mathcal{R}^{\mathbb{Z}}$ be a recurrent rule distribution. If H_θ is not surjective, then it is not pre-injective.*

Proof. Let $r \in \mathbb{Z}_+$ be large enough that H_θ can be defined with radius-r local rules. Let $s = |\Sigma|$. Suppose that H_θ is not surjective. Then by Lemma 2 there are $i, j \in \mathbb{Z}$ such that $H_{\theta|[i,j]}$ is not surjective. Let $n = |j - i| + 1$.

Let $q \in \Sigma$ and $k \in \mathbb{Z}_+$. Let $C \subseteq \mathbb{Z}$ be a segment of width kn and C' a segment of width $kn - 2r$ centred on C. Let

$$K = \{c \in \Sigma^{\mathbb{Z}} \mid \mathrm{supp}_q(c) \subseteq C'\}.$$

Now $|K| = s^{|C'|} = s^{kn-2r}$.

Because θ is recurrent, it has infinitely many translated copies of the pattern $\theta_{|[i,j]}$. Then there are also infinitely many copies of $\theta_{|[i,j]}$ separated by a multiple of n. Let $m \in \mathbb{Z}_+$ be the number of such copies in $\theta_{|C}$. Because there are infinitely many such copies in θ, choosing sufficiently large k, the number m can be arbitrarily large.

Consider now $H_\theta(K)$. Because $H_{\theta|[i,j]}$ is not surjective, there is a finite pattern $p \in \Sigma^{[i,j]}$ with no $H_{\theta|[i,j]}$ pre-image. Then no translated copy can appear in the same position as a copy of $\theta_{|[i,j]}$ in any configuration in $H_\theta(K)$. Then there are at most $(s^n - 1)^m s^{n(k-m)}$ configurations in $H_\theta(K)$. Now by Lemma 6,

$$|H_\theta(K)| \le (s^n - 1)^m s^{n(k-m)} < s^{kn-2r} = |K|$$

for sufficiently large m. Therefore there must be configurations $c_1, c_2 \in K$ such that $c_1 \ne c_2$ and $H_\theta(c_1) = H_\theta(c_2)$. Hence H_θ is not pre-injective. $\square$

Lemma 8. *Let $\theta \in \mathcal{R}^\mathbb{Z}$ be a recurrent rule distribution. If H_θ is not pre-injective, then it is not surjective.*

Proof. Let $r \in \mathbb{Z}_+$ be large enough that H_θ can be defined with radius-$\frac{r}{2}$ local rules. Let $s = |\Sigma|$. Suppose that H_θ is not pre-injective. Let $c_1, c_2 \in \Sigma^\mathbb{Z}$ be asymptotic configurations such that $c_1 \ne c_2$ and $H_\theta(c_1) = H_\theta(c_2)$.

Because c_1 and c_2 are asymptotic, there is a segment $[i+r, j-r] \subseteq \mathbb{Z}$ such that $\mathrm{diff}(c_1, c_2) \subseteq [i+r, j-r]$. Let $n = |i-j|+1$. Let $p_1 = c_{1|[i,j]}$ and $p_2 = c_{2|[i,j]}$.

Let $e_1 \in \Sigma^\mathbb{Z}$ be a configuration containing a copy of p_1 in some segment $[i+y, j+y]$ where $y \in \mathbb{Z}$ is such that $\theta_{|[i+y,j+y]}$ is a copy of $\theta_{|[i,j]}$. Let $e_2 \in \Sigma^\mathbb{Z}$ be the configuration obtained by replacing all translated copies of p_1 in e_1 with a translated copies of p_2. Consider cell $x \in \mathbb{Z}$. If $N(x) \cap \mathrm{diff}(e_1, e_2) = \emptyset$, then clearly $H_\theta(e_1)(x) = H_\theta(e_2)(x)$. If $N(x) \cap \mathrm{diff}(e_1, e_2) \ne \emptyset$ then the distance of x from a differing cell is at most $\frac{r}{2}$. Then $x \in [i+y, j+y]$, and

$$H_\theta(e_1)(x) = H_\theta(c_1)(x - y) = H_\theta(c_2)(x - y) = H_\theta(e_2)(x).$$

Therefore $H_\theta(e_1) = H_\theta(e_2)$, meaning a copy of p_1 can be replaced with a copy of p_2 without affecting the image of the configurations, provided that the copy of p_1 lies in the same cells as a copy of $\theta_{|[i,j]}$ in θ.

Let C be a segment of width kn for some $k \in \mathbb{Z}_+$ and C' a hypercube of width $kn - 2r$ centred on C. If H_θ is surjective, then $H_{\theta|C'}$ is surjective, meaning every pattern in the domain C' has a pre-image in the domain C. Because θ is recurrent, it contains infinitely many copies of $\theta_{|[i,j]}$. Let m be the number of such copies in $\theta_{|C}$. With sufficiently large k, the number m can be arbitrarily large.

There are s^{kn-2r} possible patterns in the domain C'. On the other hand, because each copy of pattern p_1 that shares its domain with one of the m copies of $\theta_{|[i,j]}$ can be replace with a copy of p_2 without affecting the image, each pattern in C' has a pre-image with no copies of p_1 on a copy of $\theta_{|[i,j]}$. There are $(s^n - 1)^m s^{n(k-m)}$ such patterns. According to Lemma 6, for sufficiently large k and m, $(s^n - 1)^m s^{n(k-m)} < s^{kn-2r}$, meaning there is some pattern in C' with no pre-image. Therefore $H_{\theta|C'}$ is not surjective and hence H_θ is not surjective. $\square$

Theorem 2. *Let $\theta \in \mathcal{R}^{\mathbb{Z}}$ be a recurrent rule distribution. The ν-CA H_θ is surjective if and only if it is pre-injective.*

Proof. The statement follows from Lemmas 7 and 8.   □

This is not a general property of ν-CA, or indeed 1-dimensional ν-CA. There are non-recurrent 1-dimensional rule distribution templates such that for either direction of the theorem, there are assignments that contradict it. As an example we examine the rule distribution template with a single differing cell, which will later be shown to only have surjective assignments.

Notation 3. *Let $a, b \in \mathbb{Z}$. We denote $a \oplus b = a + b \mod 2$.*

Notation 4. *Let $\mathcal{R} = \{f, g\}$ be a set of local rules. We denote*

$$\phi_{f,g}(x) = \begin{cases} f, & \text{if } x = 0, \\ g, & \text{otherwise.} \end{cases}$$

Theorem 3. *There exists a set of local rules $\mathcal{R} = \{f, g\}$ such that the 1-dimensional ν-CA H_ϕ, where $\phi = \phi_{f,g}$, is pre-injective but not surjective.*

Proof. Let $\Sigma = \{0, 1\}$ and $N = (0, 1)$. Let $f : \Sigma^2 \to \Sigma$ and $g : \Sigma^2 \to \Sigma$ map

$$f(a, b) = 0,$$
$$g(a, b) = a \oplus b$$

for all $a, b \in \Sigma$. Clearly H_ϕ is not surjective, as for all $c \in \Sigma^{\mathbb{Z}}$, $H_\phi(c)(0) = 0$.

Let $c, e \in \Sigma^{\mathbb{Z}}$ be asymptotic configurations with $c \neq e$. Then there is a cell $x \in \mathbb{Z}$ such that $c(x) \neq e(x)$ and for all $y \in \mathbb{Z}, y > x$ it holds that $c(y) = e(y)$. If $x \neq 0$, then because $e(x+1) = c(x+1)$ and $e(x) = c(x) \oplus 1$,

$$H_\phi(c)(x) = c(x) \oplus c(x+1)$$
$$\neq c(x) \oplus 1 \oplus c(x+1) = e(x) \oplus e(x+1) = H_\phi(e)(x).$$

Suppose then that $x = 0$. Then there is $z \in \mathbb{Z}$ such that $c(z) \neq e(z)$ and for all $y \in \mathbb{Z}, y < z$ it holds that $c(y) = e(y)$. Clearly $z \leq x = 0$. Now because $e(z-1) = c(z-1)$ and $e(z) = c(z) \oplus 1$,

$$H_\phi(c)(z-1) = c(z-1) \oplus c(z)$$
$$\neq c(z-1) \oplus c(z) \oplus 1 = e(z-1) \oplus e(z) = H_\phi(e)(z-1).$$

So in either case, $H_\phi(c) \neq H_\phi(e)$ meaning H_ϕ is pre-injective.   □

Definition 19. *Let $n \geq 1$. A 1-dimensional blocking function $B_n : \Sigma^{\mathbb{Z}} \to (\Sigma^n)^{\mathbb{Z}}$ maps any configuration $c \in \Sigma^{\mathbb{Z}}$ to the configuration $B_n(c)$ such that*

$$B_n(c)(x) = (c(xn), c(xn+1), \dots, c(xn+n-1))$$

for all $x \in \mathbb{Z}$. Clearly B_n is a bijection.

Theorem 4. *There exists a set of local rules* $\mathcal{R} = \{f, g\}$ *such that the 1-dimensional ν-CA H_ϕ, where $\phi = \phi_{f,g}$, is surjective but not pre-injective.*

Proof. Let $\Sigma = \{0, 1\}$ and $N = (-1, 0, 1)$. Let $h_\leftrightarrow, h_\leftarrow, h_\rightarrow : \Sigma^3 \to \Sigma$ be local rules such that $h_\leftrightarrow(a, b, c) = a \oplus c$, $h_\leftarrow(a, b, c) = a \oplus b$ and $h_\rightarrow(a, b, c) = b \oplus c$ for all $a, b, c \in \Sigma$. Let $\mathcal{R}' = \{h_\leftrightarrow, h_\leftarrow, h_\rightarrow\}$ and $\psi \in \mathcal{R}'^{\mathbb{Z}}$ a rule distribution where

$$\psi(x) = \begin{cases} h_\leftarrow, & \text{if } x = 0, \\ h_\rightarrow, & \text{if } x = 2, \\ h_\leftrightarrow, & \text{otherwise.} \end{cases}$$

An illustration of the operation of H_ψ can be found in Fig. 1.

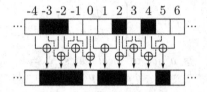

Fig. 1. Illustration of the operation of H_ψ

Let $c, e \in \Sigma^{\mathbb{Z}}$ such that $c(x) = 0$ and

$$e(x) = \begin{cases} 1, & \text{if } x = 1, \\ 0, & \text{otherwise,} \end{cases}$$

for all $x \in \mathbb{Z}$. The configurations are asymptotic and $c \neq e$, but clearly $H_\psi(c) = c = H_\psi(e)$. Therefore H_ψ is not pre-injective.

Next, we show every configuration has a pre-image. Let $c \in \Sigma^{\mathbb{Z}}$ be arbitrary, and $e \in \Sigma^{\mathbb{Z}}$ the configuration where

$$e(x) = \begin{cases} c(0) \oplus c(1), & \text{if } x = -1, \\ c(1), & \text{if } x = 0, \\ 0, & \text{if } x \in [1, 2], \\ c(2), & \text{if } x = 3, \\ e(x+2) \oplus c(x+1), & \text{if } x < -1, \\ e(x-2) \oplus c(x-1), & \text{if } x > 3, \end{cases}$$

for all $x \in \mathbb{Z}$. It holds that

$$H_\psi(e)(0) = h_\leftarrow(c(0) \oplus c(1), c(1), 0) = c(0) \oplus c(1) \oplus c(1) = c(0),$$
$$H_\psi(e)(1) = h_\leftrightarrow(c(1), 0, 0) = c(1) \oplus 0 = c(1),$$
$$H_\psi(e)(2) = h_\rightarrow(0, 0, c(2)) = 0 \oplus c(2) = c(2),$$

and for all $x < 0, y > 2$,

$$
\begin{aligned}
H_\psi(e)(x) &= h_\leftarrow(e(x+1) \oplus c(x), e(x), e(x+1)) \\
&= e(x+1) \oplus c(x) \oplus e(x+1) = c(x), \\
H_\psi(e)(y) &= h_\leftarrow(e(y-1), e(y), e(y-1) \oplus c(y)) \\
&= e(y-1) \oplus e(y-1) \oplus c(y) = c(y).
\end{aligned}
$$

Therefore $H_\psi(e) = c$, meaning H_ψ is surjective.

Let $h_0, h_1, h_2 \in \mathcal{R}'$. We denote $(h_0, h_1, h_2) : (\Sigma^3)^3 \to \Sigma^3$ as a function that maps

$$
\begin{aligned}
&((a_0, b_0, c_0), (a_1, b_1, c_1), (a_2, b_2, c_2)) \\
&\mapsto (h_0(c_0, a_1, b_1), h_1(a_1, b_1, c_1), h_2(b_1, c_1, a_2))
\end{aligned}
$$

for all $a_i, b_i, c_i \in \Sigma, i \in \{0, 1, 2\}$.

Let $f = (h_\leftarrow, h_\leftrightarrow, h_\rightarrow), g = (h_\rightarrow, h_\leftrightarrow, h_\leftarrow)$ and $\phi \in \{f, g\}^{\mathbb{Z}}$ like defined in the theorem statement. Let $B_3 : \Sigma^{\mathbb{Z}} \to (\Sigma^3)^{\mathbb{Z}}$ be a blocking function. Clearly for all $c \in \Sigma^{\mathbb{Z}}$ it holds that $H_\phi(B_3(c)) = B_3(H_\psi(c))$.

Because B_3 is bijective, H_ϕ is surjective. Additionally, clearly configurations $c, e \in \Sigma^{\mathbb{Z}}$ are asymptotic if and only if $B_3(c)$ and $B_3(e)$ are asymptotic, meaning H_ϕ is not pre-injective. $\quad\square$

5 Surjunctivity

In cellular automata, surjunctivity is the condition that injectivity implies surjectivity. Since injectivive automata are clearly pre-injective, the Garden of Eden theorem implies surjunctivity. Therefore we know that ν-CA with uniformly recurrent rule distributions are surjunctive, and that 1-dimensional ν-CA with recurrent rule distributions are surjunctive.

However, there are also non-recurrent rule distribution templates with assignments for which the Garden of Eden theorem does not hold, but whose assignments are always surjunctive. The following theorem is a special case of a result in [7], where it is shown that all rule distributions asymptotic with a uniform rule distribution are surjunctive.

Definition 20. *Let $m \in \mathbb{Z}_+$. A ν-CA over $\mathbb{Z}_m$ is the tuple $A = (\Sigma, N, \mathcal{R}, \theta)$, where Σ is a state set, $N = (n_1, \ldots, n_k)$ is a neighbourhood of cells $n_i \in \mathbb{Z}_m$, $\mathcal{R}$ is a set of local rules $f : \Sigma^k \to \Sigma$ and $\theta \in \mathcal{R}^{\mathbb{Z}_m}$ is a local rule distribution.*

The global update function of A is the function $F_\theta : \Sigma^{\mathbb{Z}_m} \to \Sigma^{\mathbb{Z}_m}$ that maps any configuration $c \in \Sigma^{\mathbb{Z}_m}$ to the configuration

$$
F_\theta(c)(x) = \theta(x)(x + n_1, \ldots, x + n_k)
$$

for all $x \in \mathbb{Z}_m$, where addition of cells is modulo m.

Notation 5. *Let u, v, v', w be finite words. The configuration $^{\omega}uv.v'w^{\omega}$ is one where infinite copies of word u are repeated to the left and infinite copies of w to the right of the word vv'. The first letter of v' is the state at cell 0.*

Theorem 5. *Let $\mathcal{R} = \{f, g\}$ be a set of local rules and $\phi = \phi_{f,g}$. If the 1-dimensional ν-CA H_ϕ is injective, then it is surjective.*

Remark 4. For the sake of clarity, in the following proof we consider patterns whose domains are finite segments as finite words, untethered from their domain.

Proof. As mentioned earlier, this theorem is a special case of a theorem from [7]. We show that if H_ϕ is not surjective then it is not injective, which is equivalent with the claim. Let Σ be the state set of H_ϕ and $r \in \mathbb{Z}_+$ large enough that $\mathcal{R}$ can be defined with radius $\frac{r}{2}$ rules. Assume H_ϕ is not surjective. Then by Theorem 2 there is a finite domain $D \subseteq \mathbb{Z}$ such that there is a pattern $p \in \Sigma^D$ with no pre-image. Let $n \in \mathbb{Z}_+$ be large enough that $D \subseteq [-n, n]$, and let $m \geq 2n + 1$. Let F_θ be the global update rule of a ν-CA over $\mathbb{Z}_m$ with the same state set, neighbourhood and local rules as H_ϕ, and

$$\theta(x) = \begin{cases} f, & \text{if } x = 0, \\ g, & \text{otherwise,} \end{cases}$$

for all $x \in \mathbb{Z}_m$

Because p has no pre-image and its domain D is a subset of $[-n, n]$, there is some configuration in $\Sigma^{\mathbb{Z}_m}$ with no F_θ pre-image. Because $\Sigma^{\mathbb{Z}_m}$ is finite, there must then be $c, e \in \Sigma^{\mathbb{Z}_m}$ such that $c \neq e$ and $F_\theta(c) = F_\theta(e)$.

For large enough m, there are $i, j \in \mathbb{Z}_m$ such that $0 \notin [i, i + r - 1], 0 \notin [j, j + r - 1], [i, i + r - 1] \cap [j, j + r - 1] = \emptyset$ and $c_{|[i,i+r-1]}, e_{|[i,i+r-1]}$ are translated copies of $c_{|[j,j+r-1]}, e_{|[j,j+r-1]}$ respectively. This is because there are only finitely many pairs of length r words. Let

$$u = c_{|[i,i+r-1]}, u_1 = c_{|[0,i-1]}, u_2 = c_{|[i+r,j-1]}, u_3 = c_{|[j+r,m-1]},$$
$$v = e_{|[i,i+r-1]}, v_1 = e_{|[0,i-1]}, v_2 = e_{|[i+r,j-1]}, v_3 = e_{|[j+r,m-1]}.$$

As remarked earlier, these patterns are treated as words. Let $c', e' \in \Sigma^{\mathbb{Z}}$ such that $c' = {}^{\omega}(u_2u)u_3.u_1(uu_2)^{\omega}$ and $e' = {}^{\omega}(v_2v)v_3.v_1(vv_2)^{\omega}$. An illustration of this definition can be found in Fig. 2.

The words u, u_1, u_2, u_3 and v, v_1, v_2, v_3 entirely cover configurations c and e respectively. Then because $c \neq e$, either $u \neq v$ or $u_k \neq v_k$ for some $k \in \{1, 2, 3\}$. Hence by definition $c' \neq e'$.

Next we show that $H_\phi(c') = H_\phi(e')$. For any given cell, its neighbourhood is at most a length r segment centred on the cell. Then the neighbourhood in c' and e' is the same as the neighbourhood of some cell in c and e respectively, because within an r-wide window the view of c' and e' is the same as c and e. Particularly at cell 0, the neighbourhood in c' and e' is the same as in c and e at cell 0. Then for all $x \in \mathbb{Z}$ there is $y \in \mathbb{Z}_m$ such that

$$H_\phi(c')(x) = F_\theta(c)(y) = F_\theta(e)(y) = H_\phi(e')(x),$$

and hence $H_\phi(c') = H_\phi(e')$. Therefore H_ϕ is not injective. $\square$

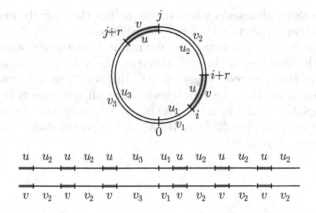

Fig. 2. Defining of the non-injective pair. Above are the configurations c and e and below the configurations c' and e'

Hence we see that every assignment to the rule distribution template with a single differing cell is surjunctive, even though the template has assignments that do not satisfy the GoE theorem, as seen before. There are also non-recurrent rule distributions which are not surjunctive.

Theorem 6. *Let* $\Sigma = \{0,1\}$, $N = (-1,0,1)$ *and* $\mathcal{R} = \{\sigma_{-1},\sigma_1\}$. *Let*

$$\theta(x) = \begin{cases} \sigma_{-1}, & \text{if } x < 0 \\ \sigma_1, & \text{if } x \geq 0. \end{cases}$$

The 1-dimensional ν-CA H_θ is injective, but not surjective.

Proof. Let $c_1, c_2 \in \Sigma^{\mathbb{Z}}$ such that $c_1 \neq c_2$. There is then $x \in \mathbb{Z}$ such that $c_1(x) \neq c_2(x)$. If $x < 0$, then $H_\theta(c_1)(x-1) = c_1(x) \neq c_2(x) = H_\theta(c_2)(x-1)$. If $x \geq 0$, then $H_\theta(c_1)(x+1) = c_1(x) \neq c_2(x) = H_\theta(c_2)(x+1)$. Therefore $H_\theta(c_1) \neq H_\theta(c_2)$ and hence H_θ is injective.

Then let $c \in \Sigma^{\mathbb{Z}}$ be the configuration with $c(-1) = c(0) = 1$ and $c(x) = 0$ for all $x \in \mathbb{Z}$, $x \notin [-1,0]$. Suppose there was $e \in \Sigma^{\mathbb{Z}}$ such that $H_\theta(e) = c$. Because $c(-2) = c(1) = 0$, it has to hold that $e(0) = e(1) = 0$. But then $c(0) = H_\theta(e)(0) = e(1) = 0$, which is a contradiction. Therefore c has no pre-image, meaning H_θ is not surjective. $\square$

6   Conclusions

We find that the Garden of Eden theorem holds for ν-CA if the local rule distribution is uniformly recurrent. More specifically in the one-dimensional case, the theorem holds if the local rule distribution is recurrent. We also find that there are rule distribution templates such that all rule assignments are surjunctive, but there are also assignments which do not satisfy the GoE theorem. Finally, there are also non-surjunctive local rule distributions.

We have been able to show that for any non-recurrent rule distribution template, for both directions of the GoE theorem, there always exist assignments that contradict that theorem. Together with this result, we can conclude that either direction of the GoE theorem is satisfied by all assignments to a rule distribution template, if and only if the distribution template is recurrent. Research should still be conducted to find exactly which rule distribution templates only have surjunctive assignments.

References

1. Gottschalk, W.: Some general dynamical notions. In: Beck, A. (ed.) Recent Advances in Topological Dynamics. Lecture Notes in Mathematics, vol. 318. Springer, Heidelberg (1973). https://doi.org/10.1007/BFb0061728
2. Cecchirini-Silberstein, T., Coornaert, M.: Cellular Automata and Groups. Springer, Heidelberg (2010)
3. Moore, E.F.: Machine models of self-reproduction. Proc. Symp. Appl. Math. **14**, 17–33 (1962)
4. Myhill, J.: The converse of Moore's Garden-of-Eden theorem. Proc. Am. Math. Soc. **14**, 685–686 (1963)
5. Sipper, M.: Co-evolving non-uniform cellular automata to perform computations. Physica D **92**(3–4), 198–208 (1996)
6. Dennunzio, A., Formenti, E., Provillard, J.: Non-uniform Cellular Automata: classes, dynamics, and decidability. Inf. Comput. **215**, 32–46 (2012)
7. Phung, X.K.: On invertible and stably reversible non-uniform cellular automata. Theoret. Comput. Sci. **940**(Part B), 43–59 (2023)
8. Fiorenzi, F.: The Garden of Eden theorem for sofic shifts. Pure Math. Appl. **11**(3), 471–484 (2000)
9. Hedlund, G.A.: Endomorphisms and automorphism of the shift dynamical system. Theory Comput. Syst. **3**, 320–375 (1969)
10. Dennunzio, A., Formenti, E., Provillard, J.: Local rule distributions, language complexity and non-uniform cellular automata. Theoret. Comput. Sci. **504**, 38–51 (2013)
11. Dennunzio, A., Formenti, E., Provillard, J.: Three research directions in non-uniform cellular automata. Theoret. Comput. Sci. **559**, 73–90 (2014)

Diddy: A Python Toolbox for Infinite Discrete Dynamical Systems

Ville Salo[✉][iD] and Ilkka Törmä[iD]

Department of Mathematics and Statistics, University of Turku, Turku, Finland
{vosalo,iatorm}@utu.fi

Abstract. We introduce Diddy, a collection of Python scripts for analyzing infinite discrete dynamical systems. The main focus is on generalized multidimensional shifts of finite type (SFTs). We show how Diddy can be used to easily define SFTs and cellular automata, and analyze their basic properties. We also showcase how to verify or rediscover some results from coding theory and cellular automata theory.

Keywords: Discrete dynamics · Symbolic dynamics · Cellular automata · Algorithms · Software

1 Introduction

This paper introduces and showcases *Diddy*, a new Python library and domain-specific language (DSL) for defining and analyzing infinite discrete dynamical systems. Its main purpose is to facilitate research of multidimensional shifts of finite type (SFTs) and cellular automata (CA), but the authors' intent is to extend it to encompass e.g. classes of finite graphs, geometric tilings and substitution systems. Diddy is free and open source, and available at [14].

The Diddy project arose from the authors' previous research, which has lately been characterized by computer-assisted proofs of combinatorial and dynamical properties of discrete objects [12,13,15]. Such research would greatly benefit from a flexible language for defining multidimensional subshifts and cellular automata (instead of working directly with cumbersome lists of forbidden patterns or local rules), a unified interface to a SAT solver and other auxiliary programs, and the ability to easily switch between a special-purpose language and Python when needed. Diddy can be used either as a standalone interpreted language or as a Python library; in this article, we focus on the former.

Diddy is a work in progress and under rapid development. We do not promise that future versions will be compatible with the sample code in this document. At the time of writing, the main features of Diddy are:

- The ability to define SFTs and CAs with first-order logical formulae, and by standard operations like intersection, composition and spacetime diagrams.
- Tests for SFT containment and CA equality.

© IFIP International Federation for Information Processing 2023
Published by Springer Nature Switzerland AG 2023
L. Manzoni et al. (Eds.): AUTOMATA 2023, LNCS 14152, pp. 33–47, 2023.
https://doi.org/10.1007/978-3-031-42250-8_3

– Computation of upper and lower bounds for the topological entropy and the minimum asymptotic density of a configuration of an SFT.
– A visualizer for the patterns of an SFT, with the ability to automatically complete a small pattern into a larger one.

2   Definitions

A directed graph $G = (V, E)$ is *grid-like*, or more specifically $\mathbb{Z}^d$-*like* for a dimension $d \geq 1$, if the group $\mathbb{Z}^d$ acts freely on G by graph automorphisms and the nodes are divided into finitely many $\mathbb{Z}^d$-orbits. This means that there is a finite set $R \subset V$ of *representative* nodes, and the edge set E is completely determined by the set of edges with at least one endpoint in R. For $\boldsymbol{n} \in \mathbb{Z}^d$, the translate $\boldsymbol{n} \cdot R$ of R is called a *cell*, and the cells form a partition of V.

As a nontrivial example, consider the two-dimensional *hexagonal grid* as shown in Fig. 1. It has two representative nodes, here named 0 and 1. Three cells, corresponding to $(0, 0)$, $(1, 0)$ and $(0, 1)$, are highlighted in the figure. Each node has three outgoing edges.

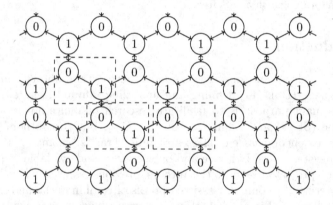

Fig. 1. The two-dimensional hexagonal grid.

Every Diddy object lives on top of some grid-like graph with a fixed set of representatives, called the *topology*. For technical reasons we always assume this graph to be undirected, meaning that for every edge (v, w) there is also an edge (w, v) in the opposite direction. For most of the definitions below, one can assume $V = \mathbb{Z}^d$ and $E = \emptyset$, which corresponds to the standard setting of symbolic dynamics used in e.g. [9]. General $\mathbb{Z}^d$-like graphs are convenient in modeling certain objects in Diddy.

Let A be a finite set, called the *alphabet*. A *configuration* on a graph $G = (V, E)$ is a function $x : V \to A$ that labels each node with an element of A. If G is a $\mathbb{Z}^d$-like graph, then $\mathbb{Z}^d$ acts on the set of all configurations A^V by translation: $(\boldsymbol{n} \cdot x)_v = x_{\boldsymbol{n} \cdot v}$ for all $x \in A^V$, $v \in V$ and $\boldsymbol{n} \in \mathbb{Z}^d$. We call A^V the *full G-shift*. A configuration $x \in A^V$ is *n-periodic*, or *periodic along* n, if $n \cdot x = x$. It is *totally periodic* if it is periodic along some vectors $n_1, \ldots, n_d \in \mathbb{Z}^d$ that span $\mathbb{R}^d$.

A *finite pattern* over A on G is given by a finite *domain* $D \subset V$ and a function $P : D \to A$. We denote $D = \mathrm{dom}(P)$. Every set F of finite patterns on G defines a *G-subshift* $X_F \subset A^V$ as the set of configurations where no element of F occurs: $X_F = \{x \in A^V \mid \forall P \in F, n \in \mathbb{Z}^d : (n \cdot x)|_{\mathrm{dom}(P)} \neq P\}$. If F is finite, then X_F is a *shift of finite type*, or SFT.

Let $X \subset A^V$ and $Y \subset B^V$ be G-subshifts. Let $R \subset V$ be the representative nodes. A *block map* is a function $f : X \to Y$ defined by a finite *neighborhood* $N \subset V$ and a *local rule* $F : A^N \to B^R$ by $f(x)_{n \cdot r} = F((n \cdot x)|_N)_r$ for all $r \in R$ and $n \in \mathbb{Z}^d$. A *cellular automaton* is a block map from a full G-shift to itself.

Let $W : A \to \mathbb{R}$ be a function, which we interpret as giving *weights* to the elements of A. The *upper density* of a configuration $x \in A^V$ is defined as

$$W(x) = \limsup_{k \to \infty} \frac{\sum_{n \in [-k,k]^d} \sum_{r \in R} W(x_{n \cdot r})}{|R|(2k+1)^d}.$$

The *minimum density* $W(X)$ of a subshift $X \subset A^V$ is $\inf_{x \in X} W(x)$. It is known that the minimum density of a subshift X can always be reached by a configuration $x \in X$ for which the limit superior in $W(x)$ is actually a limit.

Let $\mathcal{V}$ be a set of variables. A *Boolean formula* over $\mathcal{V}$ is either a variable $v \in \mathcal{V}$ or one of the forms $\neg \phi$, $\phi \vee \psi$, or $\phi \wedge \psi$, where ϕ and ψ are Boolean formulas over $\mathcal{V}$. A formula ϕ is *satisfiable*, if there is an assignment $\pi : \mathcal{V} \to \{\mathrm{True}, \mathrm{False}\}$ such that ϕ evaluates to True when its variables are substituted with their π-values. A formula is in *conjunctive normal form* (CNF), if it has the form $\bigwedge_{i=1}^{k} \bigvee_{j=1}^{n_i} a_{i,j}$, where each $a_{i,j}$ is a variable or the negation of a variable. Every formula is equivalent to a CNF formula. The *Boolean satisfiability problem* (SAT) is the following decision problem: given a Boolean formula in CNF, determine if it is satisfiable. SAT is NP-complete, but modern SAT solvers are remarkably efficient at solving many kinds of real-world SAT instances. Diddy uses the Glucose 4.1 solver [1] through the PySAT library [6].

A *(maximizing) linear program* is given by a set of *variables* $\mathcal{V}$ and a set of *constraints* of the form $a_1 v_1 + \cdots + a_n v_n \bowtie b$, where $\bowtie$ is one of $\leq$, $=$ or $\geq$, each v_i is a variable, and $a_1, \ldots, a_n, b \in \mathbb{R}$ are constants. To *solve* the linear program for a variable $v \in \mathcal{V}$ means to find a valuation $\pi : \mathcal{V} \to \mathbb{R}$ for the variables such that each constraint holds and $\pi(v)$ is maximal. There is an obvious variant that minimizes the value instead. Efficient algorithms exist for solving linear programs. Diddy uses the default solver of the Pulp library [11].

3   Representations

In this section we describe the internal representations of some objects in Diddy. In Diddy, the topology $G = (V, E)$ is defined by fixing the dimension $d \geq 1$, a finite set $R \subset V$ of representatives, and a finite set E_0 of triples $(r, s, n) \in R^2 \times \mathbb{Z}^d$. Then the nodes $V = \{(v, r) \mid n \in \mathbb{Z}^d, r \in R\}$ and edges

$E = \{((\boldsymbol{m}, r), (\boldsymbol{m} + \boldsymbol{n}, s)) \mid \boldsymbol{m} \in \mathbb{Z}^d, (r, s, \boldsymbol{n}) \in E_0\}$ of G are obtained by translating R and E_0. The action of $\mathbb{Z}^d$ is given by $\boldsymbol{n} \cdot (\boldsymbol{m}, r) = (\boldsymbol{m} + \boldsymbol{n}, r)$. For example, the two-dimensional square grid can be specified by $R = \{a\}$ and $E_0 = \{(a, a, (0, 1)), (a, a, (0, -1)), (a, a, (1, 0)), (a, a, (-1, 0))\}$; note that since we want G to be undirected, we include edges in all four cardinal directions.

In order to use SAT solvers to analyze symbolic dynamical objects, we must encode the relevant problems as SAT instances. Diddy can represent an SFT $X \subset A^V$ over G in two ways: as a concrete collection of forbidden patterns, or as a Boolean formula that represents the complement of such a collection. First, an alphabet $A = \{a_0, \ldots, a_{m-1}\}$ of size m is represented by a collection of $m - 1$ Boolean variables $v_1, \ldots v_{m-1}$ together with the formula $\phi_A(v_1, \ldots, v_{m-1}) = \bigwedge_{1 \leq i < j < m} \neg v_i \vee \neg v_j$ stating that at most one of them can be true. The interpretation is that the all-False assignment represents a_0, and the assignment of some v_i as True represents a_i. (One could just as well have a separate variable for a_0, but for $|A| = 2$ this doubles the number of variables.)

Suppose that $D \subset V$ is a finite set and ψ is a Boolean formula over a variable set $\mathcal{V}$ that includes $v_{e,i}$ for $e \in D$ and $1 \leq i < m$ and possibly some auxiliary variables. It defines an SFT $X = X_\psi \subset A^V$ as follows. A configuration $x \in A^V$ is in X if and only if for each $\boldsymbol{n} \in \mathbb{Z}^d$, there exists an assignment $\pi : \mathcal{V} \to \{\text{True}, \text{False}\}$ such that ψ evaluates to True, and for each $e \in D$, the assignment π restricted to $v_{e,1}, \ldots, v_{e,m-1}$ represents $(\boldsymbol{n} \cdot x)_e$. In other words, we set the values of the variables $v_{e,i}$ according to the local pattern of x at $\boldsymbol{n}$, and require that the partially evaluated ψ is satisfiable.

The representation by a Boolean formula is used for every SFT, and the representation by forbidden patterns only when needed. The reason is that converting a list of forbidden patterns F into a CNF formula ϕ_F is straightforward, and the size (in computer memory) of ϕ_F is linear in that of F. However, a Boolean formula may require an exponentially larger set of forbidden patterns.

To represent a block map, we need to specify the neighborhood $N \subset V$ and the local rule $F : A^N \to B^R$. It suffices to describe for each node $r \in R$ and symbol $b \in B$ the set of patterns $P \in A^N$ satisfying $F(P)_r = b$. This can be coded as a Boolean formula analogously to what we did with SFTs. Thus a block map is defined by $|R||B|$ Boolean formulas.[1]

4   Defining Topologies, SFTs and Block Maps

In this section, we detail the definition of various objects in the DSL of Diddy. Recall that a $\mathbb{Z}^d$-like topology $G = (V, E)$ is defined by specifying the set $R \subset V$ of representatives and a set E_0 of triples $(r, s, \boldsymbol{n}) \in R^2 \times \mathbb{Z}^d$. In Diddy, the triples are named, and can be referred to by these names. The syntax is also different from our definition of E_0: a triple is defined as **name source target**, where both **source** $= (\boldsymbol{m}, r)$ and **target** $= (\boldsymbol{n}, s)$ are nodes of the topology $\mathbb{Z}^d \times R$, and the definition corresponds to a triple $(r, s, \boldsymbol{n} - \boldsymbol{m}) \in E_0$. Often $\boldsymbol{m} = \boldsymbol{0}$, but this is not mandatory.

---

[1] This representation allows nondeterministic cellular automata, but Diddy always uses the first formula that applies, in the given order.

For example, the following code defines the two-dimensional hexagonal grid of Fig. 1 (which is also available via the built-in command %topology hex). The representatives are $R = \{0, 1\}$, and there are six triples, named N, S, sE, sW, nE and nW. Two triples may have equal names, if they originate from distinct vertices. We also illustrate defining alphabets, in this case $A = \{0, 1\}$.

```
%dim 2
%nodes 0 1
%topology
N (0,0,0) (0,1,1); S (0,0,1) (0,-1,0); sE (0,0,0) (0,0,1);
sW (0,0,0) (-1,0,1); nE (0,0,1) (1,0,0); nW (0,0,1) (0,0,0)
%alphabet 0 1
```

For example, N (0,0,0) (0,1,1) defines the triple $(0, 1, (0, 1)) \in E_0$, and the "upward" edge $((0, 0, 0), (0, 1, 1)) \in E$ (and all its translates) of the topology.

In Diddy, SFTs can be defined in two ways: by a list of forbidden patterns, or by a *first order formula* (FO formula) that is compiled into an intermediate circuit representation and then a SAT instance. The language of valid FO formulae, at the time of writing, consists of the following elements (which we will not define formally in this paper):

- Variables ranging over nodes of V, cells of $\mathbb{Z}^d$, symbols of A, or truth values.
- Moving along edges: If x is a node variable whose value is of the form $m = (m, r)$, and n is the name of a triple (r, s, n), then x.n is the node $(m + n, s)$. If x is a cell or node and s is the name of a node s, then x.s instead denotes the node (m, s) in the cell (of) x.
- Equality and proximity: If x and y are node variables, x @ y means they are the same node, and x ~ y means they are adjacent in G. If x is a node variable and y is a symbol variable (or a literal symbol), x = y means that x has the symbol y. If y is a node variable, it means that the nodes have the same symbol. These can be negated as x !@ y, x !~ y and x != y.
- Logical connectives: Diddy has the prefix operator ! (negation), and infix operators & (conjunction), | (disjunction), -> (implication) and <-> (equivalence) with the usual semantics.
- Restricted quantification: Ey[x2] defines a new node variable y that is existentially quantified over $B_2(x)$, the ball of radius 2 centered on the existing node variable x with respect to the path distance of G. There can be more than one restriction inside the brackets: for example, in Ez[x2y1] the variable z ranges over the union $B_2(x) \cup B_1(y)$. Ay[x2] is the analogous universal quantifier. EC and AC quantify cells instead of nodes.
- Local definitions: For example, let func a b := a @ b | a = b = 0 in defines an auxiliary two-argument formula func, checking that its two arguments are either the same node or both contain the symbol 0. In the code that follows the definition, it can be invoked as func x y. Auxiliary formulas can have any number of arguments, which can be node or symbol variables.

An SFT can be defined with the command %SFT name formula. We illustrate the syntax with examples, all of which can be directly run on the visualizer: the command `%tiler name` opens a new window containing a finite grid-shaped subgraph of the topology of the SFT `name`. The optional arguments `x_size` and `y_size` control the size of the grid. The user can zoom and pan the camera, set the values of any nodes, and ask Diddy to assign values to the remaining nodes so that the patch is locally valid in the SFT, if possible. We use the Pygame library [10] for the visualization.

Consider first the *checkerboard* SFT $X \subset \{0,1\}^{\mathbb{Z}^2}$, where all orthogonally adjacent cells must have distinct symbols. We can define this SFT on the grid topology as follows:

```
%SFT checkerboard Ao o != o.rt & o != o.up
```

There are two conditions for the universally quantified node o separated by a conjunction operator `&`: it must be different from the cell directly on its right (`o.rt`), and from the cell directly above it (`o.up`). Note that the edge labels `lt`, `rt`, `up` and `dn` correspond to left, right, up and down in several topologies.

As a second example, consider the SFT $Y \subset \{0,1,2\}^{\mathbb{Z}^2}$ where every non-2 cell must have a 1 in its radius-3 neighborhood:

```
%alphabet 0 1 2
%SFT cover Ao o != 2 -> Ep[o3] p = 1
```

The definition states that if a node o does not contain a 2, then there exists another node p within distance 3 (the restricted quantification `Ep[o3]`) that contains a 1.

For a more involved example, a *radius-r identifying code* [8] on a graph $G = (V, E)$ is a subset $C \subset V$ such that

1. All $v \in V$ satisfy $B_r(v) \cap C \neq \emptyset$, and
2. All $v \neq w \in V$ satisfy $B_r(v) \cap C \neq B_r(w) \cap C$.

The nodes in C model "sensors" that send an alert if some event occurs at any node within distance r. In case an event occurs, we would like to have at least one alert. Item 1 guarantees this by forcing every node to contain a sensor in its radius-r neighborhood. Furthermore, we would like to be able to infer the exact position of the event from the set of alerting sensors. This is guaranteed by item 2: the set of sensors that lie in the radius-r neighborhood of any given node $v \in V$ (i.e. those that will alert when an event occurs at v) is unique to v.

The SFT of radius-1 identifying codes (over the alphabet $A = \{0,1\}$, with C represented as the set of nodes containing a 1) can be defined as follows:

```
%SFT idcode Ao let cnbr u v := v=1 & u~v in
  (Ed[o1] cnbr o d) &
  (Ap[o2] p!@o -> Eq[o1p1] (cnbr o q & p!~q) | (cnbr p q & o!~q))
```

We first define an auxiliary formula `cnbr u v`, which is true if v is in C and adjacent to u. On the next line, we check that the universally quantified o, representing an arbitrary node, has a neighbor d in C. Finally, we check a condition on all nodes p within distance 2 of o: if p and o are distinct, one of them should have a neighbor q in C which is not a neighbor of the other. Note that this definition is independent of the topology G.

Diddy supports definitions of block maps between two full shifts of the same dimension. The syntax for defining a block map from a full shift to itself (i.e. a cellular automaton) is %blockmap name preimages where preimages is a list of commands of the form node symbol formula. The formula formula describes when the local rule $F : A^N \to A^R$ of the block map should write the symbol symbol in the node node, which is an element of R. Similarly as when describing SFTs, N is simply the set of nodes that the Boolean formula references. When none of the formulas applies at a particular node, the local rule writes a default symbol, which is the first element of the alphabet that does not occur in a rule, or the first element of the alphabet if they all occur. If two or more formulas apply at a node, the earliest one in the list is used, so the rules need not be mutually exclusive. The command %CA is an alias for %blockmap, and they can be used interchangeably.

As a first example, consider the elementary cellular automaton [18] rule 18, which is the one-dimensional CA $f : \{0,1\}^{\mathbb{Z}} \to \{0,1\}^{\mathbb{Z}}$ with neighborhood $\{-1,0,1\}$ defined by $f(x)_i = 1$ if and only if $x_{[i-1,i+1]} \in \{001, 100\}$. We give two overlapping and non-exhaustive rules for this CA:

```
%topology line
%CA rule18;   0 0 Ao o=1;   0 1 Ao o.lt != o.rt
```

Both rules concern the node named 0, which is the only representative node of the one-dimensional line topology. If the node contains a 1, then the result is always 0. If the first rule does not apply (i.e. the node contains a 0) and its two neighbors have different symbols, then the result is 1. In case neither rule applies, we default to the first symbol in the alphabet, which is 0.

The set of *spacetime diagrams* of a d-dimensional cellular automaton ca can be produced with the command %spacetime name ca, which saves the $(d+1)$-dimensional SFT of spacetime diagrams to name. It can then be analyzed with SFT-specific commands or visualized. Similarly, one can extract the SFT of fixed points of a CA with %fixed_points name ca.

We provide a second example with a different topology. Consider three cellular automata L, R, F with two-tracks (both with binary alphabet), i.e. $A = \{0,1\}^2$, where L and R shift the top track to the left and right respectively, and F adds the top track to the bottom track modulo 2. All three are reversible, and their compositions form a group that is isomorphic to the *lamplighter group* $\mathcal{L}$. It is the wreath product $\mathbb{Z}_2 \wr \mathbb{Z}$, i.e. semidirect product of the groups $\bigoplus_{n \in \mathbb{Z}} \mathbb{Z}_2 \rtimes \mathbb{Z}$ where $\mathbb{Z}$ acts on the infinite direct product $\bigoplus_{n \in \mathbb{Z}} \mathbb{Z}_2$ by shifting. An element of the lamplighter group can be thought of as an instruction for shifting a bi-infinite tape of bits and toggling ($0 \leftrightarrow 1$) finitely many tape cells.

```
%alphabet 0 1
%nodes top bot -- two tracks, top and bottom (-- starts a comment)
```

```
%dim 1
%topology -- rt and lt are shorthands for right and left
rt (0, top) (1, top); rt (0, bot) (1, bot);
lt (0, top) (-1, top); lt (0, bot) (-1, bot)
%CA R -- partial right shift on the top track
top 1 ACo o.top.lt=1;  bot 1 ACo o.bot=1
%CA L -- partial left shift on the top track
top 1 ACo o.top.rt=1;  bot 1 ACo o.bot=1
%CA F -- add top track to bottom track
top 1 ACo o.top=1;  bot 1 ACo o.bot != o.top
```

5   Comparing SFTs

Given two SFTs $X, Y \subset A^V$ on G, do we have $X = Y$? This problem is in general undecidable for $d \geq 2$, even when $Y = \emptyset$ is fixed, as shown by Berger in [2]. Thus we have no hope of implementing total algorithms for testing equality of SFTs. However, the following is true:

1. If $X \subseteq Y$, then it can be verified computationally. This is due to a compactness argument. Let F and F' be sets of forbidden patterns for X and Y. If $X \subseteq Y$, there must exist a finite set $N \subset \mathbb{Z}^d$ such that if $x \in A^V$ satisfies $(\boldsymbol{n} \cdot x)|_{\mathrm{dom}(P')} \neq P'$ for all $P' \in F'$ and $\boldsymbol{n} \in N$, then $x|_{\mathrm{dom}(P)} \neq P$ for all $P \in F$. It is checkable whether a given N has this property, and any such N proves $X \subseteq Y$.
2. If there exists a totally periodic configuration $x \in X \setminus Y$, then it can be found computationally, simply by enumerating totally periodic configurations and checking whether they contain forbidden patterns of X and/or Y.

This gives rise to a partial algorithm for checking the containment $X \subseteq Y$. For increasing $k = 1, 2, \ldots$, check whether condition 1 holds with $N = [-k, k]^d$, returning "yes" if it does; otherwise check condition 2 for the periods $\boldsymbol{n}_i = (0, \cdots, 0, k, 0, \cdots, 0)$, returning "no" if such a periodic configuration is found. In particular, $X \subseteq Y$ is decidable if X has dense totally periodic points (as many natural examples do).

This is essentially Wang's semi-algorithm for checking whether a set of colored square tiles can tile the infinite plane [17]. The command %equal performs the checks with a SAT solver, using the representations of SFTs by formulas. Of course, the algorithm never terminates if $X \setminus Y$ is nonempty but contains no totally periodic configurations. The command %contains can be used to check containment of SFTs. Both commands can be given the optional argument method=recognizable, which tries to find a separating configuration that is ultimately periodic in every cardinal direction. This method can separate more SFTs than the default one, but is computationally more demanding.

6   Computing and Comparing Block Maps

Given two G-SFTs $X \subseteq A^V$ and $Y \subseteq B^V$ and block maps $f, g : X \rightarrow Y$, it is undecidable whether $f = g$ for the same reason as equality checking between SFTs: if the local rules of f and g always give a different output, then $f = g$ if and only if $X = \emptyset$. However, if $X = A^V$ is a full shift, the problem becomes "merely" co-NP-complete, as we now have to check that there does not exist an input where one of the formulas defining the local rule of f evaluates to True and the corresponding one for g to False, or vice versa. Diddy provides this functionality with the `%equal` command.

In addition, one can compose block maps, either explicitly using the command `%compose name blockmap_list` which gives a name to the composition, or by enumerating all compositions of a given set of cellular automata up to a given length and reporting which of them are equal, using `%calculate_CA_ball bound filename CA_list`. The latter command writes its results into a log file. Its name refers to the fact that it essentially analyzes the shape and size of a ball in the Cayley graph of the semigroup generated by the given automata.

Continuing the lamplighter example, consider the cellular automata $\alpha = FR^3 FL^5 FR^2$ and $\beta = L^2 FR^5 FL^3 F$. In both compositions, the top track is added to the bottom track shifted by -2, 0 and 3 steps (in some order). Hence, they should be equal. We can check this relation in Diddy:

```
%compose alpha F R R R F L L L L L F R R
%compose beta  L L F R R R R R F L L L F
%equal alpha beta
```

Diddy also allows us to compute the order of cellular automata, at least if it is small. Consider the cellular automaton f on $\mathbb{Z}$ with alphabet $\{0, 1\}$ and neighborhood $\{0, 1, 2, 3, 4, 5, 6\}$ which maps

$$f(x)_0 = 1 \iff x_{[0,6]} \in \{0111000, 1000100, 0111100, 1010110, 1111110, 0010001,$$
$$0101001, 1101001, 0000101, 0010101, 0011101, 0000011,$$
$$1110011, 0011011, 1011011, 0111011, 1111011, 1000111,$$
$$1100111, 0010111, 1110111, 0001111, 0111111\}.$$

The first-named author suggested in an invited talk of the AUTOMATA 2017 conference that this CA might be nilpotent, and showed that its nildegree (first power n such that f^n maps everything to 0) is at least 7. The author has later shown with an ad hoc proof that the nildegree is at most 9.

With Diddy we can compute the nildegree directly. The cellular automaton can be translated quite directly into Diddy code (with some lines omitted):

```
%topology line
%CA f
0 1 Ao let x a b c d e f g :=
  o=a & o.rt=b & o.rt.rt=c & o.rt.rt.rt=d &
  o.rt.rt.rt.rt=e & o.rt.rt.rt.rt.rt=f & o.rt.rt.rt.rt.rt.rt=g in
x 0 1 1 1 0 0 0 | x 1 0 0 0 1 0 0 | [...] | x 0 1 1 1 1 1 1
```

Here we define a predicate x that checks whether the origin has a particular word in its neighborhood, and then take the disjunction over the set from above. Now we also define the zero CA and calculate the ball that this pair generates:

```
%CA zero 0 1 Ao 0=1
%calculate_CA_ball filename=outfile 10 f zero
```

The output file contains several lines, but the most relevant one is zero = f f f f f f. It states that the seventh power of f is the zero CA. One can also calculate this much quicker with %compose seventh f f f f f f f and %equal seventh zero, if we already know (or correctly guess) the order.

7   Minimum Density

In many applications, it is important to determine the minimum density $W(X)$ of an SFT $X \subset A^V$ with respect to some alphabet weights $W : A \to \mathbb{R}$. Diddy includes two algorithms for approximating $W(X)$, one for finding upper bounds and another one for lower bounds. Neither of them is guaranteed to find the true value, but in practice they can give good results.

7.1   Upper Bounds by Periodic Configurations

We first describe the algorithm for finding upper bounds. Choose a set of $d - 1$ vectors $K = \{n_2, n_3, \ldots, n_d\} \subset \mathbb{Z}^d$ such that $\{e_1, n_2, n_3, \ldots, n_d\}$ is a basis of $\mathbb{R}^d$, where $e_1 = (1, 0, \ldots, 0)$ is the first standard basis vector. Let $X_K \subset X$ be the set of configurations that are periodic along n_i for each $2 \le i \le d$. Then X_K is also an SFT and $W(X_K) \ge W(X)$. Moreover, we claim that $W(X_K)$ is computable in a reasonably effective and parallelizable way. In fact, we have already announced a special case in [15]. To compute upper bounds for $W(X)$ one just needs to choose suitable sets of periods K and apply the algorithm. Note that if X happens to be aperiodic, then this algorithm will never give a result for any choice of K, and in any case its performance depends on how well the density $W(X)$ is approximated by periodic configurations.

In this algorithm we use the representation of X by a set F of forbidden patterns. Let $D \subset \mathbb{Z}^d$ be a fundamental domain of the vectors $K \cup \{e_1\}$, and let $U = \{a_2 n_2 + \cdots + a_d n_d \mid a_2, \ldots, a_d \in \mathbb{Z}\}$. Let $B = \bigcup_{u \in U} u + D$ be the *border*, and call $B^+ = \{(b + pe_1) \cdot r \mid b \in B, p \ge 0, r \in R\}$ the *right side* and $B^- = \{(b + pe_1) \cdot r \mid b \in B, p \le 0, r \in R\}$ the *left side* of the vertex set V, where $R \subset V$ is the set of representatives. The set X_K is essentially a one-dimensional SFT whose alphabet is $A^{D \cdot R}$, and the dynamics is translation by e_1. We represent it as a labeled digraph $G' = (V', E')$ as follows. A vertex $v \in V'$ is a set of finite patterns $Q = m \cdot P$ where $P \in F$ and $m \in \mathbb{Z}^d$ such that:

- v is invariant under U-translation: if $Q \in v$ and $n \in U$, then $n \cdot Q \in v$; and
- for each $Q \in v$, the domain $\mathrm{dom}(Q)$ intersects both B^+ and B^-.

Note that while each $v \in V'$ is technically an infinite set of finite patterns, the U-invariance and the intersection property ensure that it can be encoded by a bounded amount of data. In particular, V' is a finite set.

Denote by v_0 the set of patterns $Q = \boldsymbol{m} \cdot P$ for $P \in F$ and $\boldsymbol{m} \in \mathbb{Z}^d$ with $\mathrm{dom}(Q) \subset B^+$ and $\mathrm{dom}(Q) \cap B^- \neq \emptyset$. For $v_1, v_2 \in V'$ and $S \in A^{D \cdot R}$, there is an edge from v_1 to v_2 with label S if and only if

$$v_2 = \{-\boldsymbol{e}_1 \cdot Q \mid Q \in v_1 \cup v_0, \nexists n \in \mathrm{dom}(Q) \cap \mathrm{dom}(S) : Q_n \neq S_n\}.$$

The intuition behind these definitions is the following. A node $v_1 \in V'$ represents the subset of configurations of X_K whose restriction to $V \backslash B^+$ is compatible with the patterns of v_1. An edge to v_2 with label S represents the action of shifting the configuration "to the left" by $\boldsymbol{e}_1$ and specifying the contents of the infinite strip $B^+ \cap B^-$ in the shifted version. Since the configuration is K-periodic, it is enough to specify the contents of $D \cdot R$, which is exactly the domain of S. Thus, a two-way infinite walk in the graph G' determines a full K-periodic configuration. Since X is an SFT defined by F, it suffices to keep track of translates of $P \in F$ whose domain intersects $B^+ \cap B^-$. The patterns are shifted to the left with the entire configuration. They are not allowed to leave B^+ before being "handled" by disagreeing with the configuration on some element of $B^+ \cap B^-$, since then they would occur in the completely specified part of the configuration.

Example 1. We illustrate this part of the algorithm with a simple example. Let $X \subset \{0,1\}^{\mathbb{Z}^2}$ be the SFT on the grid graph defined by forbidding the single pattern $P = 00$ of domain $\{((0,0),a),((1,0),a)\}$. Choose $K = \{(0,2)\}$ and take $D = \{(0,0),(0,1)\}$ as the fundamental domain of $K \cup \{\boldsymbol{e}_1\}$. Then $U = \{0\} \times 2\mathbb{Z}$ is the even part of the y-axis and $B = \{0\} \times \mathbb{Z}$ is the whole axis. The left and right sides of the border are $R^- = \{((x,y),a) \in \mathbb{Z}^2 \times R \mid x \leq 0\}$ and $B^+ = \{((x,y),a) \in \mathbb{Z}^2 \times R \mid x \geq 0\}$.

The graph $G' = (V', E')$ has the following structure. Each vertex $v \in V'$ is a set of translates $Q = (x,y) \cdot P$. Since we require $\mathrm{dom}(Q)$ to intersect B^+ and B^-, we must have $x \in \{-1, 0\}$. Also, $(x,y) \cdot P \in v$ if and only if $(x, y+2) \cdot P \in v$, so v is completely determined by its intersection with the set

$$v' = \{P, (-1,0) \cdot P, (0,1) \cdot P, (-1,1) \cdot P\}.$$

In particular, $|V'| = 2^4 = 16$.

The edge set E' is defined using the set $v_0 = \{(0,y) \cdot P \mid y \in \mathbb{Z}\}$ of patterns whose support lies inside B^+ and intersects B^-. Each $v_1 \in V'$ and $S \in \{0,1\}^{D \cdot R}$, where $D \cdot R = \{((0,0),a),((0,1),a)\}$, may define an edge $(v_1, v_2) \in E'$ as follows:

1. add all patterns of v_0 into v_1;
2. remove those that have a K-translate that is incompatible with S; and
3. shift every remaining pattern to the left; the result if v_2.
4. If there remain patterns whose domain does not intersect B^+, reject.

For example, suppose $v_1 \cap v' = \{P, (-1,1) \cdot P\}$, and $S = \frac{1}{0}$. First we add all patterns of v_0, so our intersection with v' is now $\{P, (0,1) \cdot P, (-1,1) \cdot P\}$. Then we remove all patterns that are incompatible with S; since S has a 1 at $((0,1),a)$, both $(0,1) \cdot P$ and $(-1,1) \cdot P$ are incompatible with it, so we are left with $\{P\}$. We shift it to the left, producing $\{(-1,0) \cdot P\}$. Since $(-1,0) \cdot P$ intersects B^+, we do not reject. This edge is visualized in Fig. 2. On the other hand, $S = \genfrac{}{}{0pt}{}{0}{1}$ would have resulted in the set $\{(-2,1) \cdot P, (-1,1) \cdot P, (0,1) \cdot P\}$, which we reject. Thus there is no edge from v_1 with label $\genfrac{}{}{0pt}{}{0}{1}$.

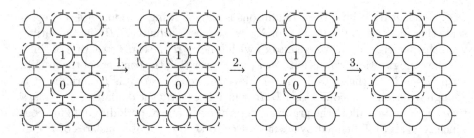

Fig. 2. An edge in the graph G' with label $\genfrac{}{}{0pt}{}{1}{0}$. The dashed boxes mark translates of the forbidden pattern P, which consists of two 0s.

All in all, we have computed a finite digraph $G' = (V', E')$ whose edges are labeled by patterns in $A^{D \cdot R}$. If we replace each label S by its density $\sum_{v \in \text{dom}(S)} W(v)/|\text{dom}(S)| \in \mathbb{R}$, then the minimum weight $W(X_K)$ equals the minimum weight of a bi-infinite walk on G'. The latter, in turn, is achieved by a simple cycle [15, Lemma 4.1], so it suffices to compute the minimum density of a simple cycle in G'. For that, we use Karp's minimum mean cycle algorithm [7], which is readily parallelizable.

We perform some additional optimizations to reduce the size of the graph G' labeled by $\mathbb{R}$ before applying Karp's algorithm. Namely, we iterate the following operations until the graph no longer changes:

1. Simplify the graph using a modified version of Hopcroft's algorithm for DFA minimization [5], resulting in a potentially smaller graph that has the same set of labels of finite (and thus bi-infinite) walks.[2]
2. For each pair of vertices $v, v' \in V'$, remove all edges from v to v' except the one with the smallest weight.

Minimization does not change the set of labels of bi-infinite walks on a graph, and the second operation does not change the minimum density of such walks, so they are safe for our purposes.

---

[2] Note that our graph is not *right resolving* in the sense of [9, Definition 3.3.1], which corresponds to being a DFA instead of an NFA. Thus the result may not be minimal in the sense of having the absolute smallest number of vertices of any graph with the same set of labels of walks. Nevertheless, the algorithm never increases the number of vertices, and in practice can substantially decrease it.

We have already used this functionality to find a new identifying code on the infinite hexagonal grid with density 53/126 [15], down from the previous record of 3/7 [3]. To reproduce the code, define the hexagonal grid and the SFT of identifying codes as in Sect. 4, and run the commands

```
%compute_forbidden_patterns radius=3 idcode
%minimum_density idcode threads=3 (5,1)
```

Here, `threads=3` is an *optional argument* specifying the number of threads (several commands accept some optional arguments, but `%minimum_density` is currently the only one to use parallel computation). The computation takes about 17 min on a laptop computer.

7.2 Lower Bounds by Discharging

We then describe the algorithm for computing lower bounds for $W(X)$. This algorithm does not depend on the existence of periodic points. Given enough computational resources, it will give arbitrarily good approximations to $W(X)$.

The theoretical background is the *discharging argument* used widely in graph theory [4]. We describe it in our context. The idea is to re-distribute the weights of the nodes using deterministic local rules, and prove by a finitary argument that the resulting configuration of weights is always at least some constant α everywhere, implying $W(X) \geq \alpha$. The *initial charge* of a configuration $x \in A^V$ is the function $C_x : \mathbb{Z}^d \to \mathbb{R}$ defined as $C_x(n) = \sum_{r \in R} W(x_{n \cdot r})/|R|$. Given a topology $G = (V, E)$ with a representative set $R \subset V$ and an alphabet A, a *discharging rule* is a triple (P, m, c) where $P \in A^D$ is a finite pattern, $m \in \mathbb{Z}^d$ and $c \in \mathbb{R}$. A finite set $\mathcal{D}$ of discharging rules defines a new charge $\mathcal{D}(C_x)$ by

$$\mathcal{D}(C_x)(n) = C_x(n) + \left(\sum_{\substack{(P,m,c) \in \mathcal{D} \\ ((n-m)\cdot x)|_{\mathrm{dom}(P)}=P}} c \right) - \left(\sum_{\substack{(P,m,c) \in \mathcal{D} \\ (n \cdot x)|_{\mathrm{dom}(P)}=P}} c \right). \quad (1)$$

Note that $\mathcal{D}$ preserves the density of a charge. Hence, if $X \subset A^V$ is a G-subshift and $\mathcal{D}(C_x)(n) \geq \alpha$ for all $x \in X$ and $n \in \mathbb{Z}^d$, then $W(X) \geq \alpha$. To prove that $\mathcal{D}(C_x)(n) \geq \alpha$ always holds, it suffices to consider every pattern $Q \in A^N$ that occurs in X, where $N \subset V$ is finite but large enough to contain the domain of P and $-m \cdot P$ for all $(P, m, c) \in \mathcal{D}$, and show that each of them satisfies $\mathcal{D}(C_x)(0) \geq \alpha$ whenever $x|_N = Q$. This is a finite computation.

Example 1. Consider again the SFT X from Example 1. For a configuration $x \in X$, the initial charge at $n \in \mathbb{Z}^2$ is $C_x(n) = 1$ if $x_{(n,a)} = 1$, and 0 otherwise. In order to prove that the minimum density of a configuration of X is at least $1/2$, we define the following discharging rule: every node that contains a 0 sends a charge of $-1/2$ to its right neighbor. Formally, it is the triple $t = (P, (1, 0), -1/2)$ where P is the pattern with domain $\{((0,0),a)\}$ containing a 0. The singleton set $\mathcal{D} = \{t\}$ defines $\mathcal{D}(C_x)$ according to (1): the new charge of n is its old charge $C_x(n)$, plus the amount of charge it received from the rules of other cells $(-1/2$

if its right neighbor is a 0, and 0 otherwise), minus the amount of charge it sent ($-1/2$ if it is a 0, and 0 otherwise). Since the right neighbor of a 0 is never a 0, the new charge of each cell containing 0 is $1/2$. The new charge of each cell containing a 1 is at least $1/2$, because at most one neighbor can send it the charge of $-1/2$. This gives a lower bound of $1/2$ for the density.

We use the idea of Stolee [16], and employ a linear program to find a good set of discharging rules automatically. First, fix a finite domain $D \subset V$ and a finite set of vectors $T \subset \mathbb{Z}^d$. Generate a set of patterns $\mathcal{P} \subset A^D$ that includes all patterns of shape D that occur in X, by enumerating all locally allowed patterns over some larger finite domain. Our triples will be $(P, m, c(P, m))$ for all $P \in \mathcal{P}$ and $m \in T$, with $c(P, m) \in \mathbb{R}$ being unconstrained variables in our linear program. We also add another variable $\alpha \in \mathbb{R}$.

Next, generate another set of patterns $\mathcal{Q} \subset A^{D'}$ over the domain $D' = \bigcup_{m \in T \cup \{0\}} -m \cdot D$ that contains all D'-shaped patterns occurring in X. Each pattern $Q \in \mathcal{Q}$ defines a constraint for the linear program, similarly to (1): the value of α must be less than or equal to the sum of $C_Q(0)$, each $c(P, m)$ for which $(-m \cdot Q)|_D = P$, and each $-c(P, m)$ for which $Q|_D = P$. Any set of values for α and the $c(P, m)$ that satisfy the constraints gives a valid lower bound for $W(X)$. Hence, we should maximize the value of α under the constraints.

A solution of the linear program is a best possible discharging strategy that transfers charge along the vectors T based on occurrences of the patterns $\mathcal{P}$, given that the SFT X may contain any of the patterns $\mathcal{Q}$. Adding more nodes to the domain D or more vectors to T, or refining the sets $\mathcal{P}$ or $\mathcal{Q}$, generally results in a better bound, but the computational cost will increase accordingly. The associated Diddy command is %density_lower_bound vectors domain. As an example, we can compute a lower bound for the density of an identifying code on the hexagonal grid by %density_lower_bound idcode (0,-1) (0,1) (1,0); (0,0,0) (0,0,1) (-1,0,1) (0,1,1) (0,-1,0) (1,0,0). In about 65 s, Diddy produces the bound 0.4, same as in the article [8] that introduced the problem. It has since been greatly improved, most recently to $23/55$ [16].

8 Future Directions

Below is a partial list of features that the authors plan to implement.

- Better support for general block maps between distinct SFTs.
- Condition 2 of the SFT comparison algorithm could be extended to e.g. semi-linear or automatic configurations.
- Many problems that are undecidable for two- and higher-dimensional SFTs can be solved effectively in the one-dimensional case, using finite automata theory and linear algebra. See e.g. [9, Sections 3.4 and 4.3]. Diddy should include total algorithms for this special case.
- The *trace* of a 2D SFT is set of infinite columns occurring in its configurations. It can be seen as a 1D subshift that can be approximated from the above (sometimes exactly) by sofic shifts. Diddy should include functionality for extracting and analyzing traces of multidimensional SFTs.

Acknowledgments. Ilkka Törmä was supported by the Academy of Finland under grant 346566.

References

1. Audemard, G., Simon, L.: Glucose 4.1 (2016). https://www.labri.fr/perso/lsimon/research/glucose/
2. Berger, R.: The undecidability of the domino problem. Mem. Amer. Math. Soc. No. **66**, 72 (1966)
3. Cohen, G.D., Honkala, I., Lobstein, A., Zémor, G.: Bounds for codes identifying vertices in the hexagonal grid. SIAM J. Discrete Math. **13**(4), 492–504 (2000). https://doi.org/10.1137/S0895480199360990
4. Cranston, D.W., West, D.B.: An introduction to the discharging method via graph coloring. Discrete Math. **340**(4), 766–793 (2017). https://doi.org/10.1016/j.disc.2016.11.022
5. Hopcroft, J.: An $n \log n$ algorithm for minimizing states in a finite automaton. In: Theory of machines and computations (Proc. Internat. Sympos., Technion, Haifa, 1971), pp. 189–196. Academic Press, New York (1971)
6. Ignatiev, A., Morgado, A., Marques-Silva, J.: PySAT: a python toolkit for prototyping with SAT oracles. In: SAT, pp. 428–437 (2018). https://doi.org/10.1007/978-3-319-94144-8_26
7. Karp, R.M.: A characterization of the minimum cycle mean in a digraph. Discrete Math. **23**(3), 309–311 (1978). https://doi.org/10.1016/0012-365X(78)90011-0
8. Karpovsky, M.G., Chakrabarty, K., Levitin, L.B.: On a new class of codes for identifying vertices in graphs. IEEE Trans. Inform. Theory **44**(2), 599–611 (1998). https://doi.org/10.1109/18.661507
9. Lind, D., Marcus, B.: An Introduction to Symbolic Dynamics and Coding. Cambridge University Press, Cambridge (1995). https://doi.org/10.1017/CBO9780511626302
10. Pygame development team: Pygame 2.3.0 (2023). https://github.com/pygame
11. Roy, J., Mitchell, S.A., Duquesne, C.M., Peschiera, F.: PuLP 2.7.0 (2022). https://github.com/coin-or/pulp
12. Salo, V., Törmä, I.: Gardens of eden in the game of life. In: Automata and complexity–essays presented to Eric Goles on the occasion of his 70th birthday, Emerg. Complex. Comput., vol. 42, pp. 399–415. Springer, Cham (2022). https://doi.org/10.1007/978-3-030-92551-2_22
13. Salo, V., Törmä, I.: What can oracles teach us about the ultimate fate of life? In: 49th EATCS International Conference on Automata, Languages, and Programming, LIPIcs. Leibniz Int. Proc. Inform., vol. 229, pp. Art. No. 131, 20. Schloss Dagstuhl. Leibniz-Zent. Inform., Wadern (2022). https://doi.org/10.4230/lipics.icalp.2022.131
14. Salo, V., Törmä, I.: Diddy (2023). https://github.com/ilkka-torma/diddy
15. Salo, V., Törmä, I.: Finding codes on infinite grids automatically (2023)
16. Stolee, D.: Automated discharging arguments for density problems in grids (2014)
17. Wang, H.: Proving theorems by pattern recognition II. Bell Syst. Tech. J. **40**, 1–42 (1961)
18. Wolfram, S.: Statistical mechanics of cellular automata. Rev. Mod. Phys. **55**(3), 601–644 (1983). https://doi.org/10.1103/RevModPhys.55.601

Convergence of Vector-Valued Fuzzy Cellular Automata with Weighted-Averaging Rules

Yuki Nishida[1]([✉])[iD], Koki Yamasaki[2], Sennosuke Watanabe[3][iD],
Akiko Fukuda[4][iD], and Yoshihide Watanabe[2]

[1] Tokyo University of Science, Katsushika, Tokyo 125-8585, Japan
ynishida@rs.tus.ac.jp
[2] Doshisha University, Kyotonabe, Kyoto 610-0394, Japan
[3] The Univeristy of Fukuchiyama, Fukuchiyama, Kyoto 620-0886, Japan
[4] Shibaura Institute of Technology, Saitama, Saitama 337-8570, Japan

Abstract. Fuzzy cellular automata are dynamical systems that are continuous counterparts of the usual cellular automata (CA). Compared with the binary case, defining a fuzzy CA with three or more states is challenging because defining mixed states is difficult. Recently, this difficulty was resolved by representing multiple states as independent vectors in higher dimensions, and the concept of vector-valued fuzzy CA (VFCA) was introduced. In this study, we theoretically analyze and discuss the asymptotic behavior of three-state, three-neighbor VFCA. First, we define the weighted-averaging rules of VFCA and show how many rules exist up to the equivalence relations. According to these rules, each state vector in the next step is determined by the weighted average of the vectors in its neighboring cells. Next, we prove that VFCA with weighted-averaging rules converge to a periodic configuration characterized by the symmetric group of order 3. In particular, the non-commutativity of the group action provides an interesting behavior that is not observed in fuzzy CA arising from binary states. These results can be extended to VFCA with more than three states and/or three neighbors.

Keywords: Fuzzy cellular automata · Vector-valued cellular automata · Weighted-averaging rule · Periodic behavior

1 Introduction

Cellular automata (CA) are dynamical systems that describe cell configurations that evolve concurrently in accordance with a local update rule based on neighboring cells. CA are used as tools for mathematical modeling in areas such as traffic flows and life sciences. One of the simplest CA is a one-dimensional two-state, three-neighbor CA, also known as the elementary CA (ECA). The local rule of an ECA can be expressed in a disjunctive normal form in Boolean algebra, which can be converted into a usual polynomial. It provides the local rule

© IFIP International Federation for Information Processing 2023
Published by Springer Nature Switzerland AG 2023
L. Manzoni et al. (Eds.): AUTOMATA 2023, LNCS 14152, pp. 48–59, 2023.
https://doi.org/10.1007/978-3-031-42250-8_4

of an elementary fuzzy CA (EFCA) [1], which is a continuous counterpart of the ECA whose state set is the closed interval $[0, 1]$. In this study, fuzzy CA does not refer to CA on fuzzy sets [2] or the fuzzy choice of local rules [3]. Although ECA rule 184 is famous for traffic models, the application of EFCA rule 184 to traffic flows was recently proposed [4].

Compared with the binary case, defining a fuzzy CA with three or more states is not easy. We previously introduced a vector-valued CA to apply fuzzification to CA with three or more states [5]. The results are briefly summarized. Let e_1, e_2, e_3 be the standard basis vectors of $\mathbb{R}^3$. The integer-valued states $2, 1, 0$ are associated with e_1, e_2, e_3, yielding the state set $Q = \{e_1, e_2, e_3\}$ of three-state vector-valued CA. For $i \in \mathbb{Z}$ and $t \in \mathbb{Z}_{\geq 0}$, where $\mathbb{Z}_{\geq 0}$ is the set of nonnegative integers, let x_i^t denote the vector in cell i at time step t. In the case of three-neighbor CA, the evolution is determined by the local rule $f : Q^3 \to Q$ as $x_i^{t+1} = f(x_{i-1}^t, x_i^t, x_{i+1}^t)$. Then, the local rule f can also be expressed as:

$$f(\boldsymbol{x}, \boldsymbol{y}, \boldsymbol{z}) = \begin{pmatrix} \sum_{f(e_j, e_k, e_\ell) = e_1} x_j y_k z_\ell \\ \sum_{f(e_j, e_k, e_\ell) = e_2} x_j y_k z_\ell \\ \sum_{f(e_j, e_k, e_\ell) = e_3} x_j y_k z_\ell \end{pmatrix}, \tag{1}$$

where $\boldsymbol{x} = (x_1, x_2, x_3)^\top, \boldsymbol{y} = (y_1, y_2, y_3)^\top$ and $\boldsymbol{z} = (z_1, z_2, z_3)^\top$. Consider the two-dimensional simplex Δ with vertices e_1, e_2, e_3:

$$\Delta = \left\{ (x_1, x_2, x_3)^\top \in \mathbb{R}^3 \mid x_1 + x_2 + x_3 = 1, \ x_1, x_2, x_3 \geq 0 \right\}.$$

The domain of function f can be expanded from Q^3 to Δ^3 through the right-hand side of (1), and f satisfies $f(\Delta^3) \subset \Delta$. Consequently, the state set Q can be expanded to Δ, and a vector-valued fuzzy CA (VFCA), which is a continuous-valued CA with local rule $f : \Delta^3 \to \Delta$, is obtained. The expression (1) is similar to the disjunctive normal form of a local rule of ECA. Thus, VFCA can be regarded as an extension of EFCA introduced in [1], which is the reason why we use the term *fuzzy*. In a recent study [6], VFCA are related to stochastic CA because vectors in Δ are considered to express the probability for each state. As in EFCA, traffic flow models in terms of VFCA were discussed in [6,7]. Thus, theoretical study of VFCA will help the analysis of both deterministic and stochastic mathematical models.

1.1 Our Contributions

In this study, we consider the asymptotic behavior of VFCA, especially the convergence of VFCA. Hereafter, all CA are assumed to satisfy the periodic boundary condition with a positive integer period L; that is, $x_i^t = x_{i+L}^t$ for $i \in \mathbb{Z}$ and $t \in \mathbb{Z}_{\geq 0}$. The local rule f of a VFCA induces the global rule $F : \Delta^L \to \Delta^L$. A VFCA with the initial configuration $\boldsymbol{X}^0 \in \Delta^L$ can be expressed as the sequence $\{\boldsymbol{X}^t\}_{t \in \mathbb{Z}_{\geq 0}}$, where $\boldsymbol{X}^{t+1} = F(\boldsymbol{X}^t)$ for $t \in \mathbb{Z}_{\geq 0}$. Let $[\boldsymbol{x}_i]_k$ denote the kth component of $\boldsymbol{x}_i$. The convergence of VFCA is defined with respect to the following metric d on Δ^L:

$$d((\boldsymbol{x}_0, \boldsymbol{x}_1, \ldots, \boldsymbol{x}_{L-1}), (\boldsymbol{y}_0, \boldsymbol{y}_1, \ldots, \boldsymbol{y}_{L-1})) = \max_{i=0,1,\ldots,L-1} \max_{k=1,2,3} |[\boldsymbol{x}_i]_k - [\boldsymbol{y}_i]_k|.$$

First, we define the weighted-averaging local rules of VFCA. In these rules, each state vector x_i^{t+1} is determined by the weighted average of two of the three neighboring vectors $x_{i-1}^t, x_i^t, x_{i+1}^t$. These rules were discussed in EFCA [8]. Because we consider a three-dimensional vector, we can permute the entries of each vector before taking the weighted average. We present a brief description of how many different weighted-averaging rules exist up to the equivalence relations. These VFCA systems exhibit asymptotically periodic behavior in both time and space. The main section provides a theoretical proof of the convergence of VFCA with weighted-averaging rules. Using a transformation of VFCA into another CA admitting different local rules for each cell, we present a proof that is applicable to many types of weighted-averaging rules. We demonstrate that the action of the symmetric group S_3 plays a crucial role in classifying the periodic pattern of behavior. In particular, the non-commutativity of S_3 induces a special type of convergence not observed in EFCA.

1.2 Related Works

The asymptotic behavior of EFCA has been discussed in several studies. For example, self-averaging rules [9] and weighted-averaging rules [8] are important classes of EFCA local rules, such that their convergence may be analytically proven. The dynamics of several specific rules have been individually studied, such as EFCA rules 90 [10] and 184 [11]. In computer simulations for some VFCA corresponding to traffic models [6,7], it was suggested that such VFCA converge to homogeneous configurations after sufficiently large steps. In contrast, this study focuses on a theoretical analysis of the convergence of VFCA.

2 Weighted-Averaging Rules in VFCA

In this section, we focus on several special rules of VFCA, called weighted-averaging rules. The formal definitions are as follows. Let us define the action of S_3 on Δ by $\sigma(x) = ([x]_{\sigma^{-1}(1)}, [x]_{\sigma^{-1}(2)}, [x]_{\sigma^{-1}(3)})^\top$ for $x \in \Delta$ and $\sigma \in S_3$. The local rule f of a VFCA is called a weighted-averaging rule if it is expressed in one of the following forms:

$$f(x, y, z) = (1 - \langle x \rangle) \cdot \sigma(y) + \langle x \rangle \cdot \tau(z), \tag{2}$$

$$f(x, y, z) = (1 - \langle z \rangle) \cdot \sigma(y) + \langle z \rangle \cdot \tau(x), \tag{3}$$

$$f(x, y, z) = (1 - \langle y \rangle) \cdot \sigma(x) + \langle y \rangle \cdot \tau(z). \tag{4}$$

Here, $\sigma, \tau \in S_3$ and $\langle x \rangle$ is one of $[x]_1, [x]_2, [x]_3, 1 - [x]_1, 1 - [x]_2, 1 - [x]_3$. Because there are six choices for σ, τ and $\langle x \rangle$, we have $6 \times 6 \times 6 = 216$ local rules for each type (2)–(4). In particular, the local rules of forms (2) and (3) are called the weighted-averaging rules of type 1, and the local rules of the form (4) are called those of type 2.

We introduce an equivalence relation for the local rules of VFCA. The action of $\rho \in S_3$ on $f : \Delta^3 \to \Delta$ is defined as

$$(\rho \circ f)(x, y, z) = \rho(f(\rho^{-1}(x), \rho^{-1}(y), \rho^{-1}(z))).$$

We also define the reflection r as

$$(r \circ f)(\boldsymbol{x}, \boldsymbol{y}, \boldsymbol{z}) = f(\boldsymbol{z}, \boldsymbol{y}, \boldsymbol{x}).$$

Then, the two local rules are said to be equivalent if one is obtained from the other by the action of $\rho \in S_3$, reflection, or their composition. Specifically, (2) and (3) provide equivalent local rules. Based on this equivalence relation, 432 weighted-averaging rules of forms (2) and (3) are divided into 40 equivalence classes. Note that some equivalence classes contain only 6 rules, whereas others contain 12 rules. For example, consider the local rule

$$f(\boldsymbol{x}, \boldsymbol{y}, \boldsymbol{z}) = (1 - [\boldsymbol{x}]_1) \cdot \sigma(\boldsymbol{y}) + [\boldsymbol{x}]_1 \cdot \boldsymbol{z}$$

with $\sigma = (2\ 3)$. It is essential that $\sigma(1) = 1$. Subsequently, for $\rho \in S_3$, we obtain

$$
\begin{aligned}
((\rho\sigma) \circ f)(\boldsymbol{x}, \boldsymbol{y}, \boldsymbol{z}) \\
&= (1 - [\boldsymbol{x}]_{\rho\sigma(1)}) \cdot \rho\sigma(\sigma(\sigma^{-1}\rho^{-1}(\boldsymbol{y}))) + [\boldsymbol{x}]_{\rho\sigma(1)} \cdot \rho\sigma(\sigma^{-1}\rho^{-1}(\boldsymbol{z})) \\
&= (1 - [\boldsymbol{x}]_{\rho(1)}) \cdot \rho(\sigma(\rho^{-1}(\boldsymbol{y}))) + [\boldsymbol{x}]_{\rho(1)} \cdot \rho(\rho^{-1}(\boldsymbol{z})) \\
&= (\rho \circ f)(\boldsymbol{x}, \boldsymbol{y}, \boldsymbol{z}).
\end{aligned}
$$

Therefore, each rule appears twice owing to the action of S_3, which reduces the number of rules in the equivalence class by half. Representatives of such types of equivalence classes are of the form (2), where $\langle \boldsymbol{x} \rangle = [\boldsymbol{x}]_1$ or $1 - [\boldsymbol{x}]_1$, and σ, τ are identities or $(2\ 3)$. Therefore, there are eight classes that contain six rules. Similarly, 216 weighted-averaging rules of the forms (4) are divided into 20 equivalence classes.

To prove the convergence of VFCA with the weighted-averaging rules, we use a general framework. Let $\mathrm{int}(\Delta)$ be the relative interior of Δ; that is

$$\mathrm{int}(\Delta) = \left\{ (x_1, x_2, x_3)^{\top} \in \mathbb{R}^3 \mid x_1 + x_2 + x_3 = 1,\ x_1, x_2, x_3 > 0 \right\}.$$

Hereafter, the indices of the cells are considered in modulo L if not specified.

Proposition 1. *Let $\{X^t\}_{t \in \mathbb{Z}_{\geq 0}}$ be a sequence in Δ^L with $X^0 \in \mathrm{int}(\Delta)^L$, where $X^t = (\boldsymbol{x}_0^t, \boldsymbol{x}_1^t, \ldots, \boldsymbol{x}_{L-1}^t)$. Suppose that the evolution can be written as*

$$\boldsymbol{x}_i^{t+1} = (1 - \gamma_i^t)\boldsymbol{x}_i^t + \gamma_i^t \boldsymbol{x}_{i+1}^t.$$

If there exists γ with $0 < \gamma < 1/2$ such that $\gamma_i^t \in [\gamma, 1 - \gamma]$ for all $i \in \mathbb{Z}$ and $t \in \mathbb{Z}_{\geq 0}$, then there exists $\boldsymbol{p} \in \Delta$ such that X^t converges to a homogeneous configuration $X^* = (\boldsymbol{p}, \boldsymbol{p}, \ldots, \boldsymbol{p})$ as $t \to \infty$.

In the proof of Proposition 1, we use the following result for EFCA:

Lemma 1 ([8]). *Let $\{X^t\}_{t \in \mathbb{Z}_{\geq 0}}$ be a sequence in $[0, 1]^L$ with $X^0 \in (0, 1)^L$, where $X^t = (x_0^t, x_1^t, \ldots, x_{L-1}^t)$. Suppose that the evolution can be written as*

$$x_i^{t+1} = (1 - \gamma_i^t)x_i^t + \gamma_i^t x_{i+1}^t.$$

If there exists γ with $0 < \gamma < 1/2$ such that $\gamma_i^t \in [\gamma, 1 - \gamma]$ for all $i \in \mathbb{Z}$ and $t \in \mathbb{Z}_{\geq 0}$, then there exists $p \in [0, 1]$ such that X^t converges to the homogeneous configuration $(p, p, \ldots, p)$ as $t \to \infty$.

Proof (Proposition 1). For each $k \in \{1, 2, 3\}$, the initial configuration satisfies $([\boldsymbol{x}_0^0]_k, [\boldsymbol{x}_1^0]_k, \ldots, [\boldsymbol{x}_{L-1}^0]_k) \in (0, 1)^L$. Moreover, the evolution can be written as

$$[\boldsymbol{x}_i^{t+1}]_k = (1 - \gamma_i^t)[\boldsymbol{x}_i^t]_k + \gamma_i^t[\boldsymbol{x}_{i+1}^t]_k.$$

Therefore, the sequence $\{X_k^t\}_{t \in \mathbb{Z}_{\geq 0}}$ where $X_k^t = ([\boldsymbol{x}_0^t]_k, [\boldsymbol{x}_1^t]_k, \ldots, [\boldsymbol{x}_{L-1}^t]_k)$ satisfies the assumption of Lemma 1. Thus, $[\boldsymbol{x}_i^t]_k$ converges to the same constant $p_k \in [0, 1]$ independent of cell i. This implies that $\boldsymbol{x}_i^t$ converges to the same vector $\boldsymbol{p} = (p_1, p_2, p_3)^\top \in \Delta$ independent of cell i. □

3   Convergence of VFCA with Weighted-Averaging Rules

We now present the convergence statement of VFCA with weighted-averaging rules. In contrast to the case of EFCA, we observe two types of convergence depending on whether σ and τ are commutative, that is, $\sigma\tau = \tau\sigma$. For simplicity, the period L is assumed to be a multiple of $|S_3| = 6$.

3.1   Commutative Case of the Weighted-Averaging Rules of Type 1

Figure 1 (left) illustrates the space-time diagram of VFCA whose local rule is

$$f(\boldsymbol{x}, \boldsymbol{y}, \boldsymbol{z}) = \begin{pmatrix} (x_2 + x_3)y_2 + x_1 z_3 \\ (x_2 + x_3)y_3 + x_1 z_1 \\ (x_2 + x_3)y_1 + x_1 z_2 \end{pmatrix} = (1 - x_1) \begin{pmatrix} y_2 \\ y_3 \\ y_1 \end{pmatrix} + x_1 \begin{pmatrix} z_3 \\ z_1 \\ z_2 \end{pmatrix}.$$

Here, $\sigma = (1\ 3\ 2)$ and $\tau = (1\ 2\ 3)$ are commutative. We observed that this VFCA exhibited periodic behavior in both time (vertical axis) and space (horizontal axis) after a sufficient number of time steps. This is stated in the following theorem. Note that $\operatorname{ord}\sigma$ is the order of a permutation σ in S_3.

Theorem 1. *Suppose* $\boldsymbol{X}^0 = (\boldsymbol{x}_0^0, \boldsymbol{x}_1^0, \ldots, \boldsymbol{x}_{L-1}^0) \in \operatorname{int}(\Delta)^L$. *If* σ *and* τ *are commutative, there exists* $\boldsymbol{p} \in \Delta$ *such that the VFCA with the weighted-averaging rule* (2) *periodically converges as follows:*

$$\boldsymbol{X}^t \to (\sigma^s(\boldsymbol{p}), \sigma^s\pi^{-1}(\boldsymbol{p}), \ldots, \sigma^s\pi^{-(L-1)}(\boldsymbol{p})), \quad t = s \bmod (\operatorname{ord}\sigma).$$

Here, $\pi = \sigma^{-1}\tau$ *and* $0 \leq s \leq \operatorname{ord}\sigma - 1$.

We note that the vector $\boldsymbol{p}$ in Theorem 1 depends on the initial configuration and is not obtained explicitly in a simple formula.

Proof. First, we verify that $m^t := \min_i \min_{k=1,2,3} [\boldsymbol{x}_i^t]_k$ is nondecreasing and $M^t := \max_i \max_{k=1,2,3} [\boldsymbol{x}_i^t]_k$ is nonincreasing. For any i and $k \in \{1, 2, 3\}$,

$$\begin{aligned}
[\boldsymbol{x}_i^{t+1}]_k &= (1 - \langle \boldsymbol{x}_{i-1}^t \rangle) \cdot [\sigma(\boldsymbol{x}_i^t)]_k + \langle \boldsymbol{x}_{i-1}^t \rangle \cdot [\tau(\boldsymbol{x}_{i+1}^t)]_k \\
&= (1 - \langle \boldsymbol{x}_{i-1}^t \rangle) \cdot [\boldsymbol{x}_i^t]_{\sigma^{-1}(k)} + \langle \boldsymbol{x}_{i-1}^t \rangle \cdot [\boldsymbol{x}_{i+1}^t]_{\tau^{-1}(k)} \\
&\geq \min([\boldsymbol{x}_i^t]_{\sigma^{-1}(k)}, [\boldsymbol{x}_{i+1}^t]_{\tau^{-1}(k)}) \\
&\geq m^t.
\end{aligned}$$

Fig. 1. To visualize the evolution of VFCA, we use the RGB color system. The states e_1, e_2, and e_3 are associated with red, green, and blue, respectively. An inner point of Δ is expressed by the mixture of the three colors. (left) Space-time diagram for a complete number-conserving rule (rule 3,226,064,485,963 by Wolfram's numbering rule [12]). (right) Space-time diagram for a weighted averaging rule (rule 3,226,250,775,339) (Color figure online)

Here, the property of the weighted average was used. Therefore, $m^{t+1} \geq m^t$. Similarly, we show that $M^{t+1} \leq M^t$. In particular, if we take $\gamma > 0$ such that $\gamma \leq m^0 \leq M^0 \leq 1 - \gamma$, then both $[\boldsymbol{x}_i^t]_k$ and $1 - [\boldsymbol{x}_i^t]_k$ are in the interval $[\gamma, 1 - \gamma]$ for all i, t, and k.

The local rule (2) can be written as

$$f(\boldsymbol{x}, \boldsymbol{y}, \boldsymbol{z}) = \sigma((1 - \langle \boldsymbol{x} \rangle) \cdot \boldsymbol{y} + \langle \boldsymbol{x} \rangle \cdot \pi(\boldsymbol{z})),$$

where $\pi = \sigma^{-1}\tau$. Let $F : \Delta^L \to \Delta^L$ be the global rule of this VFCA. For each $t \in \mathbb{Z}_{\geq 0}$ and $i = 0, 1, \ldots, L - 1$ we define the local function as

$$g_{t,i}(\boldsymbol{x}, \boldsymbol{y}, \boldsymbol{z}) = (1 - \langle \sigma^t \pi^{-(i-1)}(\boldsymbol{x}) \rangle) \cdot \boldsymbol{y} + \langle \sigma^t \pi^{-(i-1)}(\boldsymbol{x}) \rangle \cdot \boldsymbol{z}. \tag{5}$$

Note that this local function differs for each cell i and time t. In addition, we define the global map $G_t : \Delta^L \to \Delta^L$ as

$$\begin{aligned} G_t(\boldsymbol{x}_0, \boldsymbol{x}_1, \ldots, \boldsymbol{x}_{L-1}) \\ = (g_{t,0}(\boldsymbol{x}_{L-1}, \boldsymbol{x}_0, \boldsymbol{x}_1), g_{t,1}(\boldsymbol{x}_0, \boldsymbol{x}_1, \boldsymbol{x}_2), \ldots, g_{t,L-1}(\boldsymbol{x}_{L-2}, \boldsymbol{x}_{L-1}, \boldsymbol{x}_0)). \end{aligned} \tag{6}$$

We also define the bijection $h_t : \Delta^L \to \Delta^L$ as

$$h_t(\boldsymbol{x}_0, \boldsymbol{x}_1, \ldots, \boldsymbol{x}_{L-1}) = (\sigma^{-t}(\boldsymbol{x}_0), \sigma^{-t}\pi(\boldsymbol{x}_1), \ldots, \sigma^{-t}\pi^{L-1}(\boldsymbol{x}_{L-1})).$$

We then show that $h_{t+1} \circ F = G_t \circ h_t$ for all positive integers $t \in \mathbb{Z}_{\geq 0}$.

The vector at cell i of $(h_{t+1} \circ F)(\boldsymbol{x}_0, \boldsymbol{x}_1, \ldots, \boldsymbol{x}_{L-1})$ is

$$\sigma^{-(t+1)}\pi^i(\sigma((1 - \langle \boldsymbol{x}_{i-1} \rangle) \cdot \boldsymbol{x}_i + \langle \boldsymbol{x}_{i-1} \rangle \cdot \pi(\boldsymbol{x}_{i+1})))$$
$$= (1 - \langle \boldsymbol{x}_{i-1} \rangle) \cdot \sigma^{-t}\pi^i(\boldsymbol{x}_i) + \langle \boldsymbol{x}_{i-1} \rangle \cdot \sigma^{-t}\pi^{i+1}(\boldsymbol{x}_{i+1}).$$

In contrast, the vector at cell i of $(G_t \circ h_t)(\boldsymbol{x}_0, \boldsymbol{x}_1, \ldots, \boldsymbol{x}_{L-1})$ is

$$g_{t,i}(\sigma^{-t}\pi^{i-1}(\boldsymbol{x}_{i-1}), \sigma^{-t}\pi^i(\boldsymbol{x}_i), \sigma^{-t}\pi^{i+1}(\boldsymbol{x}_{i+1}))$$
$$= (1 - \langle \sigma^t \pi^{-(i-1)}(\sigma^{-t}\pi^{i-1}(\boldsymbol{x}_{i-1})) \rangle) \cdot \sigma^{-t}\pi^i(\boldsymbol{x}_i)$$
$$+ \langle \sigma^t \pi^{-(i-1)}(\sigma^{-t}\pi^{i-1}(\boldsymbol{x}_{i-1})) \rangle \cdot \sigma^{-t}\pi^{i+1}(\boldsymbol{x}_{i+1})$$
$$= (1 - \langle \boldsymbol{x}_{i-1} \rangle) \cdot \sigma^{-t}\pi^i(\boldsymbol{x}_i) + \langle \boldsymbol{x}_{i-1} \rangle \cdot \sigma^{-t}\pi^{i+1}(\boldsymbol{x}_{i+1}).$$

In both computations, we use $\sigma\pi = \pi\sigma$, which is derived from $\sigma\tau = \tau\sigma$. Because this holds for all $i = 0, 1, \ldots, L-1$, we have $h_{t+1} \circ F = G_t \circ h_t$. Using this system repeatedly, we can express t times the composition of F as

$$F^t = h_t^{-1} \circ (G_{t-1} \circ \cdots \circ G_1 \circ G_0) \circ h_0. \tag{7}$$

We set $\boldsymbol{Y}^0 := h_0(\boldsymbol{X}^0) \in \text{int}(\Delta)^L$. We define $\boldsymbol{Y}^t$ as

$$\boldsymbol{Y}^t = (G_{t-1} \circ \cdots \circ G_1 \circ G_0)(\boldsymbol{Y}^0).$$

From (5) and (6), the sequence $\{\boldsymbol{Y}^t\}_{t \in \mathbb{Z}_{\geq 0}}$ satisfies Proposition 1. Therefore, $\boldsymbol{Y}^t$ converges to a homogeneous configuration $(\boldsymbol{p}, \boldsymbol{p}, \ldots, \boldsymbol{p}) \in \Delta^L$ as $t \to \infty$. From (7), $\boldsymbol{X}^t$ converges to

$$h_t^{-1}(\boldsymbol{p}, \boldsymbol{p}, \ldots, \boldsymbol{p}) = (\sigma^t(\boldsymbol{p}), \sigma^t\pi^{-1}(\boldsymbol{p}), \ldots, \sigma^t\pi^{-(L-1)}(\boldsymbol{p})).$$

In particular, when $t = s \mod (\text{ord}\,\sigma)$, we obtain

$$\boldsymbol{X}^t \to (\sigma^s(\boldsymbol{p}), \sigma^s\pi^{-1}(\boldsymbol{p}), \ldots, \sigma^s\pi^{-(L-1)}(\boldsymbol{p}))$$

as $t \to \infty$.   □

3.2   Non-commutative Case of the Weighted-Averaging Rules of Type 1

Next, we consider the case in which σ and τ are non-commutative. The corresponding VFCA converges to a homogeneous configuration consisting of centroids whenever the initial configuration is in $\text{int}(\Delta)^L$. Figure 1(right) shows the space-time diagram of a VFCA whose local rule is

$$f(\boldsymbol{x}, \boldsymbol{y}, \boldsymbol{z}) = \begin{pmatrix} (x_2 + x_3)y_2 + x_1 z_3 \\ (x_2 + x_3)y_1 + x_1 z_1 \\ (x_2 + x_3)y_3 + x_1 z_2 \end{pmatrix} = (1 - x_1) \begin{pmatrix} y_2 \\ y_1 \\ y_3 \end{pmatrix} + x_1 \begin{pmatrix} z_3 \\ z_1 \\ z_2 \end{pmatrix}.$$

Here, $\sigma = (1\ 2)$ and $\tau = (1\ 2\ 3)$ are non-commutative. We can see that all cells converge to "gray", representing $(1/3, 1/3, 1/3)^\top$.

Theorem 2. *Suppose $X^0 = (x_0^0, x_1^0, \ldots, x_{L-1}^0) \in \text{int}(\Delta)^L$. If σ and τ are non-commutative, then the VFCA with the weighted-averaging rule (2) converges to*

$$X^* = (a, a, \ldots, a),$$

where $a = (1/3, 1/3, 1/3)^\top$.

The following two lemmas will be used in the proof of Theorem 2. Let $S(\sigma, \tau; m, n)$ be the set of all permutations in S_3 obtained from a composition of m times σ and n times τ in any order.

Lemma 2. *Let $m^t = \min_i \min_{k=1,2,3}[x_i^t]_k$, $M^t = \max_i \max_{k=1,2,3}[x_i^t]_k$. Under the assumption in Theorem 2, we consider $\gamma > 0$ such that $\gamma \leq m^0 \leq M^0 \leq 1-\gamma$. At step t, suppose $M^t = [x_i^t]_k$. Then, for any pair (j, s) with $0 \leq j \leq s$ and permutation $\rho \in S(\sigma, \tau; s - j, j)$,*

$$[x_{i-j}^{t+s}]_{\rho(k)} \geq m^t + \gamma^s(M^t - m^t).$$

Proof. As in the proof of Theorem 1, we see that m^t is nondecreasing and M^t is nonincreasing; in particular, both $\langle x_i^t \rangle$ and $1 - \langle x_i^t \rangle$ are in the interval $[\gamma, 1 - \gamma]$ for all i and t. We prove the assertion of this lemma through induction on s. The case $s = 0$ is trivial. Suppose that this assertion is true for $s - 1$. Let $\rho \in S(\sigma, \tau; s - j, j)$.

Case 1: $\rho = \sigma\rho'$ where $\rho' \in S(\sigma, \tau; s - j - 1, j)$.
Under the assumption of induction, we obtain

$$[x_{i-j}^{t+s-1}]_{\rho'(k)} \geq m^t + \gamma^{s-1}(M^t - m^t).$$

Therefore, we have

$$
\begin{aligned}
[x_{i-j}^{t+s}]_{\rho(k)} &= [\sigma^{-1}(x_{i-j}^{t+s})]_{\rho'(k)} \\
&= (1 - \langle x_{i-j-1}^{t+s-1} \rangle) \cdot [x_{i-j}^{t+s-1}]_{\rho'(k)} + \langle x_{i-j-1}^{t+s-1} \rangle \cdot [\sigma^{-1}\tau(x_{i-j+1}^{t+s-1})]_{\rho'(k)} \\
&\geq (1 - \langle x_{i-j-1}^{t+s-1} \rangle) \cdot (m^t + \gamma^{s-1}(M^t - m^t)) + \langle x_{i-j-1}^{t+s-1} \rangle \cdot m^t \\
&\geq \gamma(m^t + \gamma^{s-1}(M^t - m^t)) + (1 - \gamma)m^t \\
&= m^t + \gamma^s(M^t - m^t).
\end{aligned}
$$

In the second inequality, we use the following fact. If $a \geq b$ and $p \geq q$, then $pa + (1 - p)b \geq qa + (1 - q)b$.

Case 2: $\rho = \tau\rho'$ where $\rho' \in S(\sigma, \tau; s - j, j - 1)$.
Under the assumption of induction, we obtain

$$[x_{i-(j-1)}^{t+s-1}]_{\rho'(k)} \geq m^t + \gamma^{s-1}(M^t - m^t).$$

Therefore, we have

$$
\begin{aligned}
[x_{i-j}^{t+s}]_{\rho(k)} &= [\tau^{-1}(x_{i-j}^{t+s})]_{\rho'(k)} \\
&= (1 - \langle x_{i-j-1}^{t+s-1} \rangle) \cdot [\tau^{-1}\sigma(x_{i-j}^{t+s-1})]_{\rho'(k)} + \langle x_{i-j-1}^{t+s-1} \rangle \cdot [x_{i-j+1}^{t+s-1}]_{\rho'(k)} \\
&\geq (1 - \langle x_{i-j-1}^{t+s-1} \rangle) \cdot m^t + \langle x_{i-j-1}^{t+s-1} \rangle \cdot (m^t + \gamma^{s-1}(M^t - m^t)) \\
&\geq (1 - \gamma)m^t + \gamma(m^t + \gamma^{s-1}(M^t - m^t)) \\
&= m^t + \gamma^s(M^t - m^t).
\end{aligned}
$$

Thus, we have proven this lemma by induction. □

Lemma 3. *Suppose $\sigma, \tau \in S_3$ are non-commutative. For any $k, k' \in \{1, 2, 3\}$ and $m, n \geq 3$, there exists a permutation $\rho \in S(\sigma, \tau; m, n)$ such that $\rho(k) = k'$.*

Proof. If σ is a cycle of length 3 and τ is a transposition, we define $\rho_1, \rho_2, \rho_3 \in S(\sigma, \tau; m, n)$ as follows:

$$\rho_1 := (\sigma^{m-3}\tau^{n-2})(\sigma^3\tau^2) = (\sigma^{m-3}\tau^{n-2}),$$
$$\rho_2 := (\sigma^{m-3}\tau^{n-2})(\sigma^2\tau\sigma\tau) = (\sigma^{m-3}\tau^{n-2})\sigma,$$
$$\rho_3 := (\sigma^{m-3}\tau^{n-2})(\sigma\tau\sigma^2\tau) = (\sigma^{m-3}\tau^{n-2})\sigma^2.$$

Because one of $\rho_1(k), \rho_2(k)$ or $\rho_3(k)$ is k', we can obtain a desired permutation $\rho \in S(\sigma, \tau; m, n)$. The case in which σ and τ are distinct transpositions is proven similarly. □

Proof (Theorem 2).. We apply Lemma 2 for $s = L + 6$ and consider the case $3 \leq j \leq L + 3$. From Lemma 3, for any k', there exists $\rho \in S(\sigma, \tau; s - j, j)$ such that $\rho(k) = k'$. Here, k is the fixed index selected from Lemma 2. Then, for any $k' = 1, 2, 3$ and $3 \leq j \leq L + 3$, we have

$$[\boldsymbol{x}_{i-j}^{t+L+6}]_{k'} \geq m^t + \gamma^{L+6}(M^t - m^t).$$

Using the periodic boundary condition, we obtain

$$[\boldsymbol{x}_i^{t+L+6}]_{k'} \geq m^t + \gamma^{L+6}(M^t - m^t)$$

for $i = 0, 1, \ldots, L - 1$, yielding

$$m^{t+L+6} \geq m^t + \gamma^{L+6}(M^t - m^t).$$

Let $m^* = \lim_{t \to \infty} m^t$ and $M^* = \lim_{t \to \infty} M^t$. We demonstrate that $m^* = M^*$. In contrast, suppose $m^* < M^*$. Then, there exists $\epsilon > 0$ such that $M^t - m^t > \epsilon$ for all $t \in \mathbb{Z}_{\geq 0}$. In contrast, for all $\delta > 0$, there exists $T \in \mathbb{Z}_{\geq 0}$ such that $m^* - m^T < \delta$. Setting $\delta = \gamma^{L+6}\epsilon$, we obtain

$$m^{T+L+6} \geq m^T + \gamma^{L+6}(M^T - m^T) > m^T + \gamma^{L+6}\epsilon > m^*,$$

which is contradictory. Therefore, we have proven $m^* = M^* = 1/3$. □

3.3 Weighted-Averaging Rules of Type 2

In this subsection, we consider weighted-averaging rules of the form (4). The period of space is assumed to be $2L$, which is a multiple of 12.

Theorem 3. *Suppose $\boldsymbol{X}^0 = (\boldsymbol{x}_0^0, \boldsymbol{x}_1^0, \ldots, \boldsymbol{x}_{2L-1}^0) \in \mathrm{int}(\Delta)^{2L}$. If σ and τ are commutative, then there exists $\boldsymbol{p}, \boldsymbol{q} \in \Delta$ such that the VFCA with weighted averaging rule (4) periodically converges as follows:*

$$\boldsymbol{X}^t \to (\sigma^s\pi^r(\boldsymbol{p}), \sigma^s\pi^r(\boldsymbol{q}), \sigma^s\pi^{r-1}(\boldsymbol{p}), \sigma^s\pi^{r-1}(\boldsymbol{q}), \ldots, \sigma^s\pi^{-(L-1)}(\boldsymbol{q})),$$

when $t = s \bmod (\operatorname{ord}\sigma)$ *and* $t = 2r \bmod 2(\operatorname{ord}\pi)$ *and*

$$\boldsymbol{X}^t \to (\sigma^s\pi^{r+1}(\boldsymbol{q}), \sigma^s\pi^r(\boldsymbol{p}), \sigma^s\pi^r(\boldsymbol{q}), \sigma^s\pi^{r-1}(\boldsymbol{p}), \ldots, \sigma^s\pi^{r-(L-1)}(\boldsymbol{p}))$$

when $t = s \bmod (\operatorname{ord}\sigma)$ *and* $t = 2r+1 \bmod 2(\operatorname{ord}\pi)$, *where* $\pi = \sigma^{-1}\tau$, $0 \le s \le \operatorname{ord}\sigma - 1$ *and* $0 \le r \le \operatorname{ord}\tau - 1$.

Proof. The local rule (4) can be written as

$$f(\boldsymbol{x}, \boldsymbol{y}, \boldsymbol{z}) = \sigma((1 - \langle\boldsymbol{y}\rangle) \cdot \boldsymbol{x} + \langle\boldsymbol{y}\rangle \cdot \pi(\boldsymbol{z})).$$

Let $F : \Delta^{2L} \to \Delta^{2L}$ be the global rule. Furthermore, let $\tilde{F} : \Delta^{2L} \to \Delta^{2L}$ be the shifted global rule defined by

$$\begin{aligned}
\tilde{F}(\boldsymbol{x}_0, \boldsymbol{x}_1, \ldots, \boldsymbol{x}_{2L-1}) &:= (S \circ F)(\boldsymbol{x}_0, \boldsymbol{x}_1, \ldots, \boldsymbol{x}_{2L-1}) \\
&= (f(\boldsymbol{x}_0, \boldsymbol{x}_1, \boldsymbol{x}_2), f(\boldsymbol{x}_1, \boldsymbol{x}_2, \boldsymbol{x}_3), \ldots, f(\boldsymbol{x}_{2L-1}, \boldsymbol{x}_0, \boldsymbol{x}_1)),
\end{aligned}$$

where $S : \Delta^{2L} \to \Delta^{2L}$ denotes the left-shift map

$$S(\boldsymbol{x}_0, \boldsymbol{x}_1, \ldots, \boldsymbol{x}_{2L-1}) = (\boldsymbol{x}_1, \ldots, \boldsymbol{x}_{2L-1}, \boldsymbol{x}_0).$$

As in the case of the EFCA [8], the key idea is to divide the entire space into even and odd parts. The original VFCA can then be regarded as a direct product of the two sequences, satisfying the assumption of Proposition 1.

For $t \in \mathbb{Z}_{\ge 0}$ and $i = 0, 1, \ldots, L-1$, we define the functions as

$$\begin{aligned}
g_{t,i}^{\mathrm{e}}(\boldsymbol{x}, \boldsymbol{z}; \boldsymbol{y}) &= (1 - \langle\sigma^t\pi^{-i}(\boldsymbol{y})\rangle) \cdot \boldsymbol{x} + \langle\sigma^t\pi^{-i}(\boldsymbol{y})\rangle \cdot \boldsymbol{z}, \\
g_{t,i}^{\mathrm{o}}(\boldsymbol{x}, \boldsymbol{z}; \boldsymbol{y}) &= (1 - \langle\sigma^t\pi^{-(i+1)}(\boldsymbol{y})\rangle) \cdot \boldsymbol{x} + \langle\sigma^t\pi^{-(i+1)}(\boldsymbol{y})\rangle \cdot \boldsymbol{z},
\end{aligned}$$

and global maps $G_t^{\mathrm{e}}, G_t^{\mathrm{o}} : \Delta^L \to \Delta^L$ as

$$\begin{aligned}
&G_t^{\mathrm{e}}(\boldsymbol{x}_0, \boldsymbol{x}_1, \ldots, \boldsymbol{x}_{L-1}; \boldsymbol{y}_0, \boldsymbol{y}_1, \ldots, \boldsymbol{y}_{L-1}) \\
&\quad = (g_{t,0}^{\mathrm{e}}(\boldsymbol{x}_0, \boldsymbol{x}_1; \boldsymbol{y}_0), g_{t,1}^{\mathrm{e}}(\boldsymbol{x}_1, \boldsymbol{x}_2; \boldsymbol{y}_1), \ldots, g_{t,L-1}^{\mathrm{e}}(\boldsymbol{x}_{L-1}, \boldsymbol{x}_0, \boldsymbol{y}_{L-1})), \\
&G_t^{\mathrm{o}}(\boldsymbol{x}_0, \boldsymbol{x}_1, \ldots, \boldsymbol{x}_{L-1}; \boldsymbol{y}_0, \boldsymbol{y}_1, \ldots, \boldsymbol{y}_{L-1}) \\
&\quad = (g_{t,0}^{\mathrm{o}}(\boldsymbol{x}_0, \boldsymbol{x}_1; \boldsymbol{y}_1), g_{t,1}^{\mathrm{o}}(\boldsymbol{x}_1, \boldsymbol{x}_2; \boldsymbol{y}_2), \ldots, g_{t,L-1}^{\mathrm{o}}(\boldsymbol{x}_{L-1}, \boldsymbol{x}_0; \boldsymbol{y}_0)).
\end{aligned}$$

Here, $\boldsymbol{x}_0, \boldsymbol{x}_1, \ldots, \boldsymbol{x}_{L-1}$ are the variables considered. In addition, we define two projective maps, $h_t^{\mathrm{e}}, h_t^{\mathrm{o}} : \Delta^{2L} \to \Delta^L$, as follows:

$$\begin{aligned}
h_t^{\mathrm{e}}(\boldsymbol{x}_0, \boldsymbol{x}_1, \ldots, \boldsymbol{x}_{2L-1}) &= (\sigma^{-t}(\boldsymbol{x}_0), \sigma^{-t}\pi(\boldsymbol{x}_2), \ldots, \sigma^{-t}\pi^{L-1}(\boldsymbol{x}_{2(L-1)})), \\
h_t^{\mathrm{o}}(\boldsymbol{x}_0, \boldsymbol{x}_1, \ldots, \boldsymbol{x}_{2L-1}) &= (\sigma^{-t}(\boldsymbol{x}_1), \sigma^{-t}\pi(\boldsymbol{x}_3), \ldots, \sigma^{-t}\pi^{L-1}(\boldsymbol{x}_{2L-1})).
\end{aligned}$$

Using these notations, we can verify

$$(h_{t+1}^{\mathrm{e}} \circ \tilde{F})(\boldsymbol{X}) = G_t^{\mathrm{e}}(h_t^{\mathrm{e}}(\boldsymbol{X}); h_t^{\mathrm{o}}(\boldsymbol{X})), \quad (h_{t+1}^{\mathrm{o}} \circ \tilde{F})(\boldsymbol{X}) = G_t^{\mathrm{o}}(h_t^{\mathrm{o}}(\boldsymbol{X}); h_t^{\mathrm{e}}(\boldsymbol{X}))$$

for $t \in \mathbb{Z}_{\ge 0}$ and $\boldsymbol{X} = (\boldsymbol{x}_0, \boldsymbol{x}_1, \ldots, \boldsymbol{x}_{2L-1}) \in \Delta^{2L}$. These equalities are obtained in a manner similar to the proof of Theorem 1.

We define $h_t : \Delta^{2L} \to \Delta^L \times \Delta^L$ and $G_t : \Delta^L \times \Delta^L \to \Delta^L \times \Delta^L$ as

$$h_t(\boldsymbol{X}) = (h_t^{\mathrm{e}}(\boldsymbol{X}), h_t^{\mathrm{o}}(\boldsymbol{X})) \quad \text{and} \quad G_t((\boldsymbol{Y}, \boldsymbol{Z})) = (G_t^{\mathrm{e}}(\boldsymbol{Y}; \boldsymbol{Z}), G_t^{\mathrm{o}}(\boldsymbol{Z}; \boldsymbol{Y})).$$

Then, h_t is a bijection, and

$$(h_t \circ \tilde{F})(\boldsymbol{X}) = (G_t^{\mathrm{e}}(h_t^{\mathrm{e}}(\boldsymbol{X}); h_t^{\mathrm{o}}(\boldsymbol{X})), G_t^{\mathrm{o}}(h_t^{\mathrm{o}}(\boldsymbol{X}); h_t^{\mathrm{e}}(\boldsymbol{X}))) = (G_t \circ h_t)(\boldsymbol{X}).$$

Therefore, the t-times composition of $\tilde{F}$ can be expressed as

$$\tilde{F}^t = h_t^{-1} \circ (G_{t-1} \circ G_{t-2} \circ \cdots \circ G_0) \circ h_0.$$

Using the commutativity of F and left-shift map S, we have

$$F^t = (S^t)^{-1} \circ h_t^{-1} \circ (G_{t-1} \circ G_{t-1} \circ \cdots \circ G_0) \circ h_0.$$

We set $(\boldsymbol{Y}^0, \boldsymbol{Z}^0) := h_0(\boldsymbol{X}^0) \in \mathrm{int}(\Delta)^L \times \mathrm{int}(\Delta)^L$. If we define

$$(\boldsymbol{Y}^t, \boldsymbol{Z}^t) = (G_{t-1} \circ G_{t-2} \circ \cdots \circ G_0)(\boldsymbol{Y}^0, \boldsymbol{Z}^0),$$

both $\{\boldsymbol{Y}^t\}_{t \in \mathbb{Z}_{\geq 0}}$ and $\{\boldsymbol{Z}^t\}_{t \in \mathbb{Z}_{\geq 0}}$ satisfy the assumption of Proposition 1. Therefore, $\boldsymbol{Y}^t$ and $\boldsymbol{Z}^t$ converge to configurations $(\boldsymbol{p}, \boldsymbol{p}, \ldots, \boldsymbol{p})$ and $(\boldsymbol{q}, \boldsymbol{q}, \ldots, \boldsymbol{q})$ as $t \to \infty$, respectively. Then, $\boldsymbol{X}^t$ converges to

$$((S^{-1})^t \circ h_t^{-1})((\boldsymbol{p}, \boldsymbol{p}, \ldots, \boldsymbol{p}), (\boldsymbol{q}, \boldsymbol{q}, \ldots, \boldsymbol{q}))$$
$$= (S^{-1})^t((\sigma^t(\boldsymbol{p}), \sigma^t(\boldsymbol{q}), \sigma^t \pi^{-1}(\boldsymbol{p}), \sigma^t \pi^{-1}(\boldsymbol{q}) \ldots, \sigma^t \pi^{-(L-1)}(\boldsymbol{p}), \sigma^t \pi^{-(L-1)}(\boldsymbol{q})))$$
$$= \begin{cases} (\sigma^t \pi^{\frac{t}{2}}(\boldsymbol{p}), \sigma^t \pi^{\frac{t}{2}}(\boldsymbol{q}), \sigma^t \pi^{\frac{t}{2}-1}(\boldsymbol{p}), \sigma^t \pi^{\frac{t}{2}-1}(\boldsymbol{q}), \ldots \\ \quad \ldots, \sigma^t \pi^{\frac{t}{2}-(L-1)}(\boldsymbol{p}), \sigma^t \pi^{\frac{t}{2}-(L-1)}(\boldsymbol{q})) & \text{if } t \text{ is even,} \\ (\sigma^t \pi^{\frac{t+1}{2}}(\boldsymbol{q}), \sigma^t \pi^{\frac{t-1}{2}}(\boldsymbol{p}), \sigma^t \pi^{\frac{t+1}{2}-1}(\boldsymbol{q}), \sigma^t \pi^{\frac{t-1}{2}-1}(\boldsymbol{p}), \ldots \\ \quad \ldots, \sigma^t \pi^{\frac{t+1}{2}-(L-1)}(\boldsymbol{q}), \sigma^t \pi^{\frac{t-1}{2}-(L-1)}(\boldsymbol{p})) & \text{if } t \text{ is odd.} \end{cases}$$

From the periodicities of σ and π, we may assert this theorem. $\qquad \square$

Combining the proofs of Theorems 2 and 3, we obtain the following result.

Theorem 4. *Suppose* $\boldsymbol{X}^0 = (\boldsymbol{x}_0^0, \boldsymbol{x}_1^0, \ldots, \boldsymbol{x}_{2L-1}^0) \in \mathrm{int}(\Delta)^{2L}$. *If* σ *and* τ *are non-commutative. The VFCA with the weighted-averaging rule* (4) *then converges to the homogeneous configuration with the centroid* $\boldsymbol{a} = (1/3, 1/3, 1/3)^{\top}$:

$$\boldsymbol{X}^* = (\boldsymbol{a}, \boldsymbol{a}, \ldots, \boldsymbol{a}).$$

4   Conclusion

In this study, we provide an analytical proof for the convergence of VFCA. The convergence patterns of some of the weighted-averaging rules in three-state, three-neighbor VFCA are similar to those in EFCA. However, there are weighted-averaging rules with a new type of convergence pattern in the three-state case because the symmetric group S_3 is non-commutative, whereas S_2 is commutative. Under these rules, all the components of the vectors are mixed, and each cell converges to the centroid. Moreover, this proof can be easily extended to VFCA in more than three states by considering the group S_n. Although weighted-averaging rules are a small part of all rules of three-state, three-neighbor VFCA, the proofs presented in this study may be effective for the general case. Future work will demonstrate the convergence of VFCA with other rules.

Acknowledgments. This work was supported by JSPS KAKENHI (Grant No. 21K03359).

References

1. Cattaneo, G., Flocchini, P., Mauri, G., Quaranta Vogliotti, C., Santoro, N.: Cellular automata in fuzzy backgrounds. Phys. D **105**, 105–120 (1997). https://doi.org/10.1016/S0167-2789(96)00233-3
2. Mraz, M., Zimic, N., Lapanja, I., Bajec, I.: Fuzzy cellular automata: from theory to applications. In: Proceedings 12th IEEE Internationals Conference on Tools with Artificial Intelligence, pp. 320–323. IEEE Press, New York (2000). https://doi.org/10.1109/TAI.2000.889889
3. Adamatzky, A.I.: Hierarchy of fuzzy cellular automata. Fuzzy Sets Syst. **62**, 167–174 (1994). https://doi.org/10.1016/0165-0114(94)90056-6
4. Higashi, K., Satsuma, J., Tokihiro, T.: Rule 184 fuzzy cellular automaton as a mathematical model for traffic flow. Jpn. J. Ind. Appl. Math. **38**, 579–609 (2021). https://doi.org/10.1007/s13160-021-00461-3
5. Nishida, Y., Watanabe, S., Fukuda, A., Watanabe, Y.: q-VFCA: q-state vector-valued fuzzy cellular automata. J. Cell. Autom. **15**, 207–222 (2020)
6. Nishida, Y., Watanabe, S., Fukuda, A., Yanagisawa, D.: Fuzzy cellular automata with complete number-conserving rule as traffic-flow models with bottleneck. JSIAM Lett. **14**, 143–146 (2022). https://doi.org/10.14495/jsiaml.14.143
7. Nishida, Y., Watanabe, S., Fukuda, A., Watanabe, Y.: Traffic flow models with two kinds of vehicles in terms of the vector-valued cellular automata and their fuzzification, In: Mufid, M.S., Adzkiya, D. (eds.) Proceedings of the AIP Conference, ICoMPAC 2021, vol. 2641. AIP Publishing, Melville (2022). Article no. 20006. https://doi.org/10.1063/5.0114966
8. Betel, H., Flocchini, P.: On the asymptotic behaviour of circular fuzzy cellular automata. J. Cell. Autom. **6**, 25–52 (2011)
9. Betel, H., Flocchini, P.: Fluctuations of fuzzy cellular automata around their convergence point. In: Proceedings of 2009 International Symposium on Nonlinear Theory and its Applications, pp. 655–658. IEICE, Tokyo (2009). https://doi.org/10.34385/proc.43.C3L-B2
10. Flocchini, P., Geurts, F., Mingarelli, A.B., Santoro, N.: Convergence and aperiodicity in fuzzy cellular automata: revisiting rule 90. Phys. D **142**, 20–28 (2000). https://doi.org/10.1016/S0167-2789(00)00052-X
11. Mingarelli, A.B., El Yacoubi, S.: On the decidability of the evolution of the fuzzy cellular automaton 184. In: Alexandrov, V.N., van Albada, G.D., Sloot, P.M.A., Dongarra, J. (eds.) ICCS 2006. LNCS, vol. 3993, pp. 360–366. Springer, Heidelberg (2006). https://doi.org/10.1007/11758532_49
12. Wolfram, S.: A New Kind of Science. Wolfram Media, Champaign (2002)

A Decentralised Diagnosis Method with Probabilistic Cellular Automata

Nazim Fatès[1]([⊠]), Régine Marchand[2], and Irène Marcovici[2]

[1] Université de Lorraine, CNRS, Inria, LORIA, 54000 Nancy, France
nazim.fates@loria.fr
[2] Université de Lorraine, CNRS, Inria, IECL, 54000 Nancy, France
{regine.marchand,irene.marcovici}@univ-lorraine.fr

Abstract. The decentralised diagnosis problem consists in the detection of a certain amount of defects in a distributed network. Here, we tackle this problem in the context of two-dimensional cellular automata with three states : neutral, alert and defect. When the density of defects is below a given threshold, we want the alert state to coexist with the neutral state while when this density is above the threshold, we want the alert state to invade the whole grid. We present two probabilistic rules to answer this problem. The first one is isotropic and is studied with numerical simulations. The second one is defined on Toom's neighbourhood and is examined with an analytical point of view. These solutions constitute a first step towards a broader study of the decentralised diagnosis problem on more general networks.

Keywords: decentralised diagnosis · consensus problems · probabilistic cellular automata

1 Introduction

Consider the following problem. We have a system of interconnected components that interact in discrete time steps according to a local rule. At each time step, each component can fail with a given probability, in which case it becomes *defective*. The non-defective components see their defective neighbours and they may switch from their normal state, or *neutral state*, to an *alert* state. We would like such a system to detect the presence of a given number of failures in a totally decentralised way. More precisely, when the density of failures is below a given threshold, some components should still operate in the neutral state, while when this density crosses this threshold, all the components should be in the alert state, and remain so.

We call this problem the *decentralised diagnosis problem* and we investigate it in the cellular automata framework, that is, when the components, which are called the *cells*, are arranged according to a regular spatial structure (a grid) and all obey the same uniform transition rule.

As we aim to work with a minimal model, we will consider only ternary cellular automata with the three states mentioned above (neutral, alert, defect).

© IFIP International Federation for Information Processing 2023
Published by Springer Nature Switzerland AG 2023
L. Manzoni et al. (Eds.): AUTOMATA 2023, LNCS 14152, pp. 60–73, 2023.
https://doi.org/10.1007/978-3-031-42250-8_5

The main idea of our proposition is to use the phase transition phenomenon, observed in some probabilistic cellular automata where a qualitative change of behaviour may be triggered by a small variation in the local transition probabilities. For example, it is well known that the probabilistic version of the Greenberg-Hastings model exhibits such a phase transition between an active regime where cells change their state regularly and an extinction regime where all activity disappears [1]. Interestingly enough, it was noticed that the presence of defects in the grid modifies the position of the critical threshold [1,7,8] and the idea to take advantage of this drift of threshold to build a diagnosis process was formulated.

Some preliminary investigations on the decentralised diagnosis problem were carried out by Gauville et al., who examined different models and compared their advantages and drawbacks [5]. The current paper aims to deepen these investigations by examining two simple ternary models. The first one, named QuorumD, is inspired from the Ising model and uses the von Neumann neighbourhood ; the second model is even simpler and uses Toom's size-3 neighbourhood: this neighbourhood breaks the isotropy and installs a direction in which information travels. Indeed, while this may seem a drawback for concrete applications, it has the advantage to allow us to derive a more formal analysis of the behaviour of the model. Note that as a first step, we consider only the case of static defects, which are already present in the initial condition, leaving the case where they gradually appear for future work.

2 The Isotropic Model

The cells are arranged on the two-dimensional lattice $\mathcal{L}$, which can be infinite $(\mathcal{L} = \mathbb{Z}^2)$, or can take the form of a finite square lattice of length L with periodic boundary conditions in which case we have $\mathcal{L} = (\mathbb{Z}/L\mathbb{Z}) \times (\mathbb{Z}/L\mathbb{Z})$.

The set of states is $Q = \{0, 1, D\}$ where 0 stands for the neutral state, 1 for the alert state, and D represents a defective cell. The set of configurations is $Q^{\mathcal{L}}$.

Let us now introduce the QuorumDrule. It is inspired by Ising model of ferromagnetic interactions of spins. We assimilate one spin to the neutral state 0 and the other spin to the states 1 and D, grouped together. Indeed, we want the defect state to generate alert states, and we want these alert states to propagate from neighbour to neighbour and to invade the whole grid only if their number is sufficiently high. We thus propose to consider the following rule [5]. For a cell in state q, its new state is given by $f(q, n, a, d)$ where n, a, d are respectively the number of states 0, 1, D found in the neighbourhood of this cell. In this section, we will restrict our scope to the von Neumann neighbourhood: $\mathcal{N} = \{(0,0), (0,1), (1,0), (0,-1), (-1,0)\}$.

We define the local transitions by steps. First, we express the fact that the defect state is inert: $f(D, ., ., .) = D$. Second, for $q \neq D$, we express the quiescence of the neutral and alert state by: $n = 0$ implies that $f(q, n, a, d) = 1$ and by $a = d = 0$ implies that $f(q, n, a, d) = 0$. Last, we give the general case: for $q \neq D, n > 0$ and $a + d > 0$, we have:

$$f(q, n, a, d) = \begin{cases} 1 & \text{with prob.} \, \pi(n, a, d) \\ 0 & \text{with prob.} \, 1 - \pi(n, a, d), \end{cases}$$

where

$$\pi(n, a, d) = \frac{\exp \lambda(a + d)}{\exp \lambda n + \exp \lambda(a + d)}.$$

The parameter λ, which could be called the resistivity of the environment, controls the ease with which the alert state propagates. It can also be seen as the inverse of a temperature: when λ is high, the cells tend to follow the majority state in their neighbourhood, which makes it difficult for the alert state to diffuse; reciprocally, when λ is low, more noise is introduced and a group of alerts can travel at a greater distance from the defect cell which created it (see Fig. 1 and 2).

To define the global dynamics of our cellular automaton, let us introduce the functions $C_q(\eta, x, y) = \text{card}\{(i, j) \in \mathcal{N} : \eta(x + i, y + j) = q\}$, which, for a configuration η, count the number of cells in state $q \in \{0, 1, \mathtt{D}\}$ in the neighbourhood of a given cell $(x, y) \in \mathcal{L}$. Then, starting from an initial configuration η_0, the system evolves according to the sequence of configurations $(\eta_t)_{t \in \mathbb{N}}$ defined by:

$$\forall (x, y) \in \mathcal{L}, \eta_{t+1}(x, y) = f(\eta_t(x, y), C_0(\eta_t, x, y), C_1(\eta_t, x, y), C_\mathtt{D}(\eta_t, x, y))$$

where the probabilities for f are drawn independently for each cell and at each time step.

2.1   Numerical Experiments

The dynamics of the `QuorumD` rule can be observed on Fig. 1. In this example, we took a small grid ($L = 32$) and arbitrarily fixed the value of the resistivity to $\lambda = 1$. Each cell was initially set as a defect with probability κ and to neutral state with probability $1 - \kappa$. It can be observed that for a defect density $\kappa = 0.10$ the alert states invades the grid in a few hundred steps, while for a smaller defect density $\kappa = 0.02$, the alert state remains contained in some regions, even after a several thousands of steps. Figure 2 also shows the transition from the coexistence regime to the invasion regime, but with a fixed density of defects $\kappa = 0.02$, and a resistivity of $\lambda = 0.05$ and $\lambda = 1$.

The distinction between these two qualitative states can be measured by the density of neutral states $d_0(t)$, that is, the ratio of neutral states over the total number of cells of the grid. We define the *coexistence regime* as the behaviour of the system where the diffusion of the alert states remains bounded, which means that $d_0(t)$ will remain stable around a non-zero value for a long time. Conversely, the *invasion regime* corresponds to the behaviour where the alert state diffuses everywhere, and where $d_0(t)$ will quickly decrease.

Figure 3 shows the temporal evolution of d_0 for different values of λ and κ. We here took a large grid ($L = 100$) and an observation time of $10\,000$ time steps. On the top plots of this figure, it can be observed that for $\kappa = 0.03$, the transition between the coexistence and invasion regime occurs for $\lambda \in [0.8, 1.6]$,

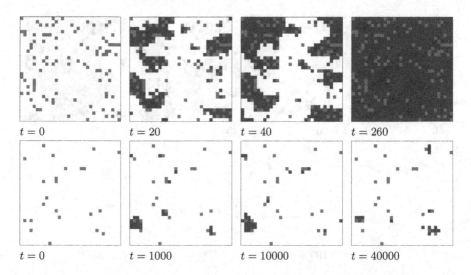

Fig. 1. Evolution of a random configuration with $L = 32$, and $\lambda = 1$. The states n, a, d are respectively in white, blue and purple. The upper line shows an evolution with a density of defects $\kappa = 0.1$: the alert state diffuses in the whole grid. The bottom line shows a long-term evolution for $\kappa = 0.02$: the diffusion of the alert state remains bounded. (Color figure online)

while for $\kappa = 0.05$ it occurs in the interval $[1.6, 2.4]$. Reciprocally, if we fix the value of the resistivity, we see that for $\lambda = 8$, progressively increasing the defect rate by steps of 0.04 makes the system evolve from the coexistence state to the invasion regime, which corresponds to the desired behaviour for a decentralised diagnosis.

These observations are rather encouraging for a practical use. We leave for future work a more detailed analysis, where the defects would dynamically appear on the grid. It also necessary to evaluate how the grid size influences the behaviour of the system. Ideally, when the resistivity λ is fixed, one would like to have a fixed threshold for the value of κ for large grid sizes. Unfortunately, the observations we made for larger grids and larger times revealed that the separation between the coexistence and the invasion regime does depend on the lattice size, although in a limited fashion. Also note that in the coexistence regime, the system is always in a metastable state: we know that on a finite time scale, there is always a non-zero probability to reach the configuration where all cells are in alert. This means that this event will always eventually happen, but in an average time that will be extremely high, that is, exponential in the size of the grid.

By analysing the behaviour of the rule at a local scale, we observed that the dynamics of the alerts in some cases closely behaves as the *bootstrap percolation* process [2]. In this model, cells have a binary state, healthy or infected, and a healthy cell gets infected if two or more neighbours are infected, after which

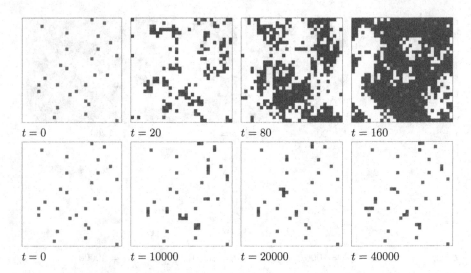

Fig. 2. Evolution of a random configuration with $L = 32$, and $\kappa = 0.02$ (same initial position of defects). The upper line shows an evolution with a density of defects $\lambda = 0.5$: the alert state diffuses rapidly everywhere and eventually invades the whole grid. The bottom line shows a long-term evolution for $\lambda = 1.0$: the diffusion of the alert state remains bounded during a long time.

it remains infected for ever. Although the QuorumD rule is stochastic and the bootstrap percolation rule is deterministic, the two dynamics have many common characteristics. In particular, in both models, rectangular zones of cells which are infected (in the bootstrap percolation) or in the alert state (in QuorumD) are stable. We leave as an open question to determine more precisely to which extent the two rules have comparable dynamics. This is why we now present a simpler rule where the use of a non-isotropic neighbourhood induces a direction for the flow of information and makes the model more tractable.

3   A Directional Model: The Biased-Quiescent Rule

3.1   Definition of the Rule

We now consider a simplification of the previous model. The new model still has three states 0, 1 and D, but, on the non-defective cells, the local rule is applied on a neighbourhood of size two, which consists of the North and East neighbours of a cell. The transitions are simplified: the two states 0 and 1 are still quiescent, and when a cell sees the two states, it becomes a 1 (alert) with probability p, whatever its initial state. We call this rule the biased-quiescent rule, or the BQ rule for short, as the rule has the quiescence property and also has a bias towards 1 with probability p.

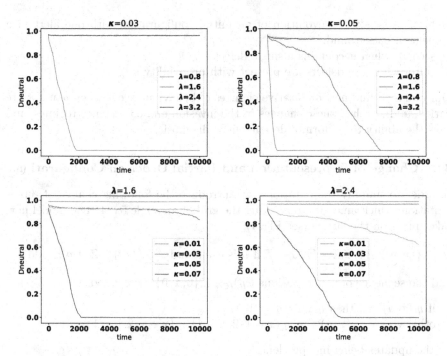

Fig. 3. Temporal evolution of the density of neutral sites as function of time for different values of κ and λ, for a grid of size $L = 100$. On the two top plots, we set $\kappa = 0.03$ (top-left) or $\kappa = 0.05$ (top-right), and vary λ. On the two bottom plots, we set $\lambda = 1.6$ (bottom-left) or $\lambda = 2.4$ (bottom-right), and vary κ.

Formally, for $p \in (0, 1)$, let ϕ be the probabilistic function defined by:

(a) the neutral state is quiescent: $\phi(0, 0) = 0$;
(b) the alert state is quiescent: if $q, q' \in \{1, D\}$ then $\phi(q, q') = 1$; and,

(c) biased breaking-ties: otherwise, $\phi(q, q') = \begin{cases} 1 & \text{with prob. } p \\ 0 & \text{with prob. } 1 - p. \end{cases}$

Starting from a (random or deterministic) initial configuration $\eta_0 \in \{0, 1, D\}^{\mathbb{Z}^2}$, we denote by $(\eta_t)_{t \in \mathbb{N}}$ the sequence of random configurations obtained as follows:

$$\forall t \in \mathbb{N}, \; \forall (x, y) \in \mathbb{Z}^2, \; \eta_{t+1}(x, y) = \begin{cases} D & \text{if } \eta_t(x, y) = D \\ \phi(\eta_t(x + 1, y), \eta_t(x, y + 1)) & \text{otherwise,} \end{cases}$$

all the updates being independent.

In the sequel, we work on the infinite grid $\mathbb{Z}^2$ and we say that a configuration η has a *neutral background* if the number its non-neutral cells is finite. The main interest of this simplified and directional model is that it is analytically tractable. We now study how its asymptotic behaviour depends on the initial configuration η_0; we proceed in three steps:

- first, we study the evolution of an initial configuration with one alert in a neutral background,
- second, when it contains a single defect,
- third, when the defects are present with probability κ.

Our aim is to find how qualitative changes of behaviour occur when p and κ are varied, and to relate these changes to the invasion and coexistence regimes, and thus the ability to perform a decentralised diagnosis.

3.2 Change of Representation and Partial Order on Configurations

In order to simplify the notations, we introduce the following change of representation, which amounts to rotating the grid of an angle $5\pi/4$. The model now takes place on the lattice (see Fig. 4):

$$\mathcal{L} = \{(x, n) \in (1/2)\mathbb{Z} \times \mathbb{Z} : x \in \mathbb{Z} \text{ if } n \text{ is even, and } x \in (1/2) + \mathbb{Z} \text{ if } n \text{ is odd}\},$$

and the sequence of configurations $(\eta_t)_{t\in\mathbb{N}} \in \{0, 1, D\}^{\mathcal{L}}$ is defined by:

- if $\eta_t(x, n) = D$ then $\eta_{t+1}(x, n) = D$,
- otherwise, $\eta_{t+1}(x, n) = \phi(\eta_t(x - 1/2, n - 1), \eta_t(x + 1/2, n - 1))$,

all the updates being independent.

On $\{0, 1, D\}$, we consider the order $0 \leq 1 \leq D$, which naturally induces a partial order on $\{0, 1, D\}^{\mathcal{L}}$ in the following manner: we say that

$$\eta \preceq \eta' \text{ if for any } (x, n) \in \mathcal{L}, \eta(x, n) \leq \eta'(x, n).$$

By using the same Bernoulli random variables to update the processes starting from two comparable (deterministic or random) initial configurations, it is easy to see that:

Fact 1. *If $\eta_0 \preceq \eta_0'$, then we can couple the evolutions $(\eta_t)_{t\in\mathbb{N}}$ and $(\eta_t')_{t\in\mathbb{N}}$ in such a way that: $\forall t \in \mathbb{N}, \eta_t \preceq \eta_t'$.*

3.3 Initial Configuration with only One Alert and No Defect

In a first step, we consider the case where one alert is set in a neutral background. How will the alerts evolve as function of p? To answer this question, we prove the following theorem.

Theorem 1. *For the BQ rule, starting from a configuration η_0 with only one cell in state 1 and no cell in state D in a neutral background, the extinction time of the alert cells $T = \inf\{t \in \mathbb{N} : \eta_t = 0^{\mathbb{Z}^2}\}$ verifies:*

- *For $p < 1/2$, then T is almost surely finite, and it is integrable ($\mathbb{E}(T) < \infty$);*
- *for $p = 1/2$, then T is almost surely finite, and $\mathbb{E}(T) = \infty$;*
- *for $p > 1/2$, T can be infinite with a positive probability ($\mathbb{P}(T = \infty) > 0$).*

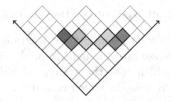

Fig. 4. The configuration η_6 with, in grey, the alert states forming a horizontal segment at time $t = 6$, with its two extremal cells in darker grey. Their possible evolutions at time $t = 7$ are shown in colour. (Color figure online)

Proof. We assume that initially, the origin $(0, 0)$ is the only cell in state 1, all the other cells are in state 0. By induction, it is clear that at any time $t \in \mathbb{N}$, the configuration η_t is either the empty configuration $0^{\mathcal{L}}$, or a *horizontal segment*, that is, a configuration where all the cells in state 1 have their second coordinate equal to t and have consecutive first coordinates. Let us denote by $L(t)$ the set of first coordinates of alert cells at time t:

$$L(t) = \{x : \eta_t(x, t) = 1\},$$
$$d(t) = \max L(t) - \min L(t) + 1, \text{ with the convention } d(t) = 0 \text{ if } L(t) = \varnothing,$$
$$T = \inf\{t \in \mathbb{N} : L(t) = \varnothing\} = \inf\{t \in \mathbb{N} : d(t) = 0\}.$$

Note that $d(t)$ is also the cardinal of $L(t)$. Moreover, as long as $L(t) \neq \varnothing$, $(\max L(t))_{t \in \mathbb{N}}$ evolves as a random walk with steps $1/2$ with probability p and $-1/2$ with probability $1 - p$. Symmetrically, $(\min L(t))_{t \in \mathbb{N}}$ evolves as a random walk with steps $-1/2$ with probability $1-p$ and $1/2$ with probability p. Moreover, as long as $d(t) > 1$, these two random walks are independent.

Consequently, one can check that $(d(t))_{t \geq 0}$ is a random walk on $\mathbb{N}$, starting from 1, absorbed in 0, with the following transition probabilities: for $i \geq 1$,

$$\begin{aligned} p_{i,i-1} &= (1 - p)^2, \\ p_{i,i} &= 2p(1 - p), \\ p_{i,i+1} &= p^2. \end{aligned} \tag{1}$$

and T is its absorption time. We thus have that [3]:

- for $p < 1/2$, then $p^2 < (1 - p)^2$, the random walk $(d(t))_{t \geq 0}$ has a negative bias, thus T is almost surely finite and has a finite expectation;
- for $p = 1/2$, then the random walk $(d(t))_{t \geq 0}$ is symmetric so T is almost surely finite and has an infinite expectation;
- for $p > 1/2$, then $p^2 > (1 - p)^2$, the random walk $(d(t))_{t \geq 0}$ has a positive bias and thus, starting from $d(0) = 1$, it has a strictly positive probability of never hitting 0. So $\mathbb{P}(T = +\infty) > 0$.

□

Theorem 1 can directly be extended to all initial configurations containing only neutral cells and a finite number of alert cells.

3.4 Initial Configuration with only One Defect

In a second step, we consider the simple case where only one defect exists on the grid. Our aim is to analyse how the density of alerts evolves asymptotically. Will it grow for ever, in which case the system is said to be *transient* or will the system reach a stable regime, in which case it will visit infinitely often the same configurations and thus will said to be *recurrent?* The following theorem answers this question.

Theorem 2. *For the BQ rule, starting from the configuration η_0 with a single defect and no alert cells in a neutral background, the first return time $T = \inf\{t \geq 1 : \eta_t = \eta_0\}$ satisfies:*

- *For $p \in (0, 1/2)$, T is almost surely finite, $\mathbb{E}(T) < +\infty$ and thus the process $(\eta_t)_{t \in \mathbb{N}}$ is positive recurrent.*
- *For $p \in [1/2, 1)$, $\mathbb{P}(T = +\infty) > 0$ and the process $(\eta_t)_{t \in \mathbb{N}}$ is transient.*

Proof. In the previous case of a single alert cell at time 0, at any time the process was either empty or one *horizontal segment*. Now, the single alert cell is replaced by a single defect cell, which generates at each time step a new horizontal segment, and these horizontal segments then evolve independently.

Let us define the *lines* of the process and their life times: for every $i \geq 1$, we define the i-th line L_i as the horizontal segment of alert states which appears at time i on the set $\{(-1/2, 1), (1/2, 1)\}$, and which then travels up by one cell at each time step until it disappears. More formally, for $t \geq 0$,

$$L_i(t) = \{x : \eta_{i+t}(x, t+1) = 1\},$$
$$d_i(t) = \max L_i(t) - \min L_i(t) + 1, \text{ with the convention } d_i(t) = 0 \text{ if } L_i(t) = \varnothing,$$
$$\tau_i = \inf\{t \in \mathbb{N} : d_i(t) = 0\}. \tag{2}$$

Note that at time i, the i-th line can either be empty (and remain so) or a horizontal segment with one or two cells, in which case it will remain a horizontal segment until it disappears. The quantity $d_i(t)$ is the length of the i-th line after t time steps and τ_i is its life time (see Fig. 5).

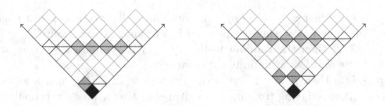

Fig. 5. The single defect is at the origin and shown in black. On the left, $t = 6$: the first line is born at time 1, and is now $L_1(5)$ in blue, while the sixth line $L_6(0)$ is just born in pink. On the right, $t = 7$, the first line has evolved in $L_1(6)$, it is displayed in blue, and the sixth line $L_6(1)$ is shown in pink (Color figure online)

Moreover, for $i \geq 1$, the processes $(d_i(t))_{t \geq 0}$ are independent and identically distributed random walks; their transition probabilities are given by Eq. (1).

To study the recurrence of our process $(\eta_t)_{t \in \mathbb{N}}$, we now introduce a queue $(R_t)_{t \geq 0}$. We start from an empty queue and we say that at each time $t \geq 1$, the line L_t enters the queue, and it leaves the queue at time $t + \tau_t$. For $t \geq 0$, we denote by R_t the maximal remaining living time of the lines that are in the queue at time t: it is a Markov process with values in $\mathbb{N}$, which satisfies the recursion relation $R_0 = 0$ and $\forall t \geq 0$, $R_{t+1} = \max(R_t - 1, \tau_{t+1})$ where $(\tau_i)_{i \geq 1}$ are the independent and identically distributed random variables defined in (2). The first return time T of the process $(\eta_t)_{t \in \mathbb{N}}$ to the state η_0 corresponds to the first return time of the Markov chain $(R_t)_{t \geq 0}$ to the state 0.

Lemma 1. *Assume that τ_1 is integrable, and that $\mathbb{P}(\tau_1 = 0) > 0$, then $(R_t)_{t \geq 0}$ is positive recurrent, that is, the expected amount of time to return to $R_t = 0$ is finite.*

Proof. It is not difficult to check that $(R_t)_{t \geq 0}$ is irreducible. Let us denote by $\mathbb{E}_a$ the expectation of this Markov chain conditionally to starting in state a. To prove the positive recurrence, we apply Foster's theorem, that we recall now in this context: if we can find a function $f : \mathbb{N} \to \mathbb{R}_+$ such that

- $\forall a \in E$, $\mathbb{E}_a(f(R_1)) < +\infty$,
- there exists $\varepsilon > 0$ and a *finite* subset F of $\mathbb{N}$ such that $\forall a \in \mathbb{N} \backslash F$, $\mathbb{E}_a(f(R_1)) \leq f(a) - \varepsilon$,

then $(R_t)_{t \geq 0}$ is positive recurrent. In our case, we simply take f as the identity on $\mathbb{N}$. Since τ_1 is integrable, we have:

$$\mathbb{E}_a(R_1) = \mathbb{E}\left(\max(a - 1, \tau_1)\right) < +\infty,$$

and

$$\begin{aligned}
\mathbb{E}_a(R_1) - a &= \mathbb{E}(\max(a - 1, \tau_1)) - a \\
&= \mathbb{E}(\tau_1 \mathbf{1}_{\tau_1 \geq a}) + (a - 1)\mathbb{P}(\tau_1 \leq a - 1) - a \\
&= \mathbb{E}(\tau_1 \mathbf{1}_{\tau_1 \geq a}) + a(\mathbb{P}(\tau_1 \leq a - 1) - 1) - \mathbb{P}(\tau_1 \leq a - 1) \\
&\leq \mathbb{E}(\tau_1 \mathbf{1}_{\tau_1 \geq a}) - \mathbb{P}(\tau_1 \leq a - 1).
\end{aligned}$$

This last upper bound goes to -1 when a tends to $+\infty$. Taking $\epsilon = 1/2$, we fix $v > 0$ such that for any $a \geq v$, $\mathbb{E}_a(R_1) - a \leq -1/2$, and set $F = \{0, \ldots, v\}$: it is a finite set and Foster's theorem applies [4].   □

- If $p < 1/2$, as noticed before, the random walk $(d_1(t))_{t \geq 0}$ has a negative bias and its absorption time τ_1 has a finite expectation. The previous lemma ensures thus that $(R_t)_{t \geq 0}$ is positive recurrent, and so is $(\eta_t)_{t \geq 0}$.
- If $p > 1/2$, the transience of $(\eta_t)_{t \geq 0}$ follows from Theorem 1 and from Fact 1.

- If $p = 1/2$, $\mathbb{P}(\tau_1 = 0) = 1/4$ and it is a classical result for the symmetric random walk that (in the following lines, C denotes some strictly positive constant whose precise value can change from line to line)

$$\mathbb{P}(\tau_1 = k | \tau_1 > 0) \sim \frac{C}{k^{3/2}} \text{ and } G(k) \overset{\text{def}}{=} \mathbb{P}(\tau_1 \geq k) \sim \frac{C}{k^{1/2}}.$$

Now, for $t > 0$ we have:

$$\mathbb{P}(R_t = 0) = \prod_{i=1}^{t} \mathbb{P}(\tau_i \leq t - i) = \prod_{i=0}^{t-1} \mathbb{P}(\tau_1 \leq i)$$

$$= \exp\left(\sum_{i=1}^{t} \ln(1 - G(i)) \right).$$

As $\ln(1 - G(i))$ is equivalent to $-C/i^{1/2}$, this yields: $\mathbb{P}(R_t = 0) = \mathcal{O}\left(\exp(-C\sqrt{t})\right)$, since we have a diverging sum of elements of the same sign. The Borel-Cantelli lemma then ensures that the chain is transient. □

The results of the theorem can be extended to any initial configuration with a finite positive number of D's and a finite number of 1's. To return to the diagnosis problem, remark that for $p > 1/2$, the transient regime corresponds to a situation where the density of alerts always grows, which implies that we will not be able to discriminate between a small and a high density of failures. In other words, only the case $p < 1/2$ is interesting.

3.5 Initial Configuration with a Positive Density of Defects

For some $\kappa \in (0, 1)$, let us denote by π_κ the probability distribution on $\{0, 1, \mathtt{D}\}^{\mathbb{Z}^2}$ for which cells are in state D with probability κ, and in state 0 with probability $1 - \kappa$, independently for different cells. In this section, we study the evolution of the BQ rule from an initial configuration η_0 distributed according to π_κ, and show (Theorem 3) that there exists a threshold value $\kappa^* > 0$ such that if $\kappa > \kappa^*$, then state 1 invades the grid (invasion regime), while it is not the case if $\kappa < \kappa^*$ (coexistence regime).

The proof of this theorem strongly relies on a comparison of the BQ rule with the *bootstrap process* $(\eta_t')_{t \in \mathbb{N}}$, defined on $\{0, 1\}^{\mathcal{L}}$ as follows:

$\eta_{t+1}'(x, n) = 1$ if and only if $\eta_t'(x, n) = 1$
$$\text{or } \eta_t'(x - 1/2, n - 1) = \eta_t'(x + 1/2, n - 1) = 1.$$

It is known that there exists a threshold $\beta^* \in (0, 1)$ such that from an initial configuration η_0' where each cell, independently, has a probability β to be in state 1:

- for $\beta > \beta^*$, state 1 invades the grid, meaning that for all $(x, n) \in \mathcal{L}$, $\lim_{n \to \infty} \mathbb{P}(\eta_t'(x, n) = 0) = 0$.

- for $\beta < \beta^*$, state 1 does not invade the grid, meaning that for all $(x, n) \in \mathcal{L}$, $\lim_{n \to \infty} \mathbb{P}(\eta_t'(x, n) = 0) > 0$.

The bootstrap rule is related to directed percolation, and it can be proven that $\beta^* = 1 - p_c$, where p_c is the probability threshold for directed site percolation on the square lattice [9]. The exact value of β^* is not known analytically, and numerical simulations give $\beta^* \approx 0.29$ [6].

We are now able to state the following result.

Theorem 3. *For $p \in (0, \beta^*)$, there exists $\kappa^*(p) \in (0, 1)$ such that from an initial configuration η_0 distributed according to π_κ,*

- *for $\kappa > \kappa^*(p)$, state 1 invades the grid, meaning that*

$$\forall(x, n) \in \mathcal{L}, \quad \lim_{n \to \infty} \mathbb{P}(\eta_t(x, n) = 0) = 0,$$

- *for $\kappa < \kappa^*(p)$, state 1 does not invade the grid.*

Proof. For the above bootstrap rule with initial density κ, the state $\eta_n'(\cdot, n)$ of line n at time n has the same distribution as $\omega_n'(\cdot, n)$, where the sequence of configurations $(\omega_n')_{n \in \mathbb{N}}$ is defined by

$$\omega_n'(x, n) = \psi'(\omega_{n-1}'(x - 1/2, n - 1), \omega_{n-1}'(x + 1/2, n - 1)), \text{ with:}$$

- if $q = q' = 1$ then $\psi'(q, q') = 1$,
- otherwise, $\psi'(q, q') = \begin{cases} 1 & \text{with prob. } \kappa, \\ 0 & \text{with prob. } 1 - \kappa. \end{cases}$

and with an initial configuration ω_0' where cells are in state 1 with probability κ on line 0. This follows from the observation that for the bootstrap rule, the state of line $n + 1$ at time $n + 1$ only depends on the state of line n at time n and of the positions of the cells initially in state 1 on line $n + 1$. For each cell independently, this event has a probability κ.

The process $(\omega_n'(\cdot, n))_{n \in \mathbb{N}}$ corresponds to the evolution of a one-dimensional probabilistic cellular automaton, known under the name of *Stavskaya's rule* [10].

We are interested in the evolution of the BQ rule from an initial configuration $\eta_0 \sim \pi_d$. In the same way as for the bootstrap rule, the state $\eta_n(\cdot, n)$ of line n at time n has the same distribution as $\omega_n(\cdot, n)$, where the sequence of configurations $(\omega_n)_{n \in \mathbb{N}}$ is defined by

$$\omega_n(x, n) = \psi(\omega_{n-1}(x - 1/2, n - 1), \omega_{n-1}(x + 1/2, n - 1)), \text{ with:}$$

- if $q, q' \in \{1, D\}$ then $\psi(q, q') = \begin{cases} D & \text{with prob. } \kappa, \\ 1 & \text{with prob. } 1 - \kappa, \end{cases}$
- if $q = q' = 0$ then $\psi(q, q') = \begin{cases} D & \text{with prob. } \kappa, \\ 0 & \text{with prob. } 1 - \kappa, \end{cases}$

$$- \text{ otherwise, } \psi(q, q') = \begin{cases} \text{D} & \text{with prob. } \kappa, \\ 1 & \text{with prob. } (1 - \kappa)p, \\ 0 & \text{with prob. } (1 - \kappa)(1 - p) \end{cases},$$

and with an initial configuration ω_0 where cells are in state D with probability κ on line 0. Furthermore, by stationarity, for any $n \in \mathbb{N}$, the distribution of η_n on line n is the same as the distribution of η_n on line 0.

We can identify states 1 and D into a joined state denoted by $\underline{1}$. The local rule is then rewritten as follows:

$$\psi(\underline{1}, \underline{1}) = \underline{1}, \qquad \psi(0, 0) = \begin{cases} \underline{1} & \text{with prob. } \kappa, \\ 0 & \text{with prob. } 1 - \kappa, \end{cases}$$

$$\psi(0, \underline{1}) = \psi(\underline{1}, 0) = \begin{cases} \underline{1} & \text{with prob. } \kappa + (1 - \kappa)p, \\ 0 & \text{with prob. } (1 - \kappa)(1 - p). \end{cases}$$

This rule dominates the bootstrap rule ψ' in the following sense: one can couple the evolutions of the two processes in such a way that there are more $\underline{1}$'s in ω than 1's in ω'. Consequently, if $\kappa > \beta^*$, this implies that the $\underline{1}$'s invade the grid.

Conversely, if $\kappa + (1 - \kappa)p < \beta^*$, the comparison with the bootstrap rule of parameter $\kappa + (1 - \kappa)p$ implies that the $\underline{1}$'s do not invade the grid.

Furthermore, by Fact 1, the BQ rule is stochastically increasing with κ. It follows that for a fixed $p \in (0, \beta^*)$, increasing κ takes us from the coexistence regime, where 1's do not invade the grid (valid at least as long as $\kappa + (1 - \kappa)p < \beta^*$), to the invasion regime, where 1's invade the grid (valid at least when $\kappa > \beta^*$), which ends the proof.   □

As a byproduct of the proof above, we know that for $p \in (0, \beta^*)$, the critical value $\kappa^*(p)$ is sandwiched between $(\beta^* - p)/(1 - p)$ and β^*. It follows that $\lim_{p \to 0} \kappa^*(p) = \beta^*$. We conjecture that Theorem 3 still holds for $p \in (0, 1/2)$, and that $\lim_{p \to 1/2} \kappa^*(p) = 0$. In other words, this would mean that the BQ rule allows one to detect any threshold of defects between 0 and β^*.

To sum up, we presented two different rules to answer the decentralised diagnosis problem. The first one, the QuorumD rule, has the advantage to be isotropic, which makes us believe that it could be applied to various other networks, in particular to irregular graphs where the number of neighbours varies from cell to cell. On the other hand, its formal analysis is quite difficult and it is an open problem to understand precisely how the density of alerts evolves according to the different parameters. By contrast, the BQ rule introduces an artificial direction for the flow of information but this anisotropy makes the model tractable and we were able to show analytically that a qualitative change of behaviour occurs as the density of defects increases. In both cases, the study needs to be deepened and other local rules need to be studied to understand more clearly how to implement distributed consensus algorithms that would realise a form of self-diagnosis.

References

1. Berry, H., Fatès, N.: Robustness of the critical behaviour in the stochastic Greenberg-Hastings cellular automaton model. Int. J. Unconv. Comput. **7**(1–2), 65–85 (2011)
2. Chalupa, J., Leath, P.L., Reich, G.R.: Bootstrap percolation on a Bethe lattice. J. Phys. C: Solid State Phys. **12**(1), L31 (1979). https://doi.org/10.1088/0022-3719/12/1/008
3. Durrett, R.: .: Probability. Theory and Examples, Cambridge Series in Statistical and Probabilistic Mathematics, vol. 49, 5th edn. Cambridge University Press, Cambridge (2019). https://doi.org/10.1017/9781108591034
4. Foster, F.G.: On the stochastic matrices associated with certain queuing processes. Ann. Math. Statist. **24**, 355–360 (1953). https://doi.org/10.1214/aoms/1177728976
5. Gauville, N., Fatès, N., Marcovici, I.: Diagnostic décentralisé à l'aide d'automates cellulaires. In: Simonin, O., Combettes, S. (eds.) Systèmes Multi-Agents et simulation - Vingt-septièmes journées francophones sur les systèmes multi-agents, JFSMA 2019, pp. 107–116. Cépaduès (2019)
6. Ramos, A.D., Sousa, C.S., Rodriguez, P.M., Cadavid, P.: An improved lower bound for the critical parameter of Stavskaya's process. Bull. Aust. Math. Soc. **102**(3), 517–524 (2020). https://doi.org/10.1017/S0004972720000404
7. Reyes, L., Laroze, D.: Cellular automata for excitable media on a complex network: the effect of network disorder in the collective dynamics. Phys. A: Statist. Mech. Appl. **588**, 126552 (2022). https://doi.org/10.1016/j.physa.2021.126552
8. Reyes, L.I.: Greenberg-Hastings dynamics on a small-world network: the collective extinct-active transition (2017). arXiv:1505.00182
9. Schonmann, R.H.: On the behavior of some cellular automata related to bootstrap percolation. Ann. Probab. **20**(1), 174–193 (1992). https://doi.org/10.1214/aop/1176989923
10. Taggi, L.: Critical probabilities and convergence time of percolation probabilistic cellular automata. J. Statist. Phys. **159**, 853–892 (2015). https://doi.org/10.1007/s10955-015-1199-8

Optimized Reversible Cellular Automata Based Clustering

Viswonathan Manoranjan, Ganta Sneha Rao,
Subramanian Vishnumangalam Vaidhianathan,
and Kamalika Bhattacharjee[(✉)]

Department of Computer Science and Engineering, National Institute of Technology,
Tiruchirappalli 620015, Tamil Nadu, India
kamalika.it@gmail.com

Abstract. The research optimizes reversible cellular automata based clustering technique for any high dimensional dataset. The reversible rules are characterized using the cycle structure properties of each rule to identify *effective* rules for clustering. This essentially reduces the rule search space for a given neighborhood size. A novel encoding technique (BiNCE Encoding) that encodes any dataset into binary form without significant data loss is also introduced for our algorithm. Finally, the algorithm and implementation is transformed into a package which is applicable on various datasets, split sizes and cluster sizes for ease of accessibility and reproducibility. While compared against the state-of-the-art methods using benchmark clustering metrics, it is shown that our algorithm is at par or beating the scores for certain datasets and settings.

Keywords: Reversible Cellular Automata (RCAs) · Clustering · Cycle · Encoding Technique · Silhouette Score · Intra-cluster distance · Package

1 Introduction

Clustering is a significant data analysis approach that involves grouping together comparable data points based on specific criteria. Clustering has grown more crucial than ever before, with the increasing need for effective data handling and the advent of big data. It enables data analysts to detect patterns and relationships in data, resulting in insights that guide decision-making and drive innovation.

There are various algorithms that are used to determine the clusters for a particular dataset. The widely used state-of-the-art algorithms are K-means, Birch Clustering and Hierarchical clustering. These traditional clustering techniques work based on distance-based cluster formation by computing centroids and repeating until the optimal centroid is found.

This work is partially supported by Start-up Research Grant (File number: SRG/2022/002098), SERB, Govt. of India.

L. Manzoni et al. (Eds.): AUTOMATA 2023, LNCS 14152, pp. 74–89, 2023.
https://doi.org/10.1007/978-3-031-42250-8_6

Recent research focusing on non-traditional clustering algorithms has discovered the use of *Reversible Cellular Automata (RCAs)*, which uses the reversibility property to create a better clustering algorithm that performs at par with other state-of-the-art algorithms and sometimes even better than most of them [1,2]. In this paper, we intend to extend the existing works and provide optimizations to improve this largely unexplored natural clustering technique.

2   Related Works and Our Contribution

The reversible cellular automaton (RCA) - a natural clustering technique was introduced in Ref. [1,2]. A reversible cellular automaton is a cellular automaton (CA) in which every configuration has a unique predecessor; so, for each starting configuration, after a number of iterations it is reached again forming a *cycle*. In Ref. [1,2], the authors exploit this property of RCAs for grouping similar entities for clustering. Elements (represented as RCA configurations) which belong to the same cycle become part of the same cluster and each cycle corresponds to a unique cluster. The 'closeness' among entities is represented as entities belonging to the same cycle, that are *reachable* from each other.

The reversible property of the cellular automaton is important for clustering as it allows for accurate analysis of data and enables reversal of the state to ensure richer clustering results. Using this cycle-based clustering technique, past researches have been able to create a better algorithm that performs at par with other state-of-the-art algorithms and sometimes even better than most of them [1–3].

In Ref. [3], the authors are the first to propose a framework to cluster any real-world high-dimensional datasets using 1-dimensional 5-neighborhood binary reversible cellular automata having null boundary conditions (RCA)[1], taking the dataset and the number of clusters as input. As the RCA is binary, datasets need to be encoded and binarized. Thus, they use Frequency-based (FB) encoder [20] to encode and binarize their dataset. The encoded data is split vertically for the *rule application algorithm*, where each split is restricted by a predefined *split_size*[2]. After splitting the encoded binary strings, they cluster the datasets in two stages using two different rules. In the first stage, each vertical split is clustered by the *rule application algorithm* mentioned in Ref. [3]. After getting the initial clusters, each data element is assigned the index of its position in the returned cluster. The returned cluster is converted to binary using the same bit order as the k bit encoding used for the FB encoder. The encoded bit strings of each vertical split are appended to get a single vertical split of size $k * s$, where k is the bit size of FB encoding, and s is the number of vertical splits. This new compressed dataset is fed into Stage 2 of the algorithm, which clusters the single

---

[1] Henceforth in this article, RCA will refer to a 1-dimensional 5-neighborhood binary reversible cellular automaton having null boundary conditions.

[2] The split size has no relation with the dataset size and is related to the computational time. The value of *split_size* can remain the same for larger datasets resulting in a larger number of splits which can be run in parallel.

vertical split into initial clusters using the *rule application algorithm* again. The number of clusters provided by this stage may not be equal to the input number of desired clusters. Thus, the next step involves either – (1) extracting the smallest cluster and merging this cluster with another cluster which is selected based on the Silhouette score until the desired number is reached, or (2) dividing clusters selected based on the Silhouette score into the input number clusters k.

There also exist other non-traditional clustering techniques which are inspired from natural clustering properties of nature and biology. Ant colony optimization [7] is a swarm intelligence [9] based artificial intelligence technique used in the partitioning problem for improving solutions of the K-means method. This technique is inspired by some insects living in collaborative colonies looking for food which makes it a very intuitive and effective method. Bacterial foraging optimization [8] is inspired by another natural methodology for clustering problems in which a group of bacteria forage converges to certain positions as final cluster centers by minimizing the fitness function. Genetics-based clustering [10] uses the searching capability of the natural genetics methodology of taking the chromosomes, which are represented as strings of real numbers, and encode the centers of a fixed number of clusters to search for appropriate cluster centers. Using these methods, numerous clustering algorithms were developed. However, here, we concentrate over the RCA based approach which, in recent years, has been shown to be at par with the state-of-the-art clustering algorithms.

As Reversible Cellular Automata remain mostly unexplored in the area of clustering with a large potential for improvement, it served as our motivation to research them further. The existing works on RCA take an intuitive approach towards clustering, but lack refinement in terms of computation time, data encoding technique, and have scope for flexibility and expandability. The approach taken by Ref. [3] takes a long time to find the optimal clusters due to an exhaustive search of the rule space to find the best set of 2 rules which give optimal results for each dataset. As this proposed clustering algorithm's run-time depends on the length of the encoded string, there is a need to encode the data efficiently. Moreover, the existing algorithms lack the flexibility needed to accommodate any change in RCA configuration, dataset sizes, taking user input for the number of clusters and support for multi-threading to improve performance.

To address these points, we extend the work of Ref. [3] and compare our results with the current state-of-the-art clustering techniques. Our contributions are four-fold that optimize and increase the efficiency of clustering using RCA as follows:

- Characterization of rules to find the efficient set of rules for clustering. Proposing a new rule search algorithm that avoids exhaustive search for rules for any dataset.
- Devising a new encoding algorithm to avoid loss in data and improve the clustering performance scores.

- Providing flexibility for multiple datasets with varying numbers of records and features by saving their optimal rules set for ease of computation when the algorithm is used again for the same dataset.
- Packaging the whole algorithm for ease of replication and development, integrating multi-threading and user input for changing configurations.

3 Methodology

This section describes our methodology of selecting appropriate rules which are effective for clustering and proposes a new encoding technique that minimizes loss of properties of the datasets used for the clustering.

3.1 Selection of Proper Rules

As mentioned in Sect. 2, the proposed RCA algorithm uses a set of 2 unique rules to cluster a dataset, with the condition that these rules are reversible. There are a total of 226 RCA rules which are reversible for some $n \in \mathbb{N}$. A list of those rules is given in Ref. [1]. Out of these, only some rules follow *strict locality* property. For these rules, there is less amount of *information flow* from one neighboring cell to another during the evolution. That means when there is a change in state value in the neighboring cells, that change may not always reflect in an update of the state in the cell under consideration. Consequently, between any two consecutive configurations, there is less number of changes in states that results in the *similar* objects becoming part of the same cycle, that is, of the same cluster. Considering the cell under consideration itself as a neighbor, replication of its state into the next configuration is also essential for maintaining less intra-cluster distance. So, in Ref. [3], an approach has been taken to select only those rules for clustering in which information flow corresponding to every neighbor is $\leq 75\%$ except the self-neighborhood, where the information flow is $\geq 75\%$. This condition, when imposed over a restriction of not taking every neighbor's information flow rate not equal to 0 or 75%, reduces the effective rule set from 226 to 162.

The RCA clustering algorithm of Ref. [3] works with these 162 rules. However, the main problem with this approach and the algorithm of Ref. [3] is, to find the clusters with optimal fit, one needs to exhaustively test all 162 rules and find the clusters with the highest benchmark scores. As our clustering algorithm involves applying the rules in a 2-stage process with a unique combination of rules such that different rules are applied in each stage, a total of $^{162}C_2 = 13041$ combinations of rules are to be exhaustively applied to find the best rules that give good results. This approach is infeasible to be of any practical usage. To reduce the search space and optimize the RCA clustering algorithm, we characterize the RCA rules further.

As in a RCA clustering algorithm, the cycles are directly mapped to the clusters, to have effective clustering with less number of clusters, the RCA needs to have a limited number of cycles. So, the 162 RCA rules which can lead to less intra-cluster distance are filtered out based on their cycle structure. The rules having more cycles are discarded as they lead to poor clustering. For our work, we exhaustively test all 162 rules for each of the cell sizes $n = \{8, \cdots, 13\}$ which user can take as the split sizes and generate the cycle structures for each of the cell sizes separately. The reason for choosing these specific sizes is, as the RCAs under consideration are of 5 neighborhood dependency having null boundary condition, the minimum size of the split can be 7. We start with the next number and conduct experiments till the split size is 13. As running time is exponential to the split size, we restrict the size to 13 for computational limitation. User with higher computational power may choose a larger split size. However, as per our observation, this range is efficient for any high-dimensional datasets in use as it provides a balance between the run time and accuracy of the algorithm. Through these exhaustive experiments run for all the 13041 combinations, the following property is observed:

Property 1. Let $\mathcal{R}$ be the set of reversible rules for a given neighborhood and state and N_{cyc_i} be the number of cycles of rule R_i, $R_i \in \mathcal{R}$. Then, in the given reversible rule set $\mathcal{R}$, there exists rule $R_i \in \mathcal{R}$ with low N_{cyc_i} which performs better at clustering in comparison to $R_j \in \mathcal{R}$ with high N_{cyc_j}.

This indicates that the rules which cluster the maximum number of elements in each cycle, resulting in a lesser number of cycles on applying the rule application algorithm, perform better for clustering, than the other rules. After getting the cycle structures of each rule for a given size n, the rules with the smallest number of cycles are filtered out and labelled as the best rules, $\mathcal{R}_n^{\mathcal{B}}$. This process can be shown as Algorithm 1. Note that the set of rules is unique to a certain split-size, i.e. $\mathcal{R}_{13}^{\mathcal{B}}$ may not contain the same rules as $\mathcal{R}_{12}^{\mathcal{B}}$. However, the same algorithm can be used to generate the best rule set $\mathcal{R}_n^{\mathcal{B}}$ for any size of n.

Algorithm 1: Rule Selection algorithm

Data: $\mathcal{R}$ ▷ set of all rules for a window size ;
n ▷ window size ;
l ▷ limit on length of cycle length
Result: $\mathcal{R}_n^{\mathcal{B}}$ ▷ set of best rules for a window size
$cyc\_str \leftarrow []$;
$\mathcal{R}_n^{\mathcal{B}} \leftarrow []$;
while $i \in len(\mathcal{R})$ **do**
    $cyc\_str = ruleApply(\mathcal{R}[i], n)$;
    while $j \in len(cyc\_str)$ **do**
        if $len(cyc\_str[j]) \geq l$ **then**
            $\mathcal{R}_n^{\mathcal{B}}.append(\mathcal{R}[i])$;   /*here l is an experimental variable limit on the number of cycles based on cycle structure*/
        end
    end
end

After the rule selection algorithm is applied, the number of rules for each split size is reduced greatly which exponentially decreases the number of trials that are needed to run to find the best result. For example, for our chosen range, there are only 20 rules to be included in the best rule-set $\mathcal{R}_n^{\mathcal{B}}$ (see Table 2(a) for the best rules of $n = 13$ considering number of cycles $l \leq 45$) resulting only 190 trials at maximum for exhaustive searching. It is important to notice that the property is not dataset specific, that is, every dataset is most likely to get clustered efficiently in at least one of the 190 trials of rule combinations through the RCA. Thus, the best rule set $\mathcal{R}_n^{\mathcal{B}}$ is universal and can be applied to any dataset, considering the encoding used to convert elements to configuration of the RCA, split size n and neighborhood condition remain the same. Our approach drastically reduces the execution time of the existing RCA algorithm of Ref. [3] even for an exhaustive testing, see Table 4 for a comparison.

3.2 A New Encoding Technique: BiNCE Encoding

Real-valued data cannot be processed by a binary RCA. Hence, encoding is necessary to convert the data into binary values. A variety of encoding algorithms have previously been used to encode datasets such as Gödel number encoding [5], Entropy-based dimensionality reduction [4] and hashing. However, as our algorithm's complexity is proportional to the length of the encoded string, Gödel number encoding is infeasible to use due to the size of encoded string. In the case of hashing using Python's inbuilt hash function SipHash [6] after Entropy-based dimensionality reduction [4], the outcome is that similar data points transform into vastly different strings, affecting the clustering performance. Thus, this method is also infeasible to apply to our algorithm. Few other encoding algorithms, although efficient, result in the loss of features, hence, performing poorly in terms of silhouette scores for the RCA clustering. Thus, there was a necessity for a new custom encoding technique that is efficient without significant loss in performance for clustering using RCA.

We propose a novel encoding technique named Binary Normalised Ceiling Encoding (**BiNCE**), a fixed-width encoding technique to encode numerical and categorical datasets into binarized datasets without sacrificing performance in comparison to the state-of-the-art techniques. The overall encoding algorithm is shown in Algorithm 2. Here, let m be the number of rows in the dataset. The following steps are taken to encode the dataset.

- **Step 1:** Dataset is preprocessed to ensure correct format, removal of garbage values and structural errors, and handling of missing data.
- **Step 2:** Normalize the dataset using Min-Max normalization to scale the score between 0 and 1.
- **Step 3:** Given the bit size of encoding for each feature, split the 0-1 region into the corresponding parts. For e.g., if a 2-bit encoding is used, the 0-1 region is then separated into $2^2 = 4$ regions, that is, 0–0.25, 0.25–0.5, 0.5–0.75 and 0.75–1. Similarly, for an k-bit encoding, the 0-1 region is split into 2^k regions.

Algorithm 2: BiNCE Encoding algorithm

Data: $data \triangleright$ raw numerical data ;
$bit\_size \triangleright$ number of bits to represent a single data point in a row
Result: $enc\_data \triangleright$ encoded data;
$encoded\_data \leftarrow$ [];
while $cols \in data.columns$ **do**
    $data[cols] = minmaxscale(data[cols])$;
    $x = pow(bit\_size, 2)$;
    $splits = intervals\ of\ x \in \{0, 1\}$;
    for $i = 0; i <= len(cols)$ **do**
        $ge = next\ greater\ element\ of\ data[i][cols] \in splits$;   `/*Assigning the`
        `next greater split value to each data element*/`
        $data[i][cols] = ge$;
    end
end
for $i = 0; i <= len(data.rows)$ **do**
    $app\_string ="$;
    for $j = 0; j <= len(data.columns$ **do**
        $app\_string.append(data[i][j])$;   `/*appending the encoded values of`
        `each column in a row to get encoded string*/`
    end
    $enc\_data.append(app\_string)$;
end

- **Step 4:** Each of these regions is assigned an k-bit binary code in ascending order of value. For e.g.

(a)	$0 - 0.25 : \mathbf{00}$	(b)	$0.25 - 0.5 : \mathbf{01}$
(c)	$0.5 - 0.75 : \mathbf{10}$	(d)	$0.75 - 1 : \mathbf{11}$

- **Step 5:** The features are then concatenated horizontally to get a bit string representing one single data. The length of the bit string n will be $k * f$, where k is the bit size of each feature in step 2, and f is the number of features of each data.

Using the above encoding technique, we get the binary string representation for each data point in the dataset for clustering by a RCA. An example can be seen in Fig. 1 with the IRIS dataset [15] before and after BiNCE Encoding (only the header of the dataset is shown). This BiNCE encoding algorithm also results in multiple data points being grouped into similarly encoded representations, that results in a preliminary clustering of data points. The data points once grouped are then inserted into a dictionary that stores the mapping with their encoded data strings. This mapping is exploited at the end to decode the data point back from the encoding.

Id	SepalLengthCm	SepalWidthCm	PetalLengthCm	PetalWidthCm			
0	1	5.1	3.5	1.4	0.2	0	00100000
1	2	4.9	3.0	1.4	0.2	1	00010000
2	3	4.7	3.2	1.3	0.2	2	00010000
3	4	4.6	3.1	1.5	0.2	3	00010000
4	5	5.0	3.6	1.4	0.2	4	00100000

(a) Original Dataset   (b) Encoded Dataset

Fig. 1. BiNCE Encoding on IRIS Dataset. (a) shows the original dataset. (b) shows the encoded dataset (after normalization, encoding and concatenating all 2-bit representations of each column)

4   Implementation and Results

Our implementation of the RCA algorithm considers the BiNCE encoder for encoding the original dataset to the bit strings suitable for RCA and takes only the best rule set $\mathcal{R}_n^{\mathcal{B}}$ for selecting a rule for a certain split size n. To compare the performance of our algorithm to the state-of-the-art clustering techniques, we find the optimal number of clusters for each method using Silhouette coefficient or Silhouette score and compare them using different benchmark clustering metrics. Figure 2 depicts the overall architecture of our proposed methodology.

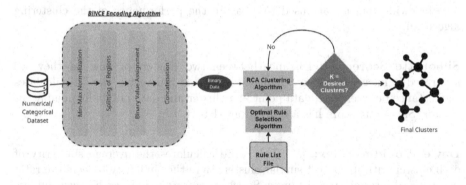

Fig. 2. Design Diagram

4.1   Packaging as a Python Module

No open-source packages are currently available to use RCA for clustering. So, we convert our code into a Python module for easy access, usage and reproduction. The packaged Reverse Cellular Automata Clustering (RCAC) module (along with our BiNCE encoding technique)[3] has the flexibility to handle changes in

---

[3] GitHub repository: https://github.com/Viswonathan06/Reversible-Cellular-Automata-Clustering.

datasets, variable split-sizes, and also takes the number of desired clusters as user input. Conversion of the core and helper functions ensures that our method can be easily imported and used similar to that of K-means and other state-of-the-art clustering techniques.

Saved States: As our clustering algorithm tries different combinations of the reduced rule set $\mathcal{R}_n^\mathcal{B}$, the package saves the best possible rule set that gives the best clustering score for a certain dataset at every point. It creates a *.config* directory and stores the best rule-pair as state for every dataset. If the algorithm has already processed a dataset, it applies that rule-pair and provides the result instantly. However, if such a rule-pair is not found, our algorithm runs for all possible rules in the best rules set and saves the best state for the next run.

Multi-threading: Additionally, the clustering algorithm is multi-threaded, where the combinations of rules to be tried are separated into the number of threads (default threads = 4) and run simultaneously. Multi-threading the algorithm streamlines the efficient utilization of resources as the threads share the same memory and data space. As some rules take longer to apply on a vertical split, running multiple threads increases the algorithm's efficiency.

4.2   Evaluation Metrics

The following metrics are used to measure the performance of the clustering algorithms.

Silhouette Score: [11] Distance between two clusters or how far they are separated is measured using Silhouette score and Silhouette plot. It calculates the distance between each data point in a cluster and data points in an adjacent cluster. Silhouette score has a range from -1 to 1.

Davies-Bouldin Index: [12] This score calculates the average similarity of each cluster with its closest similar cluster. Here the similarity reflects the ratio of intra and inter-cluster distances. So, clusters farther from each other and less scattered will result in a better score. Zero is the minimum score, and lower values represent better clustering.

Calinski-Harabasz Index: [13] When ground truth labels are unknown, the Calinski-Harabasz (CH) index is used to analyze the model. To check whether the clustering is done properly, it uses the specific dataset's quantities and attributes. To determine the similarity between two data points, the distance between data points in a cluster and its cluster's centroid is used. Whereas, to figure out how different they are, the distance between cluster centroids and the global centroid is used.

4.3   Datasets

We test our algorithm over the following datasets: Credit Card Customer Dataset, IRIS Dataset, Heart Failure Dataset, Customer Segmentation Dataset, School District Breakdown (SDB) and Wine Dataset. The details of the datasets (with the number of rows and columns in brackets) are given in Table 1.

Table 1. Dataset Dimensions Details

#Dataset	Primary Datasets	Dimensions	#Dataset	Secondary Datasets	Dimensions
1	Credit Card Customers [14]	$(660, 6)$	4	Customer Segmentation [17]	$(2000, 7)$
2	IRIS [15]	$(150, 4)$	5	Heart Failure [18]	$(299, 12)$
3	School District Breakdown [16]	$(32, 44)$	6	Wine [19]	$(178, 13)$

While the row and column dimensions of the *School District Breakdown* dataset are nearly equal, *IRIS*'s dimensions vary largely and an even greater difference is seen in the *Credit Card Customer Dataset*. Hence, using a variety of datasets helps us to generalize how our algorithm performs for other datasets.

4.4   Results

Depending on the length of the string returned by the BiNCE encoding, vertical split sizes are varied from 8 to 13. The default number of threads is 4 for each experiment, and the system used for running the experiments is an Intel i7 11700K processor with 16M Cache, clocking up to 5.00 GHz with NVIDIA GeForce RTX 3060 graphics card and a 1TB SSD Disk. For lack of space, we report the results of only the primary datasets given in first column of Table 1 (Table 2).

Rule Selection Algorithm: In order to test Property 1, the rules that generate a small number of cycles, that is, the best rules, as well as, the rules that generate a large number of cycles, that is, the worst rules, are tested and their corresponding scores are compared. It is seen that, using the 20 best rules (190 trials) for split size 13 (Table 2(a)) on the Credit Card Customer dataset, we get scores that are comparatively higher than the scores produced by the worst rules. The 5 best and worst rules' results for this dataset are shown in Table 3. Similarly, when applied to the other datasets to get the best results, we observe that, the top 5 scorers may vary but still belong to the best rule set $\mathcal{R}_n^{\mathcal{B}}$ of 20 rules, provided that the split size and encoding method remain the same. As observed in Property 1, the best rules help with clustering most of the data points together in a lesser number of cycles in Stage 1 making Stage 2 more effective, resulting in competitive scores with state-of-the-art clustering algorithms.

Comparison with the State-of-the-Art Algorithms: After finding the optimal clusters for each dataset, we calculate the Silhouette scores, Davies-Bouldin and Calinski-Harabasz scores for each of the 3 primary datasets for

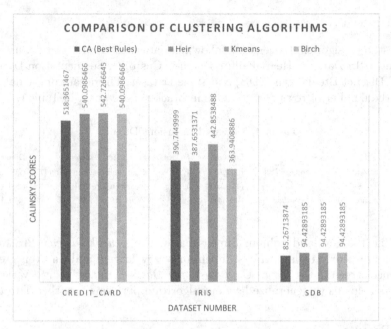

(a) Comparison using Calinski-Harabasz Scores.
*Dataset 1: Credit Card Customers, Dataset 2: IRIS Dataset, Dataset 3:
School District Dataset, Hier: Hierarchical Clustering Algorithm*

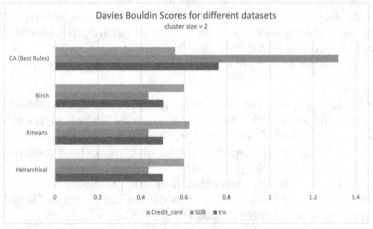

(b) Comparison using Davies-Bouldin Scores.
*Credit_card: Credit Card Customers, Iris: IRIS Dataset, SDB: School
District Dataset*

Fig. 3. Comparison using Davies-Bouldin and Calinski-Harabasz

Table 2. Best rules and State-of-the-art Algorithms' Comparison

(b) Results across multiple datasets vs state-of-the-art methods (Silhouette Score Comparison for split size = 8)

(a) List of best rules (Split size = 13)

Rule	Cycles	Rule	Cycles
3537028050	4	517140690	18
3537035730	8	2018212080	18
4031508660	8	264499440	34
3027809415	10	4039315215	34
3537972705	10	4041289185	34
3035673615	12	2019194970	34
517136850	14	2777130375	34
2018212020	14	3785744805	38
517136850	14	2783028705	40
3538955760	16	3035673780	44

Best Results For Each Dataset			
Credit Card Customer			
RCA	Hier	K-means	Birch
0.4560	0.4065	0.4156	0.4065
Customer Segmentation			
RCA	Hier	K-means	Birch
0.5845	0.5682	0.5834	0.5938
Heart Failure			
RCA	Hier	K-means	Birch
0.5816	0.6789	0.5829	0.6789
Wine Dataset			
RCA	Hier	K-means	Birch
0.4676	0.6587	0.6569	0.6587
IRIS Dataset			
RCA	Hier	K-means	Birch
0.6084	0.6002	0.6205	0.5904
SDB Dataset			
RCA	Hier	K-means	Birch
0.4358	0.4537	0.4537	0.4537

Table 3. Best vs Worst Rules Silhouette Score Results (Split size =13) (Credit Card Customer Dataset)

Best Rule Set			Worst Rule Set		
Silhouette Score	Rules	No. of Cyc	Silhouette Score	Worst Rules	No. of Cyc
0.5974	3035673780	44	−0.0335	254611245	3684
	3538955760	16		1259293455	3684
0.5367	3035673780	44	−0.0535	256577295	6096
	4027576560	64		1259293455	3684
0.5367	3035673780	44	−0.0640	755961615	5156
	3785744805	38		1924428408	5664
0.5217	3035673780	44	−0.0535	256577295	6096
	4042272240	44		1259293455	3684
0.5018	3035673780	44	−0.0335	254611245	3684
	517136850	14		1259293455	3684

comparison with the state of the art algorithms. For these datasets, we get the best scores when the desired number of clusters is given as 2. So, all our results are shown based on number of clusters as 2. Table 2(b) shows the Silhouette score comparison. We can see that our proposed algorithm performs better than all or some of the existing clustering methods. The best results can be seen using the Credit Card Customer Dataset.

Table 4. Comparison of Execution Times

Algorithm	Execution Time
RCA [3] [162 rules]	3.6 h
Optimized RCA (Ours) [20 rules]	3.167 min
K-Means	0.0162 s
Hierarchical	0.00431 s
Birch	0.0474 s

Figure 3(a) shows the Calinski-Harabasz scores for these primary datasets. Here we can see that, the scores for Dataset 1 and 3 are comparable with the preexisting algorithms although not better; whereas, Dataset 2 performs even better than the Hierarchical clustering algorithm. This may be due to lesser loss of data in the encoding phase as it has the smallest number of features amongst the three datasets. The CA algorithm, although comparable to these state-of-the-art methods, does not outperform most of them when performance is measured using Calinski-Harabasz scores.

Finally, Fig. 3(b) shows the Davies-Bouldin scores for these 3 primary datasets. Here, the scores for our algorithm are higher than that of Birch, Kmeans and Hierarchical clustering. Hence, although comparable, Davis Bouldin scores are higher for our clustering algorithm when compared to the state-of-the-art methods.

Overall, the benchmark scores are competitive with those of state-of-the-art method. Although in some cases, the score is lower, it is still comparable with the scores of the existing algorithms. We suspect that there exists some correlation between datasets and RCA rules as according to our experiments, the proposed algorithm's performance greatly depends on the type of dataset used. Also, our RCA algorithm uses silhouette scores to optimize its clustering and therefore makes clustering decisions according to the corresponding silhouette scores. So, accordingly performance with respect to the Silhouette score and the Davies-Bouldin score is better. However, as data is lost during the encoding stage, datasets with large variations in features lose performance and does not perform well using the RCA algorithm. In Table 4, we can compare the execution times of the RCA clustering algorithm with other state-of-the-art clustering algorithms. We note that although there has been an exponential improvement due to the rule selection algorithm, the optimized RCA clustering algorithm is still comparatively slower than the other state-of-the-art algorithms as it has to get the best score by navigating through the set of best rules and its corresponding cycle structures.

Table 5. BiNCE vs Frequency Based Encoding Scores

Dataset num	BiNCE Encoding	Frequency Based Encoding
1	0.4560	0.1990
2	0.6084	0.2913
3	0.4358	0.4131

Efficiency of BiNCE Encoding: Table 5 shows a comparison between the BiNCE and Frequency Based Encoding. We can see those datasets with a small number of features lose less information through BiNCE encoding and therefore achieve higher performance scores. Dataset 2 i.e. IRIS dataset has the least number of features and therefore performs the best, followed by Dataset 1, that is, the Customer Credit Card Dataset with the second least number of features and Dataset 3 which is the School District Dataset with the most number of features. This indicates the a comparative effectiveness of our proposed encoding technique.

5   Conclusion

This study aimed at improving the efficiency of the RCA based clustering algorithm by effectively characterizing and finding the best rule set for clustering. A novel encoding algorithm has been introduced, which can be used in the preprocessing stage in other fields, like feature engineering, where there is comparatively minimal data loss. The packaging of the algorithm makes it easier for users to compare the performance with the traditional clustering algorithms across different datasets with variable split sizes and desired cluster inputs. The proposed optimized RCA algorithm, coupled with the BiNCE encoding algorithm, can outperform state-of-the-art clustering methods for multiple datasets under certain settings. Overall, our optimized RCA clustering algorithm can achieve comparable performance with the state-of-the-art methods, while taking significantly lesser computation time than the existing works.

However, our assessments are primarily restricted to uniform RCA, which limits the sample space of available RCAs. Using non-uniform RCAs increases the sample space, which may provide better clustering results. Exploring this non-uniform RCA path to close the gap between the performance of our algorithm and other existing ones can be the next step in this research. From our results, we suspect a correlation exists between the rules used in Stage 1 and Stage 2 of the clustering algorithm and between the rules and the dataset, which can be a scope for future work. As we have restricted our research by fixing the neighborhood size of the rule to 5, another direction of research would be to find suitable rules for different neighborhood sizes and apply those rules.

References

1. Mukherjee, S., Bhattacharjee, K., Das, S.: Reversible cellular automata: a natural clustering technique. J. Cell. Autom. **16**, 1–38 (2021)
2. Mukherjee, S., Bhattacharjee, K., Das, S.: Clustering using cyclic spaces of reversible cellular automata. Complex Syst. **30**, 205–237 (2021). https://doi.org/10.25088/ComplexSystems.30.2.205
3. Bhattacharjee, K., Abhishek, S., Dharwish, M., Das, A.: A cellular automata-based clustering technique for high-dimensional data. In: Das, S., Martinez, G.J. (eds.) ASCAT 2023, pp. 37–51. Springer, Cham (2023). https://doi.org/10.1007/978-981-99-0688-8_4
4. He, H., Tan, Y.: Automatic pattern recognition of ECG signals using entropy-based adaptive dimensionality reduction and clustering. Appl. Soft Comput. **55**, 238–252 (2017). https://doi.org/10.1016/j.asoc.2017.02.001
5. Negadi, T.: The genetic code via Godel encoding: arXiv preprint arXiv:0805.0695 (2008)
6. Aumasson, J.-P., Bernstein, D.J.: SipHash: a fast short-input PRF. In: Galbraith, S., Nandi, M. (eds.) INDOCRYPT 2012. LNCS, vol. 7668, pp. 489–508. Springer, Heidelberg (2012). https://doi.org/10.1007/978-3-642-34931-7_28
7. Trejos, J., Murillo, A., Piza, E.: Clustering by ant colony optimization. In: Banks, D., McMorris, F.R., Arabie, P., Gaul, W. (eds.) Classification, Clustering, and Data Mining Applications. Studies in Classification, Data Analysis, and Knowledge Organisation, pp. 25–32. Springer, Heidelberg (2004). https://doi.org/10.1007/978-3-642-17103-1_3
8. Wan, M., Xiao, J., Wang, C., Yang, Y.: Data clustering using bacterial foraging optimization. J. Intell. Inf. Syst. JIIS **38**, 321–341 (2011). https://doi.org/10.1007/s10844-011-0158-3
9. Kumar, N., Abraham, A., Pant, M.: Biological and Swarm Intelligence-Based Clustering Algorithms: A Comprehensive Survey and Analysis (2017)
10. Maulik, U., Bandyopadhyay, S.: Genetic algorithm-based clustering technique. Pattern Recogn. **33**, 1455–1465 (2000). https://doi.org/10.1016/S0031-3203(99)00137-5
11. Rousseeuw, P.J.: Silhouettes: a graphical aid to the interpretation and validation of cluster analysis. J. Comput. Appl. Math. **20**, 53–65 (1987). https://doi.org/10.1016/0377-0427(87)90125-7
12. Davies, D.L., Bouldin, D.W.: A cluster separation measure. IEEE Trans. Pattern Anal. Mach. Intell. **PAMI-1**(2), 224–227 (1979). https://doi.org/10.1109/TPAMI.1979.4766909
13. Caliński, T., Harabasz, J.: A dendrite method for cluster analysis. Commun. Stat. **3**(1), 1–27 (1974). https://doi.org/10.1080/03610927408827101
14. Shah, A.: Credit Card Customer Data. https://www.kaggle.com/datasets/aryashah2k/credit-card-customer-data
15. Fisher, R.A.: IRIS. UCI Machine Learning Repository (1988). https://doi.org/10.24432/C56C76
16. Dataworldadmin, School District Breakdowns - dataset by city-of-ny — data.world. https://data.world/city-of-ny/g3vh-kbnw
17. Mahimkar, A.: Customer Segmentation. https://www.kaggle.com/code/adityamahimkar/customer-segmentation/input?select=segmentation+data.csv

18. Larxel, Heart Failure Prediction. https://www.kaggle.com/datasets/andrewmvd/heart-failure-clinical-data
19. Aeberhard, S., Forina, M.: Wine. UCI Machine Learning Repository (1991). https://doi.org/10.24432/C5PC7J
20. Dougherty, J., Kohavi, R., Sahami, M.: Supervised and unsupervised discretization of continuous features. In: Machine Learning Proceedings 1995, pp. 194–202. Morgan Kaufmann (1995)

Multiple-Stream Parallel Pseudo-Random Number Generation with Cellular Automata

Hanan Abdul Jaleel, Saran Kaarthik, Sailesh Sathish,
and Kamalika Bhattacharjee[✉]

Department of Computer Science and Engineering, National Institute of Technology,
Tiruchirappalli 620015, Tamilnadu, India
kamalika.it@gmail.com

Abstract. There exists a need to generate massive amounts of random numbers in parallel for applications like simulation, machine learning, and deep learning in a fast, reproducible, portable, and efficient manner. This work reports the first implementation of a lightweight and efficient multiple-stream parallel random number generator based on cellular automata that is an improvement on the standard CPU implementations of PRNGs like Mersenne Twister and can be parallelized to run on a GPU in order to achieve a significant speedup over all known algorithms. We use a 2-state 3-neighborhood linear maximal-length cellular automaton that acts as the underlying model for the algorithm. This PRNG also passes a majority of the benchmark empirical tests for randomness proposed by the NIST, Dieharder, and TestU01 suites.

Keywords: Pseudo-Random Number Generator (PRNG) · Maximal-Length Cellular Automata · CA (150′) · Multiple Stream Parallel Generator · Graphics Processing Unit (GPU)

1 Introduction

Pseudo-random number generation is a field of computation that concerns the generation of sequences of numbers which look like random for usage in various applications such as Monte Carlo simulations, machine learning, deep learning, and gaming. These applications require the speedy and consistent generation of random numbers which can be achieved with the help of an efficient pseudo-random number generator (PRNG). Formally defined, a PRNG is a deterministic computer algorithm which takes as input(s) a seed/(s) and outputs a sequence of numbers that appear to be random and are uniformly distributed.

One of the most efficient classes of PRNGs to be developed so far is the Mersenne Twister (MT) family of generators by Makoto Matsumoto and Takuji

This work is partially supported by Start-up Research Grant (File number: SRG/2022/002098), SERB, Govt. of India.

L. Manzoni et al. (Eds.): AUTOMATA 2023, LNCS 14152, pp. 90–104, 2023.
https://doi.org/10.1007/978-3-031-42250-8_7

Nishimura [1]. It is widely in use in many programming languages like Python, Ruby, and R. Although quite robust, the Mersenne Twister fails to pass two empirical tests from the BigCrush [2] test suite. In [4], a cellular automaton (CA) based approach has been adapted in order to improve the MT algorithm even further, and this implementation passes almost all the empirical tests. However both these implementations generate numbers in a single stream. Whereas, a single stream of random numbers often will not suffice for several applications that require a large quantity of random numbers to be generated together, especially in simulations. In such cases, there is a need for multiple independent streams of random numbers to be generated very fast.

For applications that require a large number of random numbers to be produced simultaneously, the high computation power of a GPU can be harnessed. However, only a lightweight algorithm can be used for such an implementation, hence rendering the current CPU-based PRNG algorithms ineffective for the same. In recent years, there have been some trials of generating multiple-stream PRNGs; like – recurrence-based PRNGs with period split up over multiple threads, Counter Based PRNGs, and splittable RNGs. Interested readers can see Ref. [3] for a good survey. However, none of these implementations are both fast and effective in terms of randomness quality.

The challenge now lies in developing an algorithm that is robust enough to produce results that pass all the benchmark test suites for randomness and abides by the GPU restrictions in order to produce multiple parallel streams of random numbers very fast. To tackle this, we propose a cellular automata-based approach to develop the algorithm, owing to the simplicity, reliability, and fast implementability of such a solution. We use a special linear CA, called CA (150'), also used in Ref. [4] to produce random numbers and parallelize the algorithm using two different methods in order to obtain a multiple-stream parallel PRNG with maximal period length. We show that our PRNG is several times faster than MT and passes almost all tests of Dieharder and NIST and many important tests of TestU01 library.

2 Background

2.1 Cellular Automata

A cellular automaton is a collection of cells where each cell changes its state over time in p-configuration with a specified rule. Here we consider one-dimensional three neighborhood n-bit binary CA with the null boundary condition. Cells are indexed as 0 to $n - 1$. For any n-cell CA, there are 2^n possible combinations of binary configurations that the CA can generate over a period of time. Ideally, a PRNG requires that the periodicity of the sequence generated is of the maximum possible value; so our aim is to look for a CA that produces the maximum possible set of numbers in a single cycle, that is a *maximal-length* CA. For this reason, we choose a simple CA named CA (150') [4] which uses elementary CA rule 90 in its first cell and CA 150 for all other cells as our PRNG. Let a_i denote the current state of cell i, then application of rule 90 or 150 at cell i is as follows:

$$R_{90} = a_{i-1} \oplus a_{i+1}(mod \quad 2) \tag{1}$$
$$R_{150} = a_{i-1} \oplus a_i \oplus a_{i+1}(mod \quad 2) \tag{2}$$

Rules 90 and 150 are *linear* CA rules and are effective in generating maximal-length cellular automata (CAs). It has been shown that CA (150′) can generate maximal length CA for certain values of n [5]. The nearest such value for a 32-bit GPU implementation is 35. Hence, we choose $n = 35$ in this work, which assures us of maximality directly. A direct benefit of choosing this CA is, it can be characterized by linear algebra by generating its *characteristic matrices*:

Definition 1. *The characteristic matrix T is a matrix of order $n \times n$ that is defined as follows:*

$$T[i,j] = \begin{cases} 1, & \text{if cell } i \text{ depends on cell } j \\ 0, & \text{otherwise} \end{cases}$$

For example, for a 5-cell CA (150′), the characteristic matrix would be as follows:

$$T = \begin{bmatrix} 0 & 1 & 0 & 0 & 0 \\ 1 & 1 & 1 & 0 & 0 \\ 0 & 1 & 1 & 1 & 0 \\ 0 & 0 & 1 & 1 & 1 \\ 0 & 0 & 0 & 1 & 1 \end{bmatrix} \tag{3}$$

There are some beautiful theorems reported in Ref. [5] about this special CA which uses the concept of p-configurations.

Definition 2. *A p-configuration is a configuration in which only one cell in the CA is set to 1, and all other cells are 0s. It is represented as p^i, $0 \le i \le n-1$, which means only the ith cell from the right is set to 1.*

For instance, 00001, 00010, 00100, 01000 and 10000 are the p-configurations for a 5-cell CA. In our scheme, characteristic matrix and p-configurations are used to implement parallelization.

2.2   The Temper Function in Mersenne Twister

In order to improve the randomness of our PRNG and help it perform better in the statistical tests, we use a temper function over the CA output to generate the random numbers of the PRNG. This function has been adopted from the 32-bit implementation of the Mersenne Twister [1]:

$$y = num \oplus (num >> u) \tag{4}$$
$$y = y \oplus ((y << s) \quad \& \quad b) \tag{5}$$
$$y = y \oplus ((y << t) \quad \& \quad c) \tag{6}$$
$$res = y \oplus (y >> l) \tag{7}$$

where num is the CA configuration at any time instant, $u = 11$, $s = 7$, $t = 15$, $l = 18$, $b = 0x9D2C5680$, $c = 0xEFC60000$ and res is the tempered output of the PRNG.

2.3 Testing

We test our PRNG against the rigorous set of empirical tests defined by three test beds, namely NIST, Dieharder, and TestU01. We also check how much faster our implementation is over the standard algorithms through a *speed test*. A brief overview of the empirical testing techniques is given below:

NIST. It is a test package that consists of 15 statistical tests encapsulating 188 subtests for randomness [6]. They focus on a variety of non-randomness that could exist in an arbitrary random number sequence. Some of the tests include the Frequency (Monobit) Test and the Binary Matrix Rank Test. It takes an input file of the numbers generated by the PRNG in binary or ASCII representation.

Dieharder. The Dieharder test suite is an improvement on George Marsaglia's Diehard test suite for randomness and contains 114 empirical tests for randomness [7]. Some of the tests included in the battery are the Birthdays Test, the BitStream test, and the 3D Sphere test. It takes a binary file representation of the numbers generated by the PRNG as input.

TestU01. TestU01 is a software library that is implemented in the ANSI C language and offers a collection of utilities to run the tests [2]. It consists of several batteries of tests, out of which we will mainly be focusing on the SmallCrush and BigCrush batteries. SmallCrush allows us to test our generators quickly and discard the ones that perform terribly in this battery itself, and BigCrush is a comprehensive battery comprising 106 tests. If a PRNG passes all the tests in the BigCrush suite, it is said to be crush-resistant.

Our approach is to develop a PRNG that works as a parallel stream generator but with a small 35-bit internal state. In the next section, we discuss how a CA can be used as a multiple-stream generator.

3 CA as Multiple Stream Parallel Generator

To convert a CA into a multiple stream generator running in parallel, there can be only the following two ways:

1. If the CA has multiple cycles with (almost) equal length, assign a configuration from each cycle to be the starting point of each stream generator. Each of these streams can run in parallel by assigning them to individual threads.

2. If the CA is having a cycle of a very large length, the cycle length can be divided into multiple segments and assigned to individual threads where each thread computes a segment of the cycle of numbers running in parallel.

Now, among these two approaches, the first approach is not suitable for a PRNG as in that case the period length of the PRNG will be very small making it a bad source of randomness. So, in a good PRNG, only the second option is applicable. However, for that, we need to know beforehand the sequence of the numbers that are part of the same cycle, which, in general, is not possible.

To tackle this, we can exploit the properties of a linear maximal-length CA. In a maximal-length CA, the period length is $2^n - 1$ making all non-zero numbers part of the same cycle. But in which sequence are they present in the cycle? Or, in other words, what is the distance between any two configurations? For any arbitrary CA and configuration pair, these questions may be unaddressable. So, as an initial approach, we can run n threads in parallel with each thread taking a p-configuration as the seed. The threads are allowed to run until they encounter another p-configuration, in which case, the process is terminated and the thread stops execution. The problem with such an approach is that the segment lengths are not equal, and some threads may terminate in a very short amount of time as compared to others that run for much longer. However, as we are working with a very special CA called CA $(150')$, we can use its properties to find an effective solution:

Theorem 1. *[5] The following relationship holds in CA $(150')$ with $n \geq 2$:*

$$length(p^{m_0}, p^{o_0}) = 2^0$$
$$length(p^{m_1}, p^{o_1}) = 2^1$$

$$\vdots$$

$$length(p^{m_i}, p^{o_i}) = 2^i$$

$$\vdots$$

$$length(p^{m_k}, p^{o_k}) = 2^k$$

where $m_0 = n - 1$, $o_0 = n - 2$ and the sequences $(m_i)_{0 \leq i \leq k}$, $(o_i)_{0 \leq i \leq k}$ for some $k \leq n - 1$ obeys the following relation:

$$m_{i+1} = \begin{cases} 2m_i + 1 & if 2m_i + 1 < n \\ 2(n - 1 - m_i) & otherwise \end{cases}$$

$$o_{i+1} = \begin{cases} 2o_i + 1 & if 2o_i + 1 < n \\ 2(n - 1 - o_i) & otherwise \end{cases}$$

Here $length(p^{m_i}, p^{o_i})$ indicates the number of iterations to reach the configuration p^{o_i} from p^{m_i}, that is, the distance between them. When CA $(150')$ is a maximal-length CA, all its p-configurations are part of the same cycle and

$$\sum_{0 \leq i \leq n-1} (length(p^{m_i}, p^{o_i}) = 2^n - 1$$

For example, Fig. 1 represents the consecutive p-configurations and their distance for a 5-cell CA (150′). As it is a maximal-length CA, all p-configurations are part of the same cycle and the total cycle length covered by them is $2^5 - 1$.

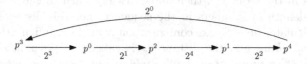

Fig. 1. Relationship among p-configurations in CA (150′) for $n = 5$

Table 1. Relation between the p-configurations for CA(150′) with $n = 35$

i	m_i	o_i	i	m_i	o_i	i	m_i	o_i	i	m_i	o_i	i	m_i	o_i
0	34	33	7	6	20	14	26	9	21	22	1	28	32	27
1	0	2	8	13	28	15	16	19	22	24	3	29	4	14
2	1	5	9	27	12	16	33	30	23	20	7	30	9	29
3	3	11	10	14	25	17	2	8	24	28	15	31	19	10
4	7	23	11	29	18	18	5	17	25	12	31	32	30	21
5	15	22	12	10	32	19	11	34	26	25	6	33	8	26
6	31	24	13	21	4	20	23	0	27	18	13	34	17	16

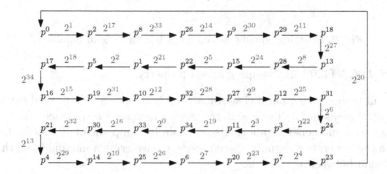

Fig. 2. Position of p-configurations in a cycle for CA (150′) with $n = 35$

For our PRNG, we have chosen $n = 35$. The relation between the p-configurations for this CA is shown in Table 1. Figure 2 shows the positions of p-configurations in the cycle for this CA along with the distance between each of the consecutive configurations. So, another solution for generating multiple-stream PRNG using this CA is to pick up the p-configurations in such a way that, a desired distance is maintained between them.

How can we ensure that the stream lengths are equal? Consider the cycle of numbers produced by the PRNG as shown in Fig. 3. If we can select initial configurations (seeds) as $s_1, s_2, \cdots, s_k$ such that they are equally spaced within the cycle, and select stream length to be equal to the distance between any two of these seeds in the sequence, then automatically, each thread would produce an equal sub-length of numbers in the sequence. Let this distance be ν. The method to calculate the νth next configuration from one configuration is named as the *jumping ahead* and the distance ν is called the *jumping ahead length*. This is essentially a property of the linear dynamical systems representable by the matrix algebra.

Definition 3. *Jumping Ahead: For any linear CA, from any current configuration* x_i, *the configuration after* ν *time steps, that is,* $x_{i+\nu}$ *can be calculated using the characteristic matrix (T) of the CA:*

$$\mathbf{x_{i+\nu}} = T^\nu \times \mathbf{x_i}$$

where $\mathbf{x_i}$ *and* $\mathbf{x_{i+\nu}}$ *are the column-matrix representations (n × 1) of the configurations* x_i *and* $x_{i+\nu}$ *and* ν *is the **jumping ahead** length for the cycle.*

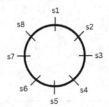

Fig. 3. Selecting equally spaced seeds from a cycle of numbers

Remark 1. CA $(150')$ has jumping ahead property.

If we want to generate k parallel streams, then take one seed. This seed can jump ahead by ν steps in the cycle and generate a new seed ν distance away. Take that new seed and generate another seed again by jump ahead of ν steps. In this way, we can generate k equally spaced seeds. Considering a maximal-length CA, the relation between ν and k is:

$$\nu = \frac{2^{n-1}}{k}$$

For any CA, once k is decided, ν is fixed. So, the next seed s_{i+1} from any seed s_i can be calculated using the characteristic matrix (T) of the CA:

$$\mathbf{s_{i+1}} = T^\nu \times \mathbf{s_i}$$

where $\mathbf{s_i}$ and $\mathbf{s_{i+1}}$ are the column-matrix representation $(n \times 1)$ of the seeds s_i and s_{i+1}. However, a computational overhead of this approach is in computing

T^{ν} where both T and ν can be large depending on n. But, for CA (150′), we can actually avoid this matrix multiplication and generate the T^{ν} directly by exploiting the following property of the T matrix:

Proposition 1. *For any $j \geq 1$, the matrix $T^{2^{j+1}}$ can be calculated from T^{2^j} as the following:*

1. *There is only a single 0 in the main diagonal of $T^{2^{j+1}}$ for any $j \geq 0$.*
2. *Apart from the main diagonal, the remaining 1s in these matrices form a diamond-like pattern. Let $(0, i)$ be the position of the first 1 from the main diagonal in row 0, where $1 \leq i \leq n - 1$. We call this position as the **first position**.*
3. *If $(0, 0)$ position in a matrix is 0, consider the first position as $(0, 0)$.*
4. *Let the first positions in T^{2^j} and $T^{2^{j+1}}$ be $(0, x)$ and $(0, y)$ respectively. Then, the following relationship holds between x and y:*

$$y = \begin{cases} 2x + 1 & \text{if } 2x + 1 < n \\ 2(n - 1 - x) & \text{otherwise} \end{cases}$$

5. *With respect to the first position $(0, i)$, the following positions have value 1 in T^{2^j} for any $j \geq 1$ when that position is a valid cell in the matrix:*
   - $(0, i), (1, i - 1), (2, i - 2), \cdots, (i, 0)$ *[the left-up edge]*
   - $(i + 1, 0), (i + 2, 1), \cdots, (n - 1, n - 2 - i)$ *[the left-down edge]*
   - $(n - 1, n - i), (n - 2, n - i + 1), \cdots, (n - i, n - 1)$ *[the right-down edge]*
   - $(n - i - 2, n - 1), (n - i - 3, n - 2), \cdots, (0, i + 1)$ *[the right-up edge]*
6. *For all $j, 0 \leq j \leq n - 1$, $(j, j) = 1$ except the case when (j, j) appears as part of the construction from Point 1 when it becomes 0. Let this position be called as the **zero position**.*

This proposition can be directly proved using linear algebra over the basic T matrix of CA (150′). For simplicity, we are avoiding the proof here. Interested reader can look into the Pages 16–18 (Appendix) of Ref. [5] for getting idea on how this can be proved. Here, Point 1 gives the base condition to start constructing the matrices. In the T matrix, $(0, 0) = 0$, that is, the first position is $(0, 0)$. Now, using this corollary, we can populate T^2, T^4, T^8, T^{16} etc. For example, let us take the T matrix of CA (150′) for $n = 5$ (Eq. 3). Then, T^2, T^4, T^8, T^{16} and $T^{32} = T$ are as follows:

$$T^2 = \begin{bmatrix} 1 & 1 & 1 & 0 & 0 \\ 1 & 1 & 0 & 1 & 0 \\ 1 & 0 & 1 & 0 & 1 \\ 0 & 1 & 0 & 1 & 0 \\ 0 & 0 & 1 & 0 & 0 \end{bmatrix} \quad T^4 = \begin{bmatrix} 1 & 0 & 0 & 1 & 1 \\ 0 & 1 & 1 & 0 & 0 \\ 0 & 1 & 1 & 0 & 1 \\ 1 & 0 & 0 & 0 & 0 \\ 1 & 0 & 1 & 0 & 1 \end{bmatrix} \quad T^8 = \begin{bmatrix} 1 & 0 & 1 & 1 & 0 \\ 0 & 0 & 0 & 0 & 1 \\ 1 & 0 & 1 & 0 & 0 \\ 1 & 0 & 0 & 1 & 1 \\ 0 & 1 & 0 & 1 & 1 \end{bmatrix} \quad T^{16} = \begin{bmatrix} 1 & 0 & 0 & 0 & 1 \\ 0 & 1 & 0 & 1 & 1 \\ 0 & 0 & 0 & 1 & 0 \\ 0 & 1 & 1 & 1 & 0 \\ 1 & 1 & 0 & 0 & 1 \end{bmatrix}$$

$$T^{32} = \begin{bmatrix} 0 & 1 & 0 & 0 & 0 \\ 1 & 1 & 1 & 0 & 0 \\ 0 & 1 & 1 & 1 & 0 \\ 0 & 0 & 1 & 1 & 1 \\ 0 & 0 & 0 & 1 & 1 \end{bmatrix}$$

Here, for T, the first position is $(0,0)$ and the zero position, where the main diagonal crosses the other patterns of Point 1, is also $(0,0)$. As per Point 1 of Proposition 1, the first position of the T^2 matrix is $(0,1)$, of the T^4 matrix is $(0,3)$, of T^8 is $(0,2)$ and for the T^{16}, the first position is at $(0,4)$. Similarly, the zero positions for these matrices are at $(4,4)$, $(3,3)$, $(1,1)$ and $(2,2)$ respectively. In the T matrix of Eq. 3 as well as in each of the above matrices, the zero position and the diamond like shape created by the 1s of the left-up, left-down, right-up and right-down edges are marked in bold. Thus, using this proposition, we can calculate the first position for any j and build up the T^{2^j} matrix directly without any matrix multiplication. However, if our desired thread length ν is not a power of 2, then we need at maximum n matrix multiplications to find the matrix T^ν:

Proposition 2. *For any $j, 0 \le j \le 2^n$, the matrix T^j can be calculated by as*

$$\prod_i T^{2^i}$$

where $i \le n - 1$ denotes the positions of 1s in the binary representation of j starting from the least signification bit as position 0 and the most significant bit as position $n - 1$.

For example, we can calculate T^{30} using the position of 1s in binary representation of 30, that is, 011110. So, $T^{30} = T^{2^4} \times T^{2^3} \times T^{2^2} \times T^{2^1}$. So, for any $k \le 2^n - 1$, T^k can be calculated by at most n products of the T^{2^j} matrices.

In this way, from one seed we can generate the other k seeds. The value of k can be set to n as the default value or taken from the user. The user can also input a seed s of their liking. The PRNG then calculate the stream length ν and the k seeds using Proposition 1 and 2. Once these k seeds are generated, each can be assigned to a thread such that k random numbers are generated at a time. Each thread generates exactly ν unique numbers without overlapping into next seed. Once ν numbers are generated, the thread stops execution.

4   CA(150′) Based Parallel PRNG

GPUs run multiple Processing Elements (PEs) that execute the same instructions over multiple data streams (SIMD). There exist SIMD restrictions for groups of threads, the number of instructions that can be run per thread and the size of the fast access private memory per thread. All of these must be accounted for while designing an algorithm to be implemented on a GPU.

However, in case of CA, it is simple enough to implement on a GPU – we can implement a CA with a small state per thread/PE and generate random numbers in parallel. The implementation details of our PRNG are as follows:

4.1   Bitwise Implementation

The internal state of our PRNG changes from one configuration to the next in accordance with the rules. For the 35-bit implementation of CA(150′), we have to apply R_{90} to the first bit and R_{150} to all consecutive bits. If this is done bit by bit (cell by cell), considering the CA configuration to be an array of 35 bits, there is a lot of calculation overhead which reduces the speed of the PRNG.

To handle this, a simple improvement can be made on the regular implementation of CA(150') as bitwise implementation that transforms a configuration to the next over a few bitwise operations. This saves a lot of time and drastically improves the running time of the algorithm. The pseudo-code for the bitwise implementation of CA(150') is as shown below:

$$firstBit = (1 << (numOfBits - 1)) \quad \& \quad num$$
$$leftShifted = num << 1$$
$$rightShifted = num >> 1$$
$$temp = leftShifted \oplus num \oplus rightShifted$$
$$newNum = firstBit \oplus temp$$

Here $numOfBits$ is 35 for our CA, num is the present configuration and $newNum$ is the next configuration. So, by using only five bitwise operations, we can generate the next configuration of the CA from its present configuration.

4.2   PRNG with Jumping Ahead

The output of the 35-bit CA (150') based PRNG is k 32-bit random numbers at each time step, considering a k-threaded implementation of the CA. There are two choices for seeds. For parallelization using the p-configurations, we initialize the seeds for each thread t_i, $1 \leq i \leq k$ as the p-configurations chosen from Fig. 2. Here the number of streams (k) can be a user-input. In the second approach, both seed (s) and k can be taken as user-input. Then, we generate the remaining $k - 1$ seeds with the help of the characteristic matrix as shown below:

1. Store all rules in a vector of size n where the ith number in the vector represents the rule applicable to cell i.
2. Store the seed s in the form of an n-sized vector $initialConfig$ where each element represents the state of a cell of the CA.
3. Initialize T to store the characteristic matrix as an $n \times n$ array in which all the elements are 0. Here each row i represents the position at which a rule is applied and each column j shows the involvement of the cells in the CA for any particular i.
4. Iterate through the rule vector and each row of T simultaneously and populate T using Definition 1:
   For the first row (first cell of the CA where rule 90 is applied), set $T[0, 1] = 1$ and for the remaining rows (applying rule 150), set $T[i, i - 1] = T[i, i] = T[i, i + 1] = 1$ where $1 \leq i \leq n - 1$. Set all other entries of T as 0.
5. For $\nu = \frac{2^{n-1}}{k}$, compute the value of $T' = T^\nu$ using Proposition 1 and 2. Set $config = initialConfig$.
6. Now, to generate each of the other $k - 1$ seeds, take the seed generated before (or given for the first case) and compute $s_i = config \times T'$.
   Store s_i in the seed array and set $config = s_i$.
   Iterate over this step to generate all k seeds.

7. Once all the seeds have been computed, initialize the k threads using the seeds from the seed array and generate random numbers using the bitwise implementation of the CA (Sect. 4.1) and tempering function of Sect. 2.2.

To test this PRNG, we need to generate binary files of random numbers which is to be given as input to the test beds. For a 35-bit CA, we generate up to 3 GB of an output file and test with the benchmark testbeds NIST and Dieharder. However, the existing testbeds are not developed for parallel streams, so we have to generate all numbers in a single thread and pass over to the testbeds.

4.3   Finding the Best Seed

Performance of any PRNG is dependent upon the seed. So to find the best seed for our PRNG we take a heuristic approach. It works on the principle that if the number of 0's and 1's in the seed are equal and uniformly distributed, then the randomness quality of the numbers generated will be better. The following algorithm is used to generate 100 such different seeds:

1. We form an array that contains all possible combinations of 4 bits in which the number of 1's and 0's are equal
2. Initialize seed as an empty string
3. Generate a random index value using the **rand** library and select the corresponding array element
4. Append the selected element to the seed, and repeat till the configuration is 35 bits long.
5. Repeat steps 2 to 4 to get 100 different seeds.

We run Dieharder tests on the files generated using these 100 seeds taking whole 35 bits as output number and compare the results in order to see which one performs best. Figure 4 and 5 plot the test results where y-axis represents the number of tests and x-axis notes the seeds. The green line shows the number of tests passed per seed, the blue line shows the number of tests that are weak, and the red line shows the number of tests that fails for each of the seeds. Here, Fig. 4 depicts the case with tempering and Fig. 5 is a graph plotted when tempering is not implemented. From these graphs, the following inferences can be made:

1. The algorithm passes many more Dieharder tests on average with tempering than without tempering.
2. The algorithm performs best for the two seeds given in Table 2 below. They pass all the tests, and show 0 failed or weak tests.

We recommend to use any of these two seeds as the default seed over the jumping ahead method to generate the other $k-1$ seeds for the k parallel threads.

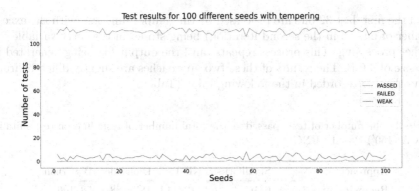

Fig. 4. Dieharder test results over 100 seeds for PRNG with tempering

Table 2. Selected Seeds for our PRNG

#Seed	Binary
1	010 1010 1110 0100 1100 1101 0110 0011 0101
2	100 1100 1101 0010 1101 0100 1011 0001 1010

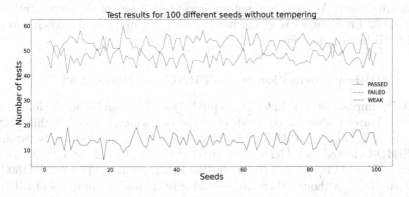

Fig. 5. Dieharder test results over 100 seeds for PRNG without tempering

4.4   The Carry Bits

Note that our 35-bit linear maximal CA produces 32-bit random numbers as output. The question arises as to how we convert the 35-bit configuration of the CA into a 32-bit random number. We have two options:

1. Remove the last 3 bits of the current state of the CA and store it in a carry variable for future processing.
2. Remove the first 3 bits of the current state of the CA and store it in a carry variable for future processing.

In both approaches, the rest of the 32 bits are tempered and output into the test file, and the carry bits are prepended/appended to the next number.

Then the first/last 32 bits are processed by the temper function, with the excess number of bits (6 in the second iteration) being stored in the carry variable for further processing. This process repeats until the output file being generated is of a size of 3 GB. The results of these two approaches are slightly different from each other, as recorded in the following table (Table 3).

Table 3. The number of tests passed vs the total number of tests in each test suite in the CA ($150'$) Based PRNG

Approach	SmallCrush	NIST	Dieharder	BigCrush
Removing first 3 bits	6/10	112/114	187/188	58/106
Removing last 3 bits	6/10	112/114	185/188	54/106

As shown in the table, the CA when tested against the NIST and Dieharder test suites passed almost all the empirical tests. However, this linear CA is not robust enough to pass the BigCrush test battery, failing about 50 tests among the total 106 in the battery, although it passes many important tests of the BigCrush library. As the scheme of removing first 3-bits of the configuration to generate 32 bit numbers is giving better result, we propose this scheme as our final GPU implementation.

4.5   GPU Implementation of the PRNG and Speed Test

The GPU implementation in CUDA is publicly available on Github [8] for anyone to use. Figures 6 shows a comparison of the performance speed of this PRNG over the MT family of PRNGs (the Mersenne Twister and two of its variants, the SIMD-Oriented Fast Mersenne Twister (SFMT) [9], and the Tiny Mersenne Twister (TinyMT) [10]) and the recent implementation of MT by CA ($150'$) of 1409 length [4]. Although there are several existing implementations of PRNGs, we chose only the MT family as they have been shown as the current best PRNGs [11]. In Ref. [11], it has also been shown that the old CA based PRNGs are not comparable to the MT family; therefore we take only the recent MTbyCA of Ref. [4] for comparison. From the figures, it can be observed that our PRNG is much faster in terms of speed than all three variations of the Mersenne Twister and the MTbyCA. This shows its effectiveness as a parallel multiple-stream generator for most of the practical applications where strict randomness is not an issue.

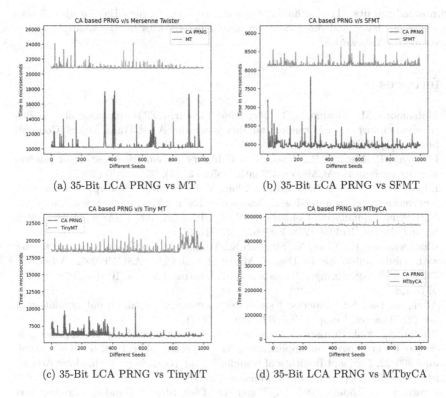

(a) 35-Bit LCA PRNG vs MT

(b) 35-Bit LCA PRNG vs SFMT

(c) 35-Bit LCA PRNG vs TinyMT

(d) 35-Bit LCA PRNG vs MTbyCA

Fig. 6. Speed Test comparison with our PRNG

5   Conclusion and Future Work

Over the course of this work, we have constructed a 32-bit multiple-stream parallel pseudo-random number generator based on a linear maximal length cellular automaton named CA (150′). This PRNG has a period length of 2^{35} which can be split into multiple streams running in parallel based on user requirements. We have taken advantage of the jumping-ahead method of generating seeds for multiple threads in order to parallelize our algorithm, and managed to accomplish a significant speedup over the normal PRNGs. Our PRNG passed most of the empirical tests from the NIST, Dieharder, and many from the TestU01 test suite.

However, there is ample room for improvement as the majority of the BigCrush tests are yet to be passed. This points to the need for further improvement in our linear rule implementation, and the most obvious step that we can take next is to inject non-linearity into the CA and test the results for the same. Non-linearity will serve to make the PRNG more cryptographically secure and may improve the randomness quality of the numbers significantly.

Acknowledgments. The authors are grateful to Prof. Sukanta Das for his valuable comments, guidance and discussions on developing theories for the multiple-stream PRNG used in this work.

References

1. Matsumoto, M., Nishimura, T.: Mersenne Twister: a 623- dimensionally equidistributed uniform pseudo-random number generator. ACM Trans. Model. Comput. Simul. **8**(1), 3–30 (1998)
2. L'Ecuyer, P., Simard, R.: TestU01: a C library for empirical testing of random number generators. ACM Trans. Math. Softw. **33**(4), 22:1-22:40 (2007)
3. L'Ecuyer, P., Nadeau-Chamard, O., Chen, Y.-F., Lebar, J.: Multiple streams with recurrence-based, counter-based, and splittable random number generators. In: 2021 Winter Simulation Conference (WSC), Phoenix, AZ, USA, pp. 1–16 (2021). https://doi.org/10.1109/WSC52266.2021.9715397
4. Bhattacharjee, K., More, N., Singh, S.K., Verma, N.: Emulating mersenne twister with cellular automata. In: Das, S., Martinez, G.J. (eds.) ASCAT 2022. AISC, vol. 1425, pp. 95–108. Springer, Singapore (2022). https://doi.org/10.1007/978-981-19-0542-1_8
5. Adak, S., Das, S.: (Imperfect) strategies to generate primitive polynomials over GF (2). Theoret. Comput. Sci. **872**, 79–96 (2021)
6. Rukhin, A., et al.: Statistical test suite for random and pseudorandom number generators for cryptographic applications, NIST special publication. revision 1a, volume 800-22. National Institute of Standards and Technology, Technology Administration, U.S. Department of Commerce (2010)
7. Brown, R.G., Eddelbuettel, D., Bauer, D.: Dieharder: A Random Number Test Suite. https://webhome.phy.duke.edu/~rgb/General/dieharder.php
8. Multiple-Stream Parallel PRNG with CA. https://github.com/ZaydenClues/CellularAutomataPRNG
9. Saito, M., Matsumoto, M.: SIMD-oriented fast mersenne twister: a 128-bit pseudorandom number generator. In: Keller, A., Heinrich, S., Niederreiter, H. (eds.) Monte Carlo and Quasi-Monte Carlo Methods in Scientific Computing, pp. 607–622. Springer, Heidelberg (2008). https://doi.org/10.1007/978-3-540-74496-2_36
10. Saito, M., Matsumoto, M.: A high quality pseudo random number generator with small internal state. IPSJ SIG Notes **3**, 1–6 (2011)
11. Bhattacharjee, K., Das, S.: A search for good pseudo-random number generators: Survey and empirical studies. Comput. Sci. Rev. **45**, 100471 (2022)

On the Minimum Distance of Subspace Codes Generated by Linear Cellular Automata

Luca Mariot$^{(\boxtimes)}$ and Federico Mazzone

Semantics, Cybersecurity and Services Group, University of Twente,
Drienerlolaan 5, 7511GG Enschede, The Netherlands
{l.mariot,f.mazzone}@utwente.nl

Abstract. Motivated by applications to noncoherent network coding, we study subspace codes defined by sets of linear cellular automata (CA). As a first remark, we show that a family of linear CA where the local rules have the same diameter—and thus the associated polynomials have the same degree—induces a Grassmannian code. Then, we prove that the minimum distance of such a code is determined by the maximum degree occurring among the pairwise greatest common divisors (GCD) of the polynomials in the family. Finally, we consider the setting where all such polynomials have the same GCD, and determine the cardinality of the corresponding Grassmannian code. As a particular case, we show that if all polynomials in the family are pairwise coprime, the resulting Grassmannian code has the highest minimum distance possible.

Keywords: cellular automata · network coding · finite fields ·
Grassmannian · greatest common divisor · Sylvester matrix

1 Introduction

The conventional way of routing packets from source to sink nodes frequently fails to exploit a network's full potential, which is a common issue in networking. The *butterfly network* [10] serves as a classic example of this problem. The field of network coding emerged around two decades ago, and seeks to solve this problem by exploiting a simple idea: instead of simply routing packets, intermediate nodes in the network can *combine* them, usually by employing linear operators [16]. In this way, more packets can be multiplexed over a single channel usage. In the *noncoherent* network coding strategy, the messages transmitted between nodes are subspaces of an ambient vector space [9]. In this scenario, the need to encode and decode subspaces in a reliable way for transmission over networks spawned a branch of coding theory that deals with *subspace codes* [8]. These codes can be seen as a generalization of classic linear error correcting codes, where the codewords are subspaces rather than vectors. By embedding the projective space of a vector space with a suitable metric, it is possible to define the minimum distance between any two codewords in a subspace code. Similarly to the usual

© IFIP International Federation for Information Processing 2023
Published by Springer Nature Switzerland AG 2023
L. Manzoni et al. (Eds.): AUTOMATA 2023, LNCS 14152, pp. 105–119, 2023.
https://doi.org/10.1007/978-3-031-42250-8_8

case of linear error correcting codes, it is desirable to define codes containing a large number of subspaces (to maximize the network's capacity) such that they are at the highest possible distance from each other (to correct as many errors and erasures as possible).

The aim of this paper is to explore the idea of using cellular automata (CA) to construct subspace codes. We consider the specific case of linear CA, motivated by the fact that the body of literature concerning them is quite extensive. Previous work [12] focused on a construction of maximal sets of mutually orthogonal Latin squares (MOLS) based on linear bipermutive CA. Such a construction is equivalent to finding a maximal family of pairwise coprime polynomials over a finite field, all having the same degree and a nonzero constant term. Here, we investigate another research question stemming from this construction: *what kind of subspace codes can be obtained by families of linear CA, if the underlying polynomials that define their local rules are not pairwise coprime?*

The main contributions of this work are listed below:

- We show that a family of linear CA with local rules of the same diameter generates a *constant dimension code*, also known as a Grassmannian code [2].
- We characterize the minimum distance of a Grassmannian code generated by a family of linear CA.
- We observe that the minimum distance of such codes is optimal when the defining polynomials are pairwise coprime. This is the case considered for MOLS and bent functions [3,4], with the resulting Grassmannian codes being a particular breed of the partial spread codes introduced in [7].
- We study the specific case where the rules of a family of linear CA are defined by polynomials that have the same GCD, and determine the number of codewords in the resulting Grassmannian code.

The remainder of this paper is organized as follows. Section 2 recalls all background notions related to cellular automata and subspace codes that are necessary to introduce our results. Section 3 formally defines the subspace code generated by a family of linear CA, and remarks that if the underlying local rules have all the same diameter, the resulting code has constant dimension. Section 4 proves the main result of the paper, namely the relationship between the minimum distance of a Grassmannian code generated by linear CA and the maximum degree occurring among the pairwise GCDs of the associated polynomials. Section 5 analyzes the cardinality of the Grassmannian codes induced by linear CA whose underlying polynomials have the same pairwise GCD. Finally, Sect. 6 summarizes the key contributions of the paper, and elaborates on several directions and open problems for future research on the topic.

2   Basic Definitions

In this section, we cover all the basic definitions and results related to cellular automata and subspace codes used throughout the paper. As a general notation, given $q \in \mathbb{N}$ a power of a prime, we denote by $\mathbb{F}_q$ the finite field of order q. For all $n \in \mathbb{N}$, the set of all n-tuples over $\mathbb{F}_q$ is denoted by $\mathbb{F}_q^n$, and we endow it with the structure of a vector space, where vector sum and multiplication by a scalar are inherited in the usual way from the sum and product operations of $\mathbb{F}_q$.

2.1   Cellular Automata

A Cellular Automaton (CA) is a type of discrete dynamical system that consists of a regular lattice of cells, which can be either finite or infinite. Each cell updates its state based on a local rule that is applied to its own state and the states of its neighboring cells. This updating process occurs simultaneously for all cells in the lattice, and it is repeated over multiple time steps, giving rise to the dynamic behavior of the system. If the lattice is finite, periodic boundary conditions are typically assumed. This ensures that each cell always has enough neighbors to evaluate the local rule.

While most research on CA focuses on their long-term dynamical behavior, in this work we consider CA as algebraic systems. Specifically, the local rule is applied only once, and only by cells that have enough neighbors to evaluate it. This leads to a CA model that can be viewed as a particular type of vectorial functions over finite fields, which we formally define below:

Definition 1. *Let* $d, n \in \mathbb{N}$ *such that* $d \leq n$, *and set* $k = d - 1$. *Further, let* $f : \mathbb{F}_q^d \to \mathbb{F}_q$ *be a d-variable function over the finite field* $\mathbb{F}_q$. *A cellular automaton of length* n, *diameter* d, *and local rule* f *is a vectorial mapping* $F : \mathbb{F}_q^n \to \mathbb{F}_q^{n-k}$ *whose i-th output coordinate is defined as:*

$$F(x_0, \cdots, x_{n-1})_i = f(x_i, \cdots, x_{i+k}) \tag{1}$$

for all $i \in \{0, \cdots, n - k - 1\}$ *and* $x \in \mathbb{F}_q^n$.

Intuitively, the output coordinate F_i consists in the application of the local rule f over the neighborhood formed by the i-th input coordinate and the k coordinates on its right. This is the reason why the function maps the vector space $\mathbb{F}_q^n$ to the smaller subspace $\mathbb{F}_q^{n-k}$: the local rule is applied as long as we have enough right neighbors, i.e., up to the $(n - k)$-th coordinate. Thus, the cellular lattice size is reduced by k coordinates after evaluating F. As we mentioned above, this is not a problem, since we consider only the one-shot application of F and we are not interested in iterating the CA over multiple time steps.

In this work we focus on *linear* CA, where the local rule is a linear combination of the input coordinates, that is, for all $x \in \mathbb{F}_q^d$ we have:

$$f(x_0, \cdots, x_k) = a_0 x_0 + a_1 x_1 + \cdots + a_k x_k \tag{2}$$

for some $a_0, \ldots, a_k \in \mathbb{F}_q$. Further, one can associate to each linear rule of the form (2) a polynomial $P_f \in \mathbb{F}_q[X]$ in a natural way as follows:

$$P_f(X) = a_0 + a_1 X + \cdots + a_k X^k. \tag{3}$$

In other words, we use the coefficients of the vector $(a_0, \cdots, a_k)$ that define the local rule as the coefficients of the monomials X^i, in increasing order of powers. In what follows, we will assume that $a_0, a_k \neq 0$, and in particular that $a_k = 1$. This implies that the local rule is *bipermutive*, since any restriction of f obtained by fixing either the first or the last k input variables induces a permutation of $\mathbb{F}_q$ respectively on the last or on the first variable [12]. Moreover, the polynomial associated to f is monic of degree k and has a nonzero constant term.

2.2   Subspace Codes

In this section we cover only the basic notions related to subspace codes. We refer the reader to [9] for a more comprehensive treatment of the subject.

We start by considering the vector space $\mathbb{F}_q^n$. We denote by $\mathcal{P}(\mathbb{F}_q^n)$ its *projective space*, i.e., the family of all subspaces of $\mathbb{F}_q^n$. Usually, in the context of network coding, the projective space is interpreted as a metric space under the following distance: for all $A, B \in \mathcal{P}(\mathbb{F}_q^n)$, we have

$$d(A, B) = dim(A) + dim(B) - 2dim(A \cap B). \tag{4}$$

We can now introduce the definition of subspace code:

Definition 2. *Let $n \in \mathbb{N}$. A subspace code $\mathcal{C}$ of parameters $[n, \ell(\mathcal{C}), \log_q |\mathcal{C}|,$ $D(\mathcal{C})]$ is a subset of $\mathcal{P}(\mathbb{F}_q^n)$ where $\ell(\mathcal{C}) = \max_{V \in \mathcal{C}} \{dim(V)\}$ and $D(\mathcal{C})$ is the minimum distance of $\mathcal{C}$, defined as:*

$$D(\mathcal{C}) = \min_{U, V \in \mathcal{C}} \{d(U, V)\}, \tag{5}$$

where $d(\cdot, \cdot)$ is computed as in (4).

This definition generalizes the concept of error-correcting codes by considering codewords that are subspaces rather than vectors. In other words, the elements of the code are not individual vectors, but sets of vectors that form a subspace of the underlying vector space.

The set of all subspaces of dimension k, for a given $0 \leq k \leq n$, is also called the *Grassmannian*, and it is denoted by $Gr(\mathbb{F}_q^n, k)$. Accordingly, a subspace code $\mathcal{C} \subseteq Gr(\mathbb{F}_q^n, k)$ is known as a *Grassmannian* code, or equivalently a *constant dimension code*, since each subspace in $\mathcal{C}$ has dimension k.

The main problem studied for subspace codes is analogous to the one studied for classic error-correcting codes: for a fixed minimum distance δ, what is the maximum cardinality achievable by a subspace code $\mathcal{C}$ with $D(\mathcal{C}) = \delta$? Intuitively, the lower the allowed minimum distance δ is, the more subspaces we can pack together in a code—and therefore, in the context of network coding, the more messages we can transmit over a network. On the other hand, one also wants that any two subspaces are as far as possible from each other for error-correction purposes, or equivalently a subspace code with the highest minimum distance possible. In the following sections we explore this trade-off for subspace codes defined by families of linear CA.

3   Subspaces Codes from Families of Linear CA

We now describe our method to construct subspace codes using sets of linear CA. Suppose that $F : \mathbb{F}_q^n \to \mathbb{F}_q^{n-k}$ is a linear CA defined by a local rule $f : \mathbb{F}_q^d \to \mathbb{F}_q$ of diameter d with associated polynomial $P_f(X) = a_0 + a_1 X + \cdots + a_k X^k$ where $k = d - 1$. This CA is a linear mapping of the form $F(x) = M_F \cdot x^\top$ for all $x \in \mathbb{F}_q^n$, where M_F is a $(n - k) \times n$ matrix over $\mathbb{F}_q$ of the following form:

$$M_F = \begin{pmatrix} a_0 \ldots a_k & 0 & 0 & \ldots & 0 \\ 0 & a_0 \ldots a_k & 0 & \ldots & 0 \\ \vdots & \ddots & \ddots & \ddots & \vdots \\ 0 \ldots & 0 & 0 & a_0 \ldots & a_k \end{pmatrix}. \tag{6}$$

The matrix M_F is called the *transition matrix* of F, and it is obtained by shifting the coefficients of P_f one place to the right per each subsequent row. As we discussed in Sect. 2.1, we assume that $a_0 \neq 0$ and $a_k = 1$. In this way, the polynomial P_f is monic of degree k with a nonzero constant term, and all the columns of M_F are nonzero.

Now, let us consider the *kernel* $ker(f)$ of the linear CA F. By definition, this is the subspace of input vectors $x \in \mathbb{F}_q^n$ such that $F(x) = \underline{0}$, and it is equivalent to the nullspace of the matrix M_F. From the rank-nullity theorem, the number of columns of M_F equals the sum of the rank of M_F and the dimension of its nullspace, that is

$$n = \mathrm{rank}(M_F) + dim(\mathrm{Null}(M_F)). \tag{7}$$

Since the matrix is already in row echelon form (recall that $a_0 \neq 0$ by assumption), we can immediately tell that its rank is $n-k$, and thus $dim(\mathrm{Null}(M_F)) = k$.

From the discussion above, we can conclude the following result:

Lemma 1. *Let $F : \mathbb{F}_q^n \to \mathbb{F}_q^{n-k}$ be a linear CA defined by a local rule $f : \mathbb{F}_q^d \to \mathbb{F}_q$ of diameter d. Then, $dim(ker(F)) = k$.*

We are now ready to define a subspace code generated by a set of linear CA.

Definition 3. *Let $n, d \in \mathbb{N}$ with $d \leq n$ and $k = d - 1$. The subspace code generated by a family $\mathcal{F}$ of t linear CA $F_1, \cdots, F_t : \mathbb{F}_q^n \to \mathbb{F}_q^{n-k}$, respectively defined by bipermutive local rules $f_1, \cdots, f_t : \mathbb{F}_q^d \to \mathbb{F}_q$ of diameter d, is the set*

$$\mathcal{C}_\mathcal{F} = \{ker(F_i) : 1 \leq i \leq t\}. \tag{8}$$

In other words, the subspace code consists of the kernels of all the t linear CA in the family $\mathcal{F}$. The reader might wonder why we choose specifically the kernels of the CA instead of, for instance, their images. This will become clearer in Sect. 4 where we exploit this fact to characterize the minimum distance of the code. Moreover, from Lemma 1 it holds that each kernel in $\mathcal{C}_\mathcal{F}$ has dimension k. Thus, we have the following result:

Lemma 2. *The subspace code $\mathcal{C}_\mathcal{F}$ defined in Eq. (8) is a Grassmannian code, i.e. $\mathcal{C}_\mathcal{F} \subseteq Gr(\mathbb{F}_q^n, k)$.*

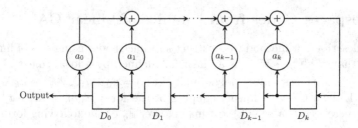

Fig. 1. Example of linear feedback shift register of order k.

3.1 Computing Preimage of Linear CA with Linear Feedback Shift Register

In this section, as a side remark, we show how to compute the kernel of a linear CA F by using a *Linear Feedback Shift Register* (LFSR). To begin, a method to construct the kernel of F is by using the following *preimage computation* procedure:

– Set the output configuration of the CA F to the null vector $\underline{0}$.
– For all $\tilde{x} = (\tilde{x}_0, \tilde{x}_1, \cdots, \tilde{x}_{k-1}) \in \mathbb{F}_q^k$, do:
   1. Set the first k coordinates of the CA input $x \in \mathbb{F}_q^n$ to $\tilde{x}$, that is, $x_0 = \tilde{x}_0$, $x_1 = \tilde{x}_1, \cdots, x_{k-1} = \tilde{x}_{k-1}$.
   2. For all $i \in \{k, \cdots, n-1\}$, compute the i-th input coordinate x_i as:

$$x_i = -(a_0 x_{i-k} + a_1 x_{i-k+1} + \cdots + a_{k-1} x_{i-1}). \tag{9}$$

Equation (9) stems from the fact that the i-th output coordinate of the CA must be zero (since the whole output configuration is the null vector $\underline{0}$). Thus, one can recover x_i from the equation of the local rule, moving all the terms $a_0 x_{i-k}, \cdots, a_{k-1} x_{i-1}$ to the left hand side and changing their sign. Since we assume $a_k = 1$, one then obtains Eq. (9).

This preimage computation procedure is equivalent to the computation of a k-th order homogeneous *Linear Recurring Sequence* (LRS) [11]. In particular, the kernel of F corresponds to all infinite sequences $x_0, x_1, \cdots$ of elements in $\mathbb{F}_q$ that satisfy the following recurrence equation:

$$a_0 x_i + a_1 x_{i+1} + \cdots + a_k x_{i+k} = 0, \tag{10}$$

and truncating such sequences to the n-th element. Thus, one can compute the kernel of F by using an LFSR of order k and with feedback polynomial P_f (see Fig. 1). The idea is to initialize the registers $D_0, \cdots, D_{k-1}$ with the starting block $\tilde{x} \in \mathbb{F}_q^k$ of the preimage x, and then run the LFSR for n clock steps. At each step $i \in \{0, \cdots, n-1\}$, the rightmost register D_k is updated with the feedback of the linear recurrence Eq. (10), while the leftmost register D_0 outputs the value of x_i. We remark that this approach has been adopted in [15] to study the period of spatially periodic preimages in linear bipermutive CA and in [13] to construct cyclic codes from linear CA.

4   Relation Between Minimum Distance and GCD

Lemma 2 prompts us with the following natural question: is it possible to charac-terize the minimum distance of a Grassmannian code generated by a family $\mathcal{F}$ of linear CA, possibly linking it with the properties of the polynomials associated to the local rules? In this section, we analyze this issue.

In the following discussion, we make the assumption that $n = 2k$. Hence, a subspace code is generated by a family of linear CA $F_1, \cdots, F_t : \mathbb{F}_q^{2k} \to \mathbb{F}_q^k$. The codewords of the Grassmannian code $\mathcal{C}_{\mathcal{F}}$ are the kernels $ker(F_i)$ for $1 \leq i \leq t$. By applying (4), and Lemma 2, the distance between any two kernels in $\mathcal{C}_{\mathcal{F}}$ equals:

$$d(ker(F), ker(G)) = dim(ker(F)) + dim(ker(G)) - 2dim(ker(F) \cap ker(G)) =$$
$$= 2k - 2dim(ker(F) \cap ker(G)). \tag{11}$$

Thus, this distance is inversely proportional to the size of the intersection of the kernels. We can then characterize the minimum distance $D(\mathcal{C}_F)$ in terms of the largest intersection between any two kernels in the subspace code. To this end, we first need some further results. Given any two CA $F, G \in \mathcal{F}$, with local rules f, g respectively, we can define their concatenation $H : \mathbb{F}_q^{2k} \to \mathbb{F}_q^{2k}$ as the map

$$H(x) := F(x) \| G(x). \tag{12}$$

Remark 1. We can easily see that H is still a linear application, and $H(x) = \underline{0}$ if and only if $F(x) = \underline{0}$ and $G(x) = \underline{0}$. So we have that the kernel of H is nothing else than the intersection $ker(F) \cap ker(G)$.

The matrix associated to H is the vertical concatenation of M_F and M_G:

$$M_H = \begin{pmatrix} a_0 & \dots & a_k & 0 & 0 & \dots & 0 \\ 0 & a_0 & \dots & a_k & 0 & \dots & 0 \\ \vdots & \dots & \ddots & \ddots & \ddots & \dots & \vdots \\ 0 & \dots & 0 & 0 & a_0 & \dots & a_k \\ b_0 & \dots & b_k & 0 & 0 & \dots & 0 \\ 0 & b_0 & \dots & b_k & 0 & \dots & 0 \\ \vdots & \dots & \ddots & \ddots & \ddots & \dots & \vdots \\ 0 & \dots & 0 & 0 & b_0 & \dots & b_k \end{pmatrix}. \tag{13}$$

We can recognize such matrix as the *Sylvester matrix* associated to the polyno-mials P_f, P_g corresponding to the local rules f, g. Notably, the determinant of this matrix is called the *resultant* of P_f and P_g, denoted by $Res(P_f, P_g)$, and it is known that $Res(P_f, P_g) \neq 0 \Leftrightarrow \gcd(P_f, P_g) = 1$ [6]. In other words, the Sylvester matrix M_H is invertible if and only if the two polynomials P_f, P_g defin-ing the local rules of F and G are relatively prime. This fact was used by the authors of [12] to construct orthogonal Latin squares from linear CA.

In our setting of Grassmannian codes, we are interested in the more general situation where the Sylvester matrix associated to F and G is not necessarily invertible. To determine the dimension of the intersection of $ker(F)$ and $ker(G)$ we need the following result that links the dimension of the null space of the Sylvester matrix to the degree of the GCD of the two polynomials[1]:

Lemma 3. *Let* $f, g \in \mathbb{F}_q[X]$ *be two polynomials, and denote by* $S_{f,g}$ *their Sylvester matrix. Then,*

$$dim(\mathrm{Null}(S_{f,g})) = \deg(\gcd(f, g)). \tag{14}$$

Proof. Notice that $S_{f,g}$ *has size* $m \times m$, *where* $m = \deg(f) + \deg(g)$. *The idea is to compute the null space* $\mathrm{Null}(S_{f,g}^\top) = \{z \in \mathbb{F}_q^m : S_{f,g}^\top z^\top = \underline{0}\}$ *of the transposed Sylvester matrix. For any* $z \in \mathrm{Null}(S_{f,g}^\top)$ *we write* $z = (w\|v)$ *as the concatenation of the vectors* $w \in \mathbb{F}_q^{\deg(g)}$ *and* $v \in \mathbb{F}_q^{\deg(f)}$. *Next, we associate to* w *and* v *two polynomials* s, t *respectively defined as:*

$$s(X) = w_0 + w_1 X + w_2 X^2 + \cdots + w_{\deg(g)} X^{\deg(g)}, \tag{15}$$

$$t(X) = v_0 + v_1 X + v_2 X^2 + \cdots + v_{\deg(f)} X^{\deg(f)}. \tag{16}$$

where clearly $\deg(s) \leq \deg(g)$ *and* $\deg(t) \leq \deg(f)$. *Then we have that* $S_{f,g}^\top z$ *can be written in polynomial form as:*

$$f(X)s(X) + g(X)t(X) = \gcd(f,g)(X)\,(f_0(X)s(X) + g_0(X)t(X)), \tag{17}$$

for suitable $f_0, g_0 \in \mathbb{F}_q[X]$ *that are relatively prime. Therefore,* z *belongs to the null space of* $S_{f,g}^\top$ *if and only if*

$$f_0(X)s(X) + g_0(X)t(X) = 0. \tag{18}$$

By taking this identity modulo g_0, *and omitting from now on the* (X) *notation, we obtain*

$$f_0 s \equiv 0 \pmod{g_0}. \tag{19}$$

Since f_0 *and* g_0 *are coprime, we have* $g_0 \mid s$, *thus* $s = g_0 p$ *for some* $p \in \mathbb{F}_q[X]$. *Further, note that* $\deg(p) = \deg(s) - \deg(g_0) \leq \deg(g) - \deg(g_0) = \deg(\gcd(f,g))$. *By replacing this in (18) we get*

$$f_0 g_0 p + g_0 t = g_0(f_0 p + t) = 0, \tag{20}$$

hence $t = -f_0 p$. *Thus,* z *belongs to the null space if and only if* (s, t) *is of the form* $(g_0 p, -f_0 p)$ *for some* p *with degree at most* $\deg(\gcd(f, g))$. *The dimension of the nullspace of (the transpose of)* $S_{f,g}$ *is then* $\deg(\gcd(f, g))$. $\qquad\square$

We can now prove our main result: the minimum distance of a Grassmannian code $\mathcal{C}_{\mathcal{F}}$ generated by a family $\mathcal{F}$ of linear CA of diameter d is determined by the largest degree of the pairwise GCD computed over the polynomials that define the local rules.

---

[1] Other proofs of this Lemma can be found in [1] (Proposition 1), or in [17] (Lemma 3.1). We report an alternative proof here to make it consistent with our notation.

Theorem 1. *Let $\mathcal{F}$ be a family of linear CA of length $2k$, each defined by a linear local rule of diameter d where $k = d - 1$. Then, the minimum distance of the Grassmannian code $\mathcal{C}_{\mathcal{F}}$ generated by $\mathcal{F}$ is equal to:*

$$D(\mathcal{C}_{\mathcal{F}}) = 2k - 2 \cdot \max_{\substack{F,G \in \mathcal{F} \\ F \neq G}} \{\deg(\gcd(P_f, P_g))\}, \tag{21}$$

where P_f, P_g are the polynomials associated to the local rules of F and G.

Proof. By Eq. (11), the distance between any two kernels $\ker(F), \ker(G)$ in $\mathcal{C}_{\mathcal{F}}$ is equal to $2k - 2dim(\ker(F) \cap \ker(G))$. Hence, to determine $D(\mathcal{C}_{\mathcal{F}})$, we need to compute

$$\max_{F,G \in \mathcal{F}} \{dim(\ker(F) \cap dim(\ker(G))\}. \tag{22}$$

Recall that, by Remark 1, the nullspace of the Sylvester matrix M_H defined by F and G is the intersection of $\ker(F)$ and $\ker(G)$. Therefore, we have

$$dim(\ker(F) \cap dim(\ker(G)) = dim(\text{Null}(M_H)). \tag{23}$$

Now, by Lemma 3, we have that $dim(\text{Null}(M_H)) = \deg(\gcd(f, g))$. We can thus rewrite (22) as:

$$\max_{F,G \in \mathcal{F}} \{dim(\ker(F) \cap dim(\ker(G))\} = \max_{F,G \in \mathcal{F}} \{\deg(\gcd(f, g))\}, \tag{24}$$

which proves our theorem. □

5   Equidistant Constant Dimension Codes from Linear CA

In the previous section we proved that the minimum distance of a Grassmannian code generated by a family of linear CA depends on the maximum degree of the pairwise GCDs of their associated polynomials. We now analyze how large such a code can be by considering some specific cases.

For a given minimum distance δ, one ideally wants to define a subspace code in such a way that it contains as many codewords as possible. To phrase it differently, we want to find the maximum number of degree k polynomials in $\mathbb{F}_q[X]$, such that their pairwise GCD has degree at most $t = k - \delta/2$.

The optimal case of the highest minimum distance occurs when $t = 0$. As a matter of fact, this happens when all polynomials that define the linear CA in the family $\mathcal{F}$ are pairwise coprime, as shown in the next result:

Lemma 4. *Let $\mathcal{C}_{\mathcal{F}}$ be a Grassmannian code generated by a set $\mathcal{F}$ of linear CA $F_1, \cdots, F_r : \mathbb{F}_q^{2k} \to \mathbb{F}_q^k$, defined by the local rules $f_1, \cdots, f_r : \mathbb{F}_q^d \to \mathbb{F}_q$ of diameter d where $k = d - 1$. Suppose that for each $F_i, F_j \in \mathcal{F}$ with $i \neq j$ the polynomials P_{f_i}, P_{f_j} associated to the local rules respectively of F_i and F_j are coprime, that is $\gcd(P_{f_i}, P_{f_j}) = 1$. Then, the minimum distance of the code is:*

$$D(\mathcal{C}_{\mathcal{F}}) = 2k. \tag{25}$$

Notice that the code in Lemma 4 is also *equidistant*: every pair of codewords in $\mathcal{C}_{\mathcal{F}}$ has distance $2k$. The maximum cardinality achievable by a subspace code of this kind corresponds to the size N_k of the largest family of pairwise coprime polynomials with degree k and nonzero constant term. This problem has already been addressed in [12], where the authors algorithmically build such sets of polynomials and prove their maximality. Specifically, N_k is equal to:

$$N_k = I_k + \sum_{j=1}^{\lfloor \frac{k}{2} \rfloor} I_j \,, \tag{26}$$

where, for all $n \in \mathbb{N}$, I_n is the cardinality of the set $\mathcal{I}_n$ of irreducible polynomials of degree n, which can be computed through *Gauss's formula* [5]:

$$I_n := |\mathcal{I}_n| = \frac{1}{n} \sum_{d|n} \mu(d) q^{n/d} \,, \tag{27}$$

with $\mu(\cdot)$ denoting the *Möbius function* [11].

If we relax the assumption on the minimum distance, allowing it for being non-optimal, we get into the generic case, where we allow the pairwise GCDs to have degree at most $t > 0$. In what follows, let us define the set of all monic polynomials of degree k with nonzero constant term as:

$$\mathrm{Poly}_k(\mathbb{F}_q) := \{f \in \mathbb{F}_q[X] : f \text{ monic}, f(0) \neq 0, \deg(f) = k\} \,. \tag{28}$$

Further, let $\mathrm{CD}_{k,t}(\mathbb{F}_q)$ be the family of subsets of $\mathrm{Poly}_k(\mathbb{F}_q)$ such that the degree of the pairwise GCDs is at most t:

$$\mathrm{CD}_{k,t}(\mathbb{F}_q) := \{S \subseteq \mathrm{Poly}_k(\mathbb{F}_q) : \forall f_1, f_2 \in S, \deg(\gcd(f_1, f_2)) \leq t\} \,. \tag{29}$$

The goal is to find a maximal element of $\mathrm{CD}_{k,t}(\mathbb{F}_q)$ and its cardinality, that is $\max_{S \in \mathrm{CD}_{k,t}(\mathbb{F}_q)} |S|$. This general case is quite tricky to handle. For this reason, here we address an intermediate problem, where we assume that *all pairs of polynomials have exactly the same GCD* $g \in \mathbb{F}_q[X]$ *with degree* t. This corresponds to finding the largest set in:

$$\mathrm{CF}_{k,g}(\mathbb{F}_q) := \{S \subseteq \mathrm{Poly}_k(\mathbb{F}_q) : \forall f_1, f_2 \in S, \gcd(f_1, f_2) = g\} \,. \tag{30}$$

Remark that the resulting Grasmannian code is again equidistant in this case, with minimum distance $2k - 2t$.

The fixed polynomial g is a common divisor of all the polynomials in the set S. So, for any polynomial $f \in \mathrm{Poly}_k(\mathbb{F}_q)$, we can find f' such that $f = gf'$, with $\deg(f') = k - t$. To build our maximal set S and compute its size, we can therefore use the same approach as in [12] applied to $\mathrm{Poly}_{k-t}(\mathbb{F}_q)$. In particular, we can build a set $S \in \mathrm{CF}_{k,g}(\mathbb{F}_q)$ by adopting a straightforward variation of the algorithm CONSTRUCTION-IRREDUCIBLE. The modified pseudocode is reported below:

CONSTRUCTION-UNIFORM-GCD(k, g)
Initialization: Initialize set T to $\mathcal{I}_{k-t}$, where $t = \deg(g)$
Loop: For all $1 \leq i \leq \lfloor \frac{k-t}{2} \rfloor$ do:
  1. Build set T_i by multiplying each polynomial in $\mathcal{I}_i$ with a distinct polynomial in $\mathcal{I}_{k-t-i}$
  2. Add set T_i to T
Final step: If $k - t$ is odd, build set $T_{(k-t-1)/2}$ by multiplying each polynomial in $\mathcal{I}_{(k-t-1)/2}$ with a distinct polynomial in $\mathcal{I}_{(k-t+1)/2}$, and add $T_{(k-t-1)/2}$ to T. If $k - t$ is even, build set $T_{(k-t)/2}$ by squaring each irreducible polynomial in $\mathcal{I}_{(k-t)/2}$, and add $T_{(k-t)/2}$ to T. Finally, define the set $S := \{gf' : f' \in T\}$.
Output: return S

It is easy to see that the set built by the above algorithm belongs to $\mathrm{CF}_{k,g}(\mathbb{F}_q)$: every element of S is monic since the product of monic polynomials, it has constant coefficient non-zero since both factors do as well, and it has degree k. Moreover, since the intermediate set T belongs to $\mathrm{CF}_{k,1}(\mathbb{F}_q)$ thanks to [12], it follows that for all $f_1', f_2' \in T$ we have $\gcd(f_1', f_2') = 1$ and thus $\gcd(gf_1', gf_2') = g$.

Therefore, by following the same arguments in [12], we can see that the cardinality of such set is:

$$|S| = I_{k-t} + \sum_{i=1}^{\lfloor \frac{k-t}{2} \rfloor} I_i. \tag{31}$$

Finally, regarding the maximality, we pick a maximal element $A \in \mathrm{CF}_{k,g}(\mathbb{F}_q)$ and define $A' := \{f/g : f \in A\}$. Then, the proof can just follow the argument of [12] by applying it to the set A'.

5.1   Example

Now, we show how to generate such subspace codes through a practical example. For the sake of simplicity, we work on the binary field $\mathbb{F}_2$, with CAs of length $n = 8$ and diameter $d = 6$. This means our linear CAs are maps $F : \mathbb{F}_2^8 \to \mathbb{F}_2^2$ defined by a local rule $f : \mathbb{F}_2^6 \to \mathbb{F}_2$ of the form

$$f(x_0, x_1, x_2, x_3, x_4, x_5) = x_0 + a_1 x_1 + a_2 x_2 + a_3 x_3 + a_4 x_4 + x_5 \tag{32}$$

for coefficients $a_1, a_2, a_3, a_4 \in \mathbb{F}_2$, with associated polynomial

$$P_f(X) = 1 + a_1 X + a_2 X^2 + a_3 X^3 + a_4 X^4 + X^5 \in \mathbb{F}_2[X]. \tag{33}$$

We fix the GCD to be the polynomial $g = X + 1 \in \mathbb{F}_2[X]$, and we apply CONSTRUCTION-UNIFORM-GCD with parameters $(5, X + 1)$. For convenience, we report in Table 1 all the irreducible binary polynomials up to degree 4. Note that, in our case, the degree of the GCD is $t = 1$, and $k = d - 1 = 5$.

We first create a maximal family of pairwise coprime polynomials of degree 4. To do so, we start by selecting all the irreducible polynomials in $\mathcal{I}_4$. Then,

Table 1. Irreducible polynomials in $\mathbb{F}_2[X]$ up to degree 4. Note that x is omitted on purpose since it has constant term zero.

$\mathcal{I}_1$	$X+1$
$\mathcal{I}_2$	X^2+X+1
$\mathcal{I}_3$	X^3+X^2+1
	X^3+X+1
$\mathcal{I}_4$	$X^4+X^3+X^2+X+1$
	X^4+X^3+1
	X^4+X+1

we multiply each polynomial in $\mathcal{I}_1$ with a distinct polynomial in $\mathcal{I}_3$, that is we select the product $(X+1)(X^3+X^2+1)$ (note that $(X+1)(X^3+X+1)$ would have worked as well). Finally, we square each polynomial in $\mathcal{I}_2$, that is, we select $(X^2+X+1)^2$. Our maximal family of pairwise coprime polynomials is then:

$$X^4+X^3+X^2+X+1$$
$$X^4+X^3+1$$
$$X^4+X+1 \tag{34}$$
$$(X+1)(X^3+X^2+1)$$
$$(X^2+X+1)^2.$$

Thus, a maximal family of degree 5 polynomial with pairwise GCD exactly $g = X+1$ is given by:

$$(X^4+X^3+X^2+X+1)(X+1) = X^5+1$$
$$(X^4+X^3+1)(X+1) = X^5+X^3+X+1$$
$$(X^4+X+1)(X+1) = X^5+X^4+X^2+1 \tag{35}$$
$$(X+1)(X^3+X^2+1)(X+1) = X^5+X^4+X^3+1$$
$$(X^2+X+1)^2(X+1) = X^5+X^4+X^3+X^2+X+1.$$

And the associated family of local rules $\mathbb{F}_2^6 \to \mathbb{F}_2$ is:

$$\begin{aligned}
f_1(x_0,x_1,x_2,x_3,x_4,x_5) &= x_0 &&&&& +x_5 \\
f_2(x_0,x_1,x_2,x_3,x_4,x_5) &= x_0+x_1 && +x_3 && +x_5 \\
f_3(x_0,x_1,x_2,x_3,x_4,x_5) &= x_0 &+ x_2 && + x_4+x_5 \\
f_4(x_0,x_1,x_2,x_3,x_4,x_5) &= x_0 &&+x_3 &+ x_4+x_5 \\
f_5(x_0,x_1,x_2,x_3,x_4,x_5) &= x_0+x_1 &+ x_2+x_3 &+ x_4+x_5\,.
\end{aligned} \tag{36}$$

By Definition 1, each local rule $f_i : \mathbb{F}_2^6 \rightarrow \mathbb{F}_2$ induces a linear CA $F_i : \mathbb{F}_2^8 \rightarrow \mathbb{F}_2^2$, which can be represented by the corresponding 3×8 transition matrix:

$$M_{F_1} = \begin{pmatrix} 1\,0\,0\,0\,0\,1\,0\,0 \\ 0\,1\,0\,0\,0\,0\,1\,0 \\ 0\,0\,1\,0\,0\,0\,0\,1 \end{pmatrix} \qquad M_{F_2} = \begin{pmatrix} 1\,1\,0\,1\,0\,1\,0\,0 \\ 0\,1\,1\,0\,1\,0\,1\,0 \\ 0\,0\,1\,1\,0\,1\,0\,1 \end{pmatrix}$$

$$M_{F_3} = \begin{pmatrix} 1\,0\,1\,0\,1\,1\,0\,0 \\ 0\,1\,0\,1\,0\,1\,1\,0 \\ 0\,0\,1\,0\,1\,0\,1\,1 \end{pmatrix} \qquad M_{F_4} = \begin{pmatrix} 1\,0\,0\,1\,1\,1\,0\,0 \\ 0\,1\,0\,0\,1\,1\,1\,0 \\ 0\,0\,1\,0\,0\,1\,1\,1 \end{pmatrix} \qquad (37)$$

$$M_{F_5} = \begin{pmatrix} 1\,1\,1\,1\,1\,1\,0\,0 \\ 0\,1\,1\,1\,1\,1\,1\,0 \\ 0\,0\,1\,1\,1\,1\,1\,1 \end{pmatrix}$$

This family of linear CAs $\mathcal{F} = \{F_1, F_2, F_3, F_4, F_5\}$ in turn gives rise to the subspace code $\mathcal{C}_{\mathcal{F}}$, whose codewords are the kernels of the CAs in $\mathcal{F}$. To compute such kernels, one could apply the technique showed in Sect. 3.1, or any standard linear algebra procedure. By Lemma 1, each kernel is a vector subspace of $\mathbb{F}_2^8$ of dimension 5, so we can represent them by a 5×8 matrices. Our subspace code is then given by:

$$\mathcal{C}_{\mathcal{F}} = \left\{ \begin{array}{l} ker(F_1) = \begin{pmatrix} 0\,0\,1\,0\,0\,0\,0\,1 \\ 0\,1\,0\,0\,0\,0\,1\,0 \\ 1\,0\,0\,0\,0\,1\,0\,0 \\ 0\,0\,0\,0\,1\,0\,0\,0 \\ 0\,0\,0\,1\,0\,0\,0\,0 \end{pmatrix}, \quad ker(F_2) = \begin{pmatrix} 1\,1\,1\,0\,0\,0\,0\,1 \\ 1\,1\,0\,0\,0\,0\,1\,0 \\ 0\,1\,1\,0\,0\,1\,0\,0 \\ 1\,1\,0\,0\,1\,0\,0\,0 \\ 0\,1\,1\,1\,0\,0\,0\,0 \end{pmatrix}, \\[3em]
ker(F_3) = \begin{pmatrix} 1\,0\,1\,0\,0\,0\,0\,1 \\ 1\,1\,1\,0\,0\,0\,1\,0 \\ 1\,1\,0\,0\,0\,1\,0\,0 \\ 0\,0\,1\,0\,1\,0\,0\,0 \\ 0\,1\,0\,1\,0\,0\,0\,0 \end{pmatrix}, \quad ker(F_4) = \begin{pmatrix} 0\,0\,1\,0\,0\,0\,0\,1 \\ 0\,1\,1\,0\,0\,0\,1\,0 \\ 1\,1\,1\,0\,0\,1\,0\,0 \\ 1\,1\,0\,0\,1\,0\,0\,0 \\ 1\,0\,0\,1\,0\,0\,0\,0 \end{pmatrix}, \\[3em]
ker(F_5) = \begin{pmatrix} 0\,1\,1\,0\,0\,0\,0\,1 \\ 1\,0\,1\,0\,0\,0\,1\,0 \\ 0\,0\,1\,0\,0\,1\,0\,0 \\ 0\,0\,1\,0\,1\,0\,0\,0 \\ 0\,0\,1\,1\,0\,0\,0\,0 \end{pmatrix} \end{array} \right\}.$$

$$(38)$$

6   Conclusions and Future Works

In this paper, we started to investigate subspace codes generated by families of linear CA. We first remarked that the subspaces codes generated by CA with uniform diameter are Grassmannian. Then, we proved that the minimum distance of such codes is determined by the maximum degree of the pairwise

GCDs of the polynomials associated to the local rules. Finally, we analyzed the maximal cardinality achievable by these subspace codes, considering two particular cases. The first one corresponds to the problem of counting how many pairwise coprime monic polynomials of fixed degree and nonzero constant term over a finite field exist, already addressed in [12], and we remarked that the resulting Grassmannian codes achieve the highest possible minimum distance $2k$. Next, we focused on the case where the polynomials have the same pairwise GCD. We presented a modified version of the algorithm in [12] to construct such a set of polynomials, and we showed that it is maximal.

There are several interesting directions to explore for future research. The most straightforward generalization would be to build Grassmannian codes from sets of linear CA where the underlying polynomials do not have the same pairwise GCD, but the degree is still fixed. The next step would then be to build and count the codes by setting an upper bound on the degree of the GCD. In this way, the cardinality of the optimal code can be determined exactly. Further, a comparison with the Grassmannian codes obtained with our method against those already published in the literature is in order, since the optimal case of our construction is a specific instance of the partial spreads codes introduced in [7]. Finally, we would like to investigate the *decoding* aspect of our subspace codes, and study if it is possible to exploit the parallel nature of the CA to build an efficient decoder. We believe that the inversion algorithm for mutually orthogonal CA presented in [14] represents a viable starting point to investigate this direction.

Acknowledgement. We would like to thank the anonymous reviewers for their useful comments and suggestions to improve the paper. We are also grateful to Giovanni Tognolini for his feedback on the preprint version of our manuscript, and also for suggesting a reference with the proof of Lemma 3.

References

1. Busé, L., Khalil, H., Mourrain, B.: Resultant-based methods for plane curves intersection problems. In: Ganzha, V.G., Mayr, E.W., Vorozhtsov, E.V. (eds.) CASC 2005. LNCS, vol. 3718, pp. 75–92. Springer, Heidelberg (2005). https://doi.org/10.1007/11555964_7
2. Etzion, T., Zhang, H.: Grassmannian codes with new distance measures for network coding. IEEE Trans. Inf. Theory **65**(7), 4131–4142 (2019)
3. Gadouleau, M., Mariot, L., Picek, S.: Bent functions from cellular automata. IACR Cryptology ePrint Archive, p. 1272 (2020)
4. Gadouleau, M., Mariot, L., Picek, S.: Bent functions in the partial spread class generated by linear recurring sequences. Des. Codes Cryptogr. **91**(1), 63–82 (2023)
5. Gauß, C.F.: Disquisitiones arithmeticae. Humboldt-Universität zu Berlin (1801)
6. Gelfand, I.M., Kapranov, M., Zelevinsky, A.: Discriminants, Resultants, and Multidimensional Determinants. Springer, New York (2008). https://doi.org/10.1007/978-0-8176-4771-1
7. Gorla, E., Ravagnani, A.: Partial spreads in random network coding. Finite Fields Their Appl. **26**, 104–115 (2014)

8. Khaleghi, A., Silva, D., Kschischang, F.R.: Subspace codes. In: Parker, M.G. (ed.) IMACC 2009. LNCS, vol. 5921, pp. 1–21. Springer, Heidelberg (2009). https://doi.org/10.1007/978-3-642-10868-6_1

9. Koetter, R., Kschischang, F.R.: Coding for errors and erasures in random network coding. IEEE Trans. Inf. Theory **54**(8), 3579–3591 (2008)

10. Kschischang, F.R.: An introduction to network coding. In: Network Coding, pp. 1–37. Elsevier (2012)

11. Lidl, R., Niederreiter, H.: Finite Fields. Cambridge University Press, Cambridge (1997)

12. Mariot, L., Gadouleau, M., Formenti, E., Leporati, A.: Mutually orthogonal Latin squares based on cellular automata. Des. Codes Cryptogr. **88**(2), 391–411 (2020)

13. Mariot, L., Leporati, A.: A cryptographic and coding-theoretic perspective on the global rules of cellular automata. Nat. Comput. **17**(3), 487–498 (2018)

14. Mariot, L., Leporati, A.: Inversion of mutually orthogonal cellular automata. In: Mauri, G., El Yacoubi, S., Dennunzio, A., Nishinari, K., Manzoni, L. (eds.) ACRI 2018. LNCS, vol. 11115, pp. 364–376. Springer, Cham (2018). https://doi.org/10.1007/978-3-319-99813-8_33

15. Mariot, L., Leporati, A., Dennunzio, A., Formenti, E.: Computing the periods of preimages in surjective cellular automata. Nat. Comput. **16**(3), 367–381 (2017)

16. Médard, M., Sprintson, A.: Network Coding: Fundamentals and Applications. Academic Press, Cambridge (2011)

17. Zeng, Z.: The numerical greatest common divisor of univariate polynomials. In: Randomization, Relaxation, and Complexity in Polynomial Equation Solving, vol. 556 (2011)

Regular Papers – AUTOMATA 2022

Triangle Solitaire

Ville Salo[1]([✉])[iD] and Juliette Schabanel[2]([✉])[iD]

[1] University of Turku, Turku, Finland
vosalo@utu.fi
[2] École Normale Supérieure PSL, 45 rue d'Ulm, 75005 Paris, France
juliette.schabanel@ens.fr

Abstract. The solitaire of independence is a reversible process (more precisely, a groupoid/group action) resembling the classical 15-puzzle, which gives information about independent sets of coordinates in a totally extremally permutive subshift. We study the solitaire with the triangle shape, which corresponds to the spacetime diagrams of bipermutive cellular automata with radius 1/2. We give a polynomial time algorithm that puts any finite subset of the plane in normal form using solitaire moves, and show that the solitaire orbit of a line of consecutive ones – the line orbit – is completely characterised by the notion of a fill matrix. We show that the diameter of the line orbit under solitaire moves is cubic.

Keywords: solitaire of independence · TEP subshift · subshift of finite type · bipermutive cellular automata

1 Introduction

Multidimensional symbolic dynamics study sets of vertex-labellings of the lattices $\mathbb{Z}^d$ under local constraints (forbidden patterns), mainly for $d \geq 2$ (the one-dimensional case being somewhat different in nature [8]). The basic object in this theory is the subshift of finite type or SFT, namely the set of $X \subset A^{\mathbb{Z}^2}$ defined by a finite alphabet A and a finite set of finite forbidden patterns, which may not appear anywhere in the configurations $x \in X$.

A typical phenomenon in this theory is undecidability, namely most basic questions, like whether a given pattern appears in the subshift or whether it is even nonempty, are undecidable [1,14]. Natural questions can be high in the arithmetical hierarchy [5] (or even analytic). Similarly, the values of invariants such as entropies [3] and periods [4] are best described by recursion theory and notions from theoretical computer science. In contrast, in the one-dimensional case simple-sounding problems tend to be solvable (with some exceptions), and there are often combinatorial and algebraic descriptions for values of invariants.

It is an interesting quest to try to find conditions on SFTs that make them less complicated and more like their one-dimensional counterparts. One such class are the totally extremally permutive (TEP) subshifts introduced in [12]. Here, we restrict to TEP subshifts defined by a triangle-shaped rule. It was

© IFIP International Federation for Information Processing 2023
Published by Springer Nature Switzerland AG 2023
L. Manzoni et al. (Eds.): AUTOMATA 2023, LNCS 14152, pp. 123–136, 2023.
https://doi.org/10.1007/978-3-031-42250-8_9

shown in [12] that these subshifts have at least two properties that set them apart from general SFTs, namely they have computable languages and admit a kind of uniform measure.

The idea of a TEP subshift arises from the theory of cellular automata. Indeed a two-dimensional TEP subshift can be seen as the spacetime subshift of a particular kind of cellular automaton. We concentrate here on the triangle shape $\{(1,1),(0,1),(1,0)\}$, equivalently the spacetime diagrams of radius-$\frac{1}{2}$ bipermutive cellular automaton (with $(0,-1)$ as the arrow of time and $\{-1,0\}$ as the neighbourhood), studied for example in [9–11,13]. For example, the spacetime subshift of the XOR cellular automaton with alphabet $\{0,1\}$ and local rule $f(a,b) = a \oplus b$, also known as the Ledrappier [7] or three-dot subshift, is TEP with this shape.

Specifically, what we study here are the independent sets of a TEP subshift with the triangle shape $\{(0,0),(0,1),(1,0)\} \subset \mathbb{Z}^2$, namely sets $A \subset \mathbb{Z}^2$ having the property that one can freely choose their content. While it remains open how to characterise such sets, we give here a complete algorithm for putting such a set in normal form in terms of the solitaire process introduced in [12], which reduces the problem of independence to independence of sufficiently disjoint triangular areas.

Our main interest is in the *line orbit*, namely the solitaire orbit of the line of n horizontally adjacent cells. We show that the line orbit corresponds exactly to the fill matrices studied previously by Gerhard Kirchner in [6].

Letting (V, E) denote the graph with this orbit as its nodes and E as the solitaire moves, from the connection with fill matrices we immediately obtain a polynomial-time algorithm for checking whether a subset of the plane belongs to V (Algorithm 1), and that the number of vertices is between $(c_1 n)^n$ and $(c_2 n)^n$ for some constants c_1, c_2 (Theorem 5). We show how to find connecting paths between elements of V in polynomial-time (Algorithm 2), and show that the diameter of (V, E) is $\Theta(n^3)$ (Theorem 4).

Algorithm 1 gives a positive answer to the last two subquestions of Question 5.36 in [12].

2   Definitions

The action we consider in this paper is the solitaire move with the triangle shape $T = \{(0,1);(1,1);(1,0)\}$ on elements of $\{0,1\}^{\mathbb{Z}^2}$. This action consists in arbitrarily permuting the three patterns depicted in Fig. 1 at some coordinates where one of them appears in the pattern.

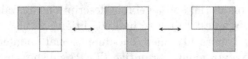

Fig. 1. The action of the triangle shape. Grey denotes 1, white denotes 0.

We call this a *solitaire move*, or more specifically a *triangle move*. The *orbit* of a pattern P, denoted $\gamma(P)$ is the set of patterns reachable from it using the triangle moves. In what follows, we only consider patterns with finitely many 1s.

The solitaire arises from the study of *TEP subshifts* [12]. We omit the general definition, and give this only for the triangle shape T: Let Σ be a finite alphabet and let $R \subset \Sigma^T$ satisfy the following, for any $\{a, b, c\} = T$: for all $p \in \Sigma^{\{a,b\}}$ there exists a unique $s \in \Sigma$ such that $p \sqcup (c \mapsto s) \in R$, where $\sqcup$ denotes disjoint union of patterns. Then R is called a *TEP family*. The set $X_R \subset \Sigma^{\mathbb{Z}^2}$, consisting of all $x \in \Sigma^{\mathbb{Z}^2}$ such that for all $v \in \mathbb{Z}^2$ the pattern $t \mapsto x_{v+t}$ is in R, is called a *triangular TEP subshift*.

Triangular TEP subshifts are precisely the spacetime subshifts (sets of spacetime diagrams) of bipermutive cellular automata, namely if $f : \Sigma^2 \to \Sigma$ satisfies that $a \mapsto f(a, b)$ and $a \mapsto f(b, a)$ are bijective for all $b \in \Sigma$, then it is easy to see that the patterns $(a, b, f(a, b)) \in \Sigma^{((0,1),(1,1),(1,0))}$ form a TEP family (and the converse holds as well).

3 Characterisation of the Orbits

In this section, we give a normal form for each γ-orbit and show a simple way to determine the orbit to which a given pattern belongs.

3.1 Notations and First Result

The *neighbourhood* of a point x is depicted Fig. 2, it corresponds to the points which can be involved in a triangle move with x. The neighbourhood of a pattern A, denoted $N(A)$ is the union of the neighbourhoods of its points. Two patterns A and B *touch* if $A \cap N(B) \neq \varnothing$ or $B \cap N(A) \neq \varnothing$.

Fig. 2. The neighbours of the orange cell are the blue ones. (Color figure online)

Let $T_n = \{(a, b) \in \{0, \ldots, n-1\}^2 \mid a + b \geq n - 1\}$ denote the size-n triangle. By its *edges* we refer to the intersections of the edges of its convex hull with the lattice $\mathbb{Z}^2$.

Proposition 1. *For every n, the three edges of T_n are in the same orbit.*

Proof. The first line of Fig. 3 explains by example how to transform the horizontal line into the diagonal, and the second one how to transform the diagonal into the vertical line (of course this is just a rotated inverse of the first transformation). □

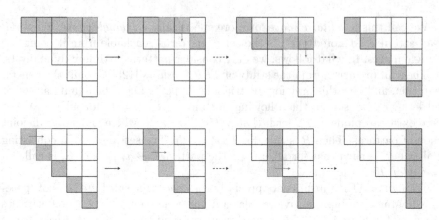

Fig. 3. How to transform one line into another for $n = 5$.

3.2 The Filling Process

The operation of *filling* a pattern P with the triangle shape was introduced in [6] to define the fill matrices. It consists in recursively adding to P the points that complete a triangle with two points of P until no more can be added. More precisely, in a single step we may add w if $P \cap |v + T| = 2$ and $w \in v + T$ (Fig. 4).

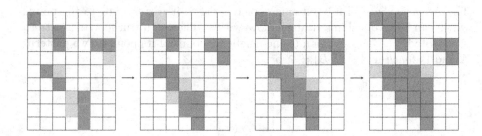

Fig. 4. An example of filling process.

Clearly this transformation is confluent and terminating, and we denote by $\varphi(P)$ its unique fixed point. Clearly $\varphi(P)$ upper bounds the set of points which can appear in patterns in the solitaire orbit of P.

We say P *fills* if $\varphi(P) = v + T_n$ for some vector v where $n = |P|$. In [6], filling sets P were called *fill matrices*. We will show that they in fact correspond to the elements of the line orbit.

Lemma 1. *If two patterns P and Q are in the same orbit, then $\varphi(P) = \varphi(Q)$.*

Proof. There is a sequence of transformation $t_1, \ldots, t_k$ that transforms P into Q. Starting with P, we can fill the triangles at position $t_1, \ldots, t_k$, thus adding all the points of Q to P, so $\varphi(Q) \subset \varphi(P)$. The other inclusion is symmetric.   □

Lemma 2. *For any pattern P, there are unique integers $k_1, \ldots k_r$ and vectors $v_1, \ldots v_r$ such that $\varphi(P) = \bigcup_{i=1}^{r} v_i + T_{k_i}$, $\sum_{i=1}^{r} k_i \leqslant |P|$ and $N(T_{k_i}) \cap T_{k_j} = \varnothing$ for each $i \neq j$.*

Proof. We prove this by induction on $|P|$. The case $|P| = 1$ is trivial.

Now assume the result is true for patterns of size at most n and let P be a pattern of size $n+1$. Then if $x \in P$, $P \backslash \{x\}$ satisfies the induction hypothesis so we can write $\varphi(P \backslash \{x\}) = \bigcup_{i=1}^{r} v_i + T_{k_i}$. We now have three cases to consider. First, if $x \in \varphi(P \backslash \{x\})$ then $\varphi(P) = \varphi(P \backslash \{x\})$. Then, if x is not in the neighbourhood of $\varphi(P \backslash \{x\})$ then no additional filling can be done with it, therefore $\varphi(P) = \varphi(P \backslash \{x\}) \cup \{x\}$ and, as $\{x\}$ is a triangle, we have the appropriate decomposition.

Finally, assume $x \in N(v_1 + T_{k_1})$, then we can extend $T_{k_1} + v_1$ as in Fig. 5. By doing so we may lose the property that the triangles do not touch, but if some do so we can merge them by repeating the extension process. Notice that if two triangles are merged, then the new triangle cannot be larger than the sum of the sizes of the initial triangle so the inequality on the triangles' sizes is still satisfied. (Merges may be triggered recursively, but nevertheless no merge can increase the sum of triangle sizes.) □

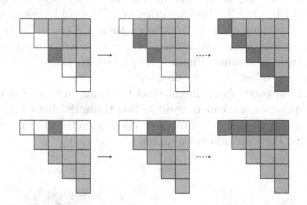

Fig. 5. How to extend a triangle with a top neighbour or a subdiagonal neighbour. The right neighbour case is symmetric to the top neighbour case.

We define the *excess* of P as the difference $e(P) = |P| - \sum_{i=1}^{r} k_i$. Note that if P is a fill matrix then it has no excess. Excess satisfies the following basic property (a proof can be found in the appendix).

Lemma 3. *If Q is a subpattern of P then $e(Q) \leqslant e(P)$.*

Proof (Proof of Lemma 3). Denote $Q = \{x_1, \ldots x_m\}$ and $P = \{x_1, \ldots, x_n\}$. Then build the fillings of the patterns $P_j = \{x_1, \ldots x_j\}$. With the proof of the previous lemma and using the same notations, we obtain that for each $1 \leqslant j \leqslant n$, either $x_j \in \varphi(P_{j-1})$ and $e(P_j) > e(P_{j-1})$ or adding x_j augments $\sum_{i=1}^{r_{j-1}} k_{i,j-1}$ by one and $e(P_j) = e(P_{j-1})$ if no merges are triggered. Merges may only increase the amount of excess, as they can only decrease the sum of triangle sizes. Thus e is monotonous. □

3.3 Characterisation of the Orbit Through the Filling

It what follow, two patterns *touch* if their fillings touch, otherwise they are *disjoint*.

Theorem 1. *A pattern P has no excess if and only if it is in the orbit of the lines that generate the $T_{k_i}s$.*

Proof. Lemmas 2 and 1 guarantee that if P is in the orbit of a set of disjoint lines then it has no excess.

We show the reverse implication by induction on $|P|$.

The base case is trivial since P can only be the line of length 1.

Now assume the implication holds for all patterns of size n and let $|P|$ be a pattern of size $n+1$ without excess, and let $x \in P$. Then $P \setminus \{x\}$ still has no excess (by Lemma 3) and has size n so we can apply the induction hypothesis. Let $v_1 + T_{k_1}, \ldots, v_r + T_{k_r}$ be the partition of $\varphi(P \setminus \{x\})$ into triangles.

We have $x \notin \bigcup_{i=1}^{r} v_i + T_{k_i}$ because otherwise P would have excess. If x is not in the union of the triangles' neighbourhoods then $\varphi(P) = \varphi(P \setminus \{x\}) \cup \{x\}$ and x cannot be moved by a triangle move. Else, x can be moved so as to extend the line of the triangle it touches. Figure 6 shows how to extend a line with a top neighbour, the two other cases are similar.

In this process, two triangle might start touching, in this case, by repeating the previous operation we can merge the two triangles' lines into one. Notice that in every merge the length of the new line is exactly the sum of the length of the two initial lines (as otherwise excess is generated). □

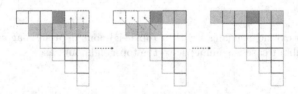

Fig. 6. How to extend a line with a top neighbour.

We denote by $P_{n,k}$ the shape composed of a line of length n to which k points were added by filling the triangle under the line from right to left and top to bottom. Examples are shown Fig. 7.

Theorem 2. *If P is a pattern, then $P \in \gamma(P_{n,k})$ if and only if $\varphi(P) = T_n$ and $e(P) = k$.*

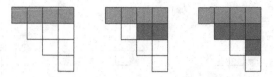

Fig. 7. From left to right: $P_{4,0}$, $P_{4,2}$ and $P_{4,4}$. The purple cells are the excess. (Color figure online)

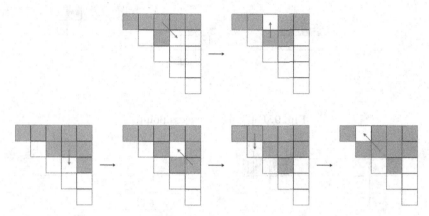

Fig. 8. Pushing the excess to the right (first line) or to the left (second line).

Proof. Triangle moves preserve fillings and excess so the direct implication holds.

First notice that any excess forming lines under an already existing full top line can be normalized to the corresponding $P_{n,k}$ using the transformations shown in Fig. 8.

Then, if the pattern is composed of a line and one additional point, the additional point can be fetched by transforming the line into the diagonal, stopping the process when one point is above the additional point, then getting back to the line, while dragging the additional point.

All that remains to do is to push the excess to the right. Figure 9 provides an example. Notice that the presence of some excess already in a good position will not cause any problem for this method, as illustrated Fig. 10.

Thus, any pattern composed of a line of length n and k excess points under it is in the orbit of $P_{n,k}$.

All that remains to prove is that a line can always be formed. This can be done using the merging process described in the proof of Theorem 1. The excess point will not disturb the merging because if one move is made impossible by their presence, say point x cannot be moved to position y, then we can just use y instead of x for the following steps. □

Combining Theorem 1 and Theorem 2, we obtain the following classification of the orbits.

Theorem 3 (Characterisation of the orbits). *If P is a finite pattern then there are integers $n_1, \ldots n_r$ and $k_1, \ldots k_r$ and vectors $v_1, \ldots v_r$ such that $P \in$*

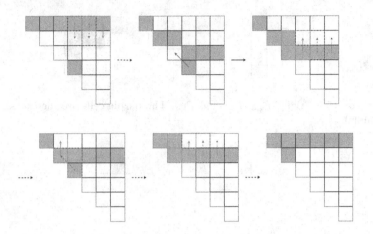

Fig. 9. Fetching an excess point.

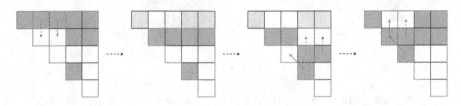

Fig. 10. Fetching an excess point with some excess already lined up.

$\gamma(\bigcup_{i=1}^{r} v_i + P_{n_i,k_i})$, the $P_{n_i,k_i} + v_i$ do not touch each other, $\sum_{i=1}^{r} n_i = |P| - e(P)$ and $\sum_{i=1}^{r} k_i = e(P)$.

Note that we now know the orbits for solitaires process with all shapes of size 3. Indeed, such a shape is either 3 aligned points (in which case orbits are easy to analyse), or it is a triangle shape on a finite index subgroup of $\mathbb{Z}^2$, and the orbits in different cosets of this subgroup are completely independent and are individually described by the triangle solitaire.

3.4   Excess Sets

It is tempting to think that if a set has excess, then we can remove some of its points to remove the excess. This turns out not to be true.

If P is a pattern, the *excess sets* of P are the subsets $Q \subset P$ such that $\varphi(P \setminus Q) = \varphi(P)$. We denote by $E(P)$ the set of all such sets.

Lemma 4. *If $U \in E(P)$ then $|U| \leqslant e(P)$.*

Proof. This is a direct consequence of Lemma 2.

However, in general there is no set $U \in E(P)$ such that $|U| = e(P)$. The pattern in Fig. 11 has excess 1 but its only excess set is the empty set.

Fig. 11. Here, $e(p) = 1$ but $E(P) = \{\varnothing\}$.

If $U \in E(P)$, then every $V \subset U$ is also an excess set. Maximal excess sets do not all have the same cardinality as shown by example in Fig. 12.

Fig. 12. The blue and orange sets are both maximal excess sets but do not have the same cardinality. (Color figure online)

4   Algorithmic Aspects

4.1   Complexity of the Identification of the Orbit of a Pattern

The proof of the characterisation of the orbits provides a polynomial time algorithm to identify to which orbit a given pattern belongs.

The algorithm is the following:

Algorithm 1 (Identify orbit). *Data: pattern P. Result: the canonical representative of the orbit of P.*

1. *Fill the pattern.*
2. *Divide the filling into triangles $v_1 + T_{k_1}, \ldots, v_r + T_{k_r}$.*
3. *Count the excess in each triangle, the canonical representative of the orbit of the pattern is $\bigcup_{i=1}^{r} v_i + P_{k_i, e(P \cap (v_i + T_{k_i}))}$.*

Let $n = |P|$. The first two steps are linear in the number of points in $\varphi(P)$ and $|\varphi(P)| \leqslant \frac{n(n+1)}{2}$ so they run in time $O(n^2)$. Step 3 is then linear so the total time complexity of the algorithm is $O(n^2)$.

4.2   Number of Steps Needed to Put a Pattern in Normal Form

The proof of the characterisation of the orbit also provides an algorithm for finding a sequence of transformations turning the pattern into the canonical representative of its orbit, following the proof of Theorem 3:

Algorithm 2 (Find a path from a pattern to its canonical form)

1. *Merge the different components and form lines using the process described in Theorem 1 (accounting for excess using the modifications described in the proof of Theorem 2).*
2. *Fetch the excess with the process described in Theorem 2.*

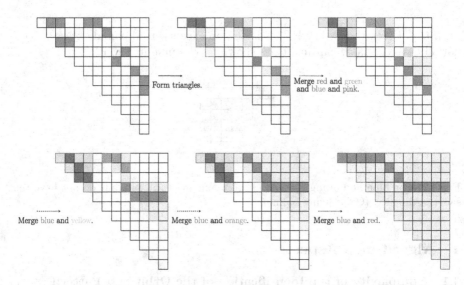

Fig. 13. An example of how to get back to the line from a random element of its orbit.

Naively implemented, this algorithm takes $O(n^2(n+k))$, where k denotes the excess: The first step takes $O(n^3)$, since each merging takes $O(n^2)$ time and we merge at most n times. The second step takes $O(n^2k)$ if we fetch the k many excess points one by one, as each fetch takes $O(n^2)$ (Fig. 13).

For $k = 0$, this is in fact optimal.

Theorem 4. *The diameter of the orbit of the line of length n, seen as a graph, is $\Theta(n^3)$.*

Proof. We are going to build an infinite family of patterns that require $\Omega(n^3)$ steps to get back to the line.

Let P_0 be the empty pattern, and P_{n+1} is inductively built by extending P_n as described in Fig. 14 where the grey triangle is the triangle in which P_n's orbit is confined. In pattern P_{n+1}, $\Omega(n^2)$ steps are required to fetch the three coloured points.

Indeed, first notice that up to renaming points, the blue point has to move right to fetch the orange one, then the orange one will have to move down to fetch the green one and finally the green one will have to go up to prepare for

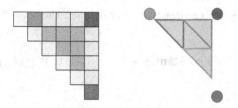

Fig. 14. Left: The extension of P_n into P_{n+1}. Right: A schematic representation of P_{n+1} used in the proof. (Color figure online)

the next extension. Now let us analyse the movement of the blue point, starting from the first moment it touches another triangle. To move a point right, one need a point in the column at its right. We'll prove that this means that at some point in the process, half of the points of the pattern have to be in the left half of the triangle.

Mark the blue point, and whenever an unmarked point is in the same column as a marked one, mark it. Consider column i from the left, and the first marked point x to reach it. Clearly the point x moves from column $i-1$ to column i, and this requires us to have an unmarked point in column i to allow this. This point was unmarked, and is now marked. Therefore, when the blue point has reached column $\frac{3n}{2}$ (the middle column), there are at least $\frac{3n}{2}$ marked points, all of which were in the blue triangle in Fig. 14 at some point during the journey of the blue point.

The same reasoning on the orange and green point gives that at some point of the process, between the first moment the blue point moves, until the point where we are ready to move the blue point of the next level, $\frac{3n}{2}$ points were in the orange triangle and the same amount in the green one. As the pattern P_n only has $3n$ points, at least $\frac{3n}{2}$ need to be moved from one subtriangle to another, therefore there is a pair of triangles that will share at least $\frac{n}{2}$ points. Those at least $\frac{n}{2}$ points will need to be moved by a mean distance of at least $\frac{n}{4}$, which requires at least $\frac{n^2}{8}$ steps. Thus pattern P_n requires $\Omega(n^3)$ moves to be transformed into a line. $\qquad\square$

5   Size of the Line Orbit

One can build an element of the orbit of the line by choosing a corner, then choosing a point on each line parallel to the edge opposed to the corner. This gives $3n! - 3$ elements of the orbit as the only patterns that can be created this way from two different corners are the lines.

If P is in the line orbit, then the number of points in P in the first k columns is at most k, and [2] gives the count $c\left(\frac{e}{2}\right)^n (n-1)^{n-\frac{5}{2}}$ with $c = \frac{4 + 2W(-2e^{-2})}{e^3 \sqrt{2\pi}}$ for patterns with this property where W is the inverse function of $f : z \mapsto ze^z$ (Lambert's W function).

Combining these, we get the following bounds on the size of the line orbit.

Theorem 5. *There are constants c_1 and c_2 such that $c_1 e^{-n} n^{n+\frac{1}{2}} \leqslant |\gamma(L_n)| \leqslant c_2 \left(\frac{e}{2}\right)^n (n-1)^{n-\frac{5}{2}}$.*

Conjecture 1. There is a constant $\frac{2}{e} \leqslant c \leqslant e$ such that $|\gamma(L_n)| = \Theta\left(\left(\frac{n}{c}\right)^n\right)$.

6   Bases

Let X_R be a TEP subshift for some $R \subset \Sigma^T$ and fix some $n \in \mathbb{N}$. Recall from [12] that the pattern $q \in \Sigma^{T_n}$ appears in X_R if and only if it does not explicitly contain a translate of a pattern in $\Sigma^T \setminus R$.

Let $P \subset T_n$. We say P is a *basis* (for the restriction of X_R to T_n) if for every $q \in \Sigma^P$, by iteratively completing partially filled triangles using the TEP rule R, we always end up with a valid pattern on T_n.

Theorem 6. *The following are equivalent for $P \subset T_n$:*

1. *P is a basis,*
2. *P is a fill matrix,*
3. *P is in the line orbit.*

Proof (Proof of Theorem 6). The equivalence of the last two items is a special case of Theorem 1. We show that (1) implies (2) and (3) implies (1).

Suppose thus first that P is a basis. Then by definition $\varphi(P) = T_n$, as the iterative steps of completing triangles correspond exactly to the basic steps of the filling process. We cannot have more than n elements in P, as the total number of valid patterns on Σ^{T_n} is n. By Lemma 2 we also cannot have less, or the set of eventually filled positions could not possibly cover T_n. We conclude that P is a fill matrix.

Suppose next that P is in the line orbit. Let $P_0 = P, P_1, P_2, \ldots, P_k$ be a sequence of successive steps in the solitaire such that P_k is an edge of T_n. It is easy to see that the property of being a basis is preserved under solitaire moves, indeed each solitaire step induces a natural bijection $\phi : \Sigma^{P_i} \to \Sigma^{P_{i+1}}$ and the unique completions of p and $\phi(p)$ are the same. Since the line is clearly a basis, P must be a basis as well. $\square$

Note that the first item talks about a specific (but arbitrary) TEP subshift, while the rest do not, i.e. the set of bases is independent of Σ and R.

The solitaire process allows us to translate patterns on one basis to ones on another, more space efficiently than the direct method suggests, indeed we give a polynomial time in-place algorithm for this.

If $P, Q \subset T_n$ are bases, any pattern $p \in \Sigma^P$ uniquely determines a pattern in $q \in \Sigma^Q$ in an obvious way, by deducing the unique extension of one pattern to T_n and then restricting to the domain of the other. If we biject P and Q with $\{1, \ldots, n\}$ we obtain a bijection $\phi : \Sigma^n \to \Sigma^n$. A *basic permutation* of Σ^n is one that ignores all but two cells. If the cells are $1, 2$, this means that for some $\hat{\pi} \in \mathrm{Sym}(\Sigma^2)$ we have $\pi(a_1 a_2 a_3 \cdots a_n)_i = \hat{\pi}(a_1 a_2) a_3 \cdots a_n$ for all $a_1 a_2 \cdots a_n \in \Sigma^n$; in general one conjugates by a reordering the cells.

Theorem 7. *The bijection ϕ can be computed with $O(n^3)$ basic permutations.*

Proof (Proof of Theorem 7). Let $P_0 = P, P_1, \ldots, P_k = Q$ be the sequence of solitaire moves, which we know can be taken of length $O(n^3)$. Keep track of an ordering of the cells in P_i so that if a solitaire move touches cells P_i with indices j_1, j_2, then only the vectors with indices j_1, j_2 differ between P_i and P_{i+1}. Then at each solitaire step, the TEP family allows us to compute the unique pattern in $\Sigma^{P_{i+1}}$ compatible with Σ^{P_i} with a single basic permutation. After k steps we obtain the pattern Σ^Q, but in a random order, and we can fix the ordering by applying $O(n)$ basic permutations with $\hat{\pi}$ of the form $ab \leftrightarrow ba$. □

7   Prospects for Future Work

Arguments similar to those of this paper work for several other shapes, but for now we have not found a general result, in particular Question 5.36 from [12] stays open.

While Theorem 6 characterises the patterns that generate the contents of a triangle, it does not characterise the maximal (or maximum cardinality) independent sets, i.e. patterns $P \subset T_n$ such that $X|_P = \Sigma^P$, where X is a TEP subshift. The characterization of such sets seems more difficult and does depend on the specific TEP subshift.

We introduced in Sect. 3.4 the notion of an excess set. What can be said about the family of excess sets as a set system? How can we determine the maximum cardinality of an excess set?

References

1. Berger, R.: The undecidability of the domino problem. Mem. Amer. Math. Soc. **66**, 72 (1966)
2. Hanna, P.D.: The On-Line Encyclopedia of Integer Sequences (2022). Sequence A101481. https://oeis.org/A101481
3. Hochman, M., Meyerovitch, T.: A characterization of the entropies of multidimensional shifts of finite type. Ann. Math. (2) **171**(3), 2011–2038 (2010). https://doi.org/10.4007/annals.2010.171.2011
4. Jeandel, E., Vanier, P.: Characterizations of periods of multi-dimensional shifts. Ergodic Theory Dynam. Syst. **35**(2), 431–460 (2015)
5. Jeandel, E., Vanier, P.: Hardness of conjugacy, embedding and factorization of multidimensional subshifts. J. Comput. Syst. Sci. **81**(8), 1648–1664 (2015)
6. Kirchner, G.: The On-Line Encyclopedia of Integer Sequences. Sequence A295928 (2022). https://oeis.org/A295928
7. Ledrappier, F.: Un champ markovien peut être d'entropie nulle et mélangeant. C. R. Acad. Sci. Paris Sér. A-B **287**(7), A561–A563 (1978)
8. Lind, D., Marcus, B.: An Introduction to Symbolic Dynamics and Coding. Cambridge University Press, Cambridge (1995). https://doi.org/10.1017/CBO9780511626302
9. Moore, C., Boykett, T.: Commuting cellular automata. Complex Syst. **11**(1), 55–64 (1997)

10. Pivato, M.: Invariant measures for bipermutative cellular automata. Discrete Contin. Dyn. Syst. **12**(4), 723–736 (2005). https://doi.org/10.3934/dcds.2005.12.723
11. Sablik, M.: Measure rigidity for algebraic bipermutative cellular automata. Ergodic Theory Dynam. Syst. **27**(6), 1965–1990 (2007). https://doi.org/10.1017/S0143385707000247
12. Salo, V.: Cutting corners. J. Comput. Syst. Sci. **128**, 35–70 (2022). https://doi.org/10.1016/j.jcss.2022.03.001
13. Salo, V., Törmä, I.: Commutators of bipermutive and affine cellular automata. In: Kari, J., Kutrib, M., Malcher, A. (eds.) AUTOMATA 2013. LNCS, vol. 8155, pp. 155–170. Springer, Heidelberg (2013). https://doi.org/10.1007/978-3-642-40867-0_11
14. Wang, H.: Proving theorems by pattern recognition II. Bell Syst. Tech. J. **40**, 1–42 (1961)

Pattern Classification with Temporally Stochastic Cellular Automata

Subrata Paul[1], Souvik Roy[2($\boxtimes$)], and Sukanta Das[1]

[1] Department of Information Technology, Indian Institute of Engineering Science and Technology, Shibpur, India
sukanta@it.iiests.ac.in
[2] C3iHub, Indian Institute of Technology, Kanpur, India
svkr89@gmail.com

Abstract. This paper introduces a new model of cellular automata where two rules (say, f and g) are applied temporally on the cells with some probability. The rule f is called default rule and g is the noise which is applied with probability τ (noise rate). This new class of automata is named as *Temporally Stochastic Cellular Automata* (TSCAs). The dynamical behaviour of these automata has been studied to identify the TSCAs that converge to fixed point from any seed. Finally, we use each of the convergent TSCAs on some standard datasets and observe the effectiveness of each TSCA as pattern classifier. It is observed that the proposed TSCA based classifier shows competitive performance in comparison with existing classifier algorithms.

Keywords: Temporally Stochastic Cellular Automata · Dynamical behaviour · Convergence · Pattern Classifier

1 Introduction

In a classical cellular automaton (CA), a rule (f) is applied to each and every cell of the lattice to evolve the CA from one configuration to its next configuration [2]. In this work, we deviate from the classical CA, and introduce another rule, say g, in the cellular structure which is applied to all the cells in a time step with probability τ. The rule g may be considered as noise of the cellular structure and τ as the noise rate. The rule f can be called as default rule, which is applied to all cells in a time step with probability $1 - \tau$. We name these cellular automata (CAs) as *Temporally Stochastic Cellular Automata* (TSCAs). In this direction, note that, stochastic cellular automata have been also investigated by several CA researchers [1,4,7,11], where the update rules are chosen randomly from a set of rules.

In this work, we take only ECAs rules as our default rule and noise to study this class of automata. We further consider the CAs as finite, which use periodic boundary condition. We first study the dynamical behaviour of these TSCAs through an extensive experiment, and classify them as Class A, Class B and

© IFIP International Federation for Information Processing 2023
Published by Springer Nature Switzerland AG 2023
L. Manzoni et al. (Eds.): AUTOMATA 2023, LNCS 14152, pp. 137–152, 2023.
https://doi.org/10.1007/978-3-031-42250-8_10

Class C by observing their behaviour following the Wolfram's [17] and Li & Packard's [9,10] classification. Then we identify a set of TSCAs that converge to fixed points from any initial configuration.

The CAs that converge to fixed point from any seed have been widely employed for the design of pattern classifier [6,12,16]. In this work we also utilize the convergent TSCAs to develop two-class pattern classifier. However, there are some convergent TSCAs which are having a single fixed point (attractor). These CAs cannot act as two-class pattern classifier. Similarly, a convergent TSCA having enormous number of fixed points (attractors) is not a good classifier. Using these criteria, we identify a set of convergent TSCAs that can act as a good classifier. To evaluate the performance of the proposed classifier, we choose standard data sets which are taken from http://www.ics.uci.edu/~mlearn/MLRepository. html. It is observed that the proposed classifier performs nicely in *training phase* as well as *testing phase*. Finally we compare the performance of the proposed classifier with that of well-known classifiers. It is found that the proposed classifier is very much competitive with the best-performing classifiers.

2   Temporally Stochastic Cellular Automata

In this work, we consider elementary cellular automata (ECAs), where the cells are arranged as a ring. The set of indices that represent the cells is denoted by $\mathcal{L} = \mathbb{Z}/n\mathbb{Z}$, where n is the number of cells. At each time step $t \in \mathbb{N}$, a cell is assigned a state from $\mathcal{Q} = \{0,1\}$. The collection of all states at a given time is called a configuration. If x is a configuration then $x = (x_i)_{i \in \mathcal{L}}$ where x_i is the state of cell $i \in \mathcal{L}$. The set of all configurations is denoted by $\mathcal{Q}^{\mathcal{L}}$.

Here, a cell changes its state depending on left neighbour, self and right neighbour. At each time step, the updates are made synchronously according to a local rule $f : \mathcal{Q}^3 \rightarrow \mathcal{Q}$. Given a local function f and a set of cells $\mathcal{L}$, one can define the global function $G : \mathcal{Q}^{\mathcal{L}} \rightarrow \mathcal{Q}^{\mathcal{L}}$ such that, the image $y = (y_i)_{i \in \mathcal{L}} = G(x)$ of a configuration $x = (x_i)_{i \in \mathcal{L}} \in \mathcal{Q}^{\mathcal{L}}$ is given by, $\forall i \in \mathcal{L}, y_i = f(x_{i-1}, x_i, x_{i+1})$. There are 256 ECA rules in two-state three-neighbourhood dependency. Through the use of left/right reflection and 0/1 complementarity, it is possible to narrow down the $2^8 = 256$ ECA rule space to 88 classes, each represented by the rule of smallest number, i.e. the minimal representative ECA rule [9].

Let us now define temporally stochastic cellular automata (TSCAs) where at a time step, a cell can be updated using one of the two rules f and g. Here, the default rule f, is spatially deterministic − at any time, it is applied over all cells uniformly, whereas, g is the noise and is applied with some probability. That is, rule g is applied with probability $\tau \in [0,1]$ whereas the rule f is applied with probability $(1 - \tau)$. We call τ as the temporal noise rate. This way of looking at these rules make the system temporally stochastic. Therefore,

$$y = \begin{cases} G_g(x) & \text{with probability } \tau \\ G_f(x) & \text{with probability } 1 - \tau \end{cases}$$

where, $G_g(x)|_i = g(x_{i-1}, x_i, x_{i+1})$ and $G_f(x)|_i = f(x_{i-1}, x_i, x_{i+1})$. We write $(f, g)[\tau]$ to denote the proposed system specification. As an evidence, let us consider a TSCA$(164, 131)[0.1]$, where $f = 164$ and $g = 131$ are applied with probability 0.9 and 0.1 at each step of the evolution. Fig 1(a) and (b) respectively show the space-time diagrams of ECA 164 and ECA 131 starting with random initial configuration. Whereas, Fig 1(c) shows the space-time diagram of TSCA$(164, 131)[0.1]$. Rule 131 is applied at the time step marked by $\leftarrow$ (arrow) in Fig 1(c). In the space-time diagrams, state one is marked by blue and red when rule f and g is applied, respectively. It is interesting to note here that the dynamical behaviour of TSCA can widely vary from that of the CAs with default rule and noise.

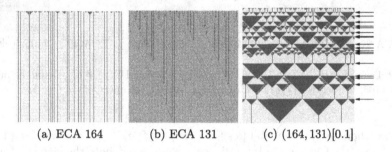

(a) ECA 164   (b) ECA 131   (c) $(164, 131)[0.1]$

Fig. 1. Dynamics of TSCA $(164, 131)[0.1]$. Here, $C((f, g)) \neq C(f)$ and $C(f) = C(g)$.

2.1 Dynamical Behaviour

Stephen Wolfram [17] introduced following general classification of the ECAs (defined over $\mathbb{Z}$) depending on their dynamical behaviour:

Class I: evolving to a homogeneous configuration;
Class II: evolving periodically;
Class III: evolving chaotically; and
Class IV: class of complex rules.

Later, Li and Packard have identified some periodic rules (Class II) as locally chaotic [9,10]. For TSCAs, we target to identify their dynamical behaviour and to classify the TSCAs as above. We take f and g from 88 minimum representative ECA rules, and then consider all possible combinations of these 88 ECAs rules. Here, total $\frac{88 \times 87}{2} = 3828$ couples of (f, g) are sufficient because, the rest are exchange symmetry of f and g.

We arrange a large number of experiments to understand dynamical behaviour of TSCAs. The results reported here are based on CA size 500 (20 initial configurations for each instance, i.e. $(f, g)[\tau]$, however, we repeat the

experiment for various other sizes to cross-verify the result. Following the qualitative visual inspection approach, we map the dynamics of TSCAs into following
three classes:

Class A: which is similar to Wolfram's Class I.
Class B: which is similar to Wolfram's Class II except locally chaotic rules.
Class C: similar to Wolfram's Class III, IV and locally chaotic rules.

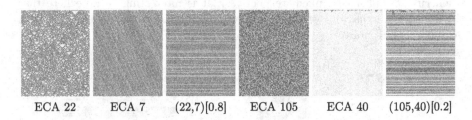

ECA 22   ECA 7   (22,7)[0.8]   ECA 105   ECA 40   (105,40)[0.2]

Fig. 2. Dynamics of CA $(22,7)[0.8]$ $(C((f,g)) = C(g)$ and $C(f) \neq C(g))$; and Dynamics
of CA $(105,40)[0.2]$ $(C((f,g)) \neq C(f), C((f,g)) \neq C(g)$ and $C(f) \neq C(g))$.

Now, there are two possibilities for a couple (f, g) - (i) f and g belong to the
same class; (ii) f and g are from different class. We denote the class of f and g
as $C(f)$ and $C(g)$, respectively, and class of (f, g) is denoted by $C((f, g))$. We
find amazing experimental outcomes:

- If $C(f) = C(g)$ in a TSCA, one option is $C((f,g)) = C(f)$, which has been
  seen in a significant number of TSCAs. The TSCA (f, g), where $C(f) = C(g)$
  = Class A, approaches to a homogeneous configuration, much like ECA f and
  ECA g. On the other hand, $C((f,g)) \neq C(f)$ could be conceivable. That is,
  the noise has a significant impact on these TSCAs(f, g) (as an evidence, see
  Fig. 1).
- Next case where $C(f) \neq C(g)$, shows the dynamics where one of the rule's
  class dominates, i.e. $C((f,g)) = C(f)$ or $C((f,g)) = C(g)$. Under this case,
  the TSCA (f, g) with $C(f)$ = Class C and $C(g)$ = Class B shows the dynamics
  as $C((f,g)) = C(g)$. Fig 2 shows an evidence of this situation. Here, ECA
  22 and ECA 7, respectively, belong to class III and II and, the CA $(22,7)$
  shows periodic behaviour (like Wolfram's Class II), see Fig 2, where the class
  of ECA 7 dominates.
- A TSCA (f, g) with $C(f) \neq C(g)$, on the other hand, depicts dynamics
  in which none of the rule's classes dominates, i.e. $C((f,g)) \neq C(f)$ and
  $C((f,g)) \neq C(g)$. The TSCA (f, g) with $C(f)$ = Class C and $C(g)$ = Class A
  displays $C((f,g))$ = Class B, with none of the rule's classes dominating, see
  Fig 2. In Fig 2, ECA 105 belongs to Class III and ECA 40 belongs to Class
  I. However, the TSCA(105,40)[0.2] shows periodic behaviour (like Wolfram's
  Class II).

Table 1. Distribution of τ-insensitive TSCAs under different classes.

Class	Conditions	Number of TSCAs
A	$\mathcal{C}(f) = \mathcal{C}(g) = \mathcal{C}((f,g)) = $ Class A	28
	$\mathcal{C}(f) = \mathcal{C}(g) = $ Class B, $\mathcal{C}((f,g)) = $ Class A	113
	$\mathcal{C}(f) = \mathcal{C}(g) = $ Class C, $\mathcal{C}((f,g)) = $ Class A	0
	$\mathcal{C}(f) = $ Class B, $\mathcal{C}(g) = $ Class A, $\mathcal{C}((f,g)) = \mathcal{C}(g)$	297
	$\mathcal{C}(f) = $ Class C, $\mathcal{C}(g) = $ Class A, $\mathcal{C}((f,g)) = \mathcal{C}(g)$	98
	$\mathcal{C}(f) = $ Class C, $\mathcal{C}(g) = $ Class B, $\mathcal{C}((f,g)) = $ Class A	57
B	$\mathcal{C}(f) = \mathcal{C}(g) = \mathcal{C}((f,g)) = $ Class B	1436
	$\mathcal{C}(f) = \mathcal{C}(g) = $ Class A, $\mathcal{C}((f,g)) = $ Class B	0
	$\mathcal{C}(f) = \mathcal{C}(g) = $ Class C, $\mathcal{C}((f,g)) = $ Class B	0
	$\mathcal{C}(f) = $ Class B, $\mathcal{C}(g) = $ Class A, $\mathcal{C}((f,g)) = \mathcal{C}(f)$	167
	$\mathcal{C}(f) = $ Class C, $\mathcal{C}(g) = $ Class B, $\mathcal{C}((f,g)) = \mathcal{C}(g)$	67
	$\mathcal{C}(f) = $ Class C, $\mathcal{C}(g) = $ Class A, $\mathcal{C}((f,g)) = $ Class B	20
C	$\mathcal{C}(f) = \mathcal{C}(g) = \mathcal{C}((f,g)) = $ Class C	149
	$\mathcal{C}(f) = \mathcal{C}(g) = $ Class A, $\mathcal{C}((f,g)) = $ Class C	0
	$\mathcal{C}(f) = \mathcal{C}(g) = $ Class B, $\mathcal{C}((f,g)) = $ Class C	18
	$\mathcal{C}(f) = $ Class C, $\mathcal{C}(g) = $ Class A, $\mathcal{C}((f,g)) = \mathcal{C}(f)$	0
	$\mathcal{C}(f) = $ Class C, $\mathcal{C}(g) = $ Class B, $\mathcal{C}((f,g)) = \mathcal{C}(f)$	89
	$\mathcal{C}(f) = $ Class B, $\mathcal{C}(g) = $ Class A, $\mathcal{C}((f,g)) = $ Class C	0

We have found that out of 3828 TSCAs, 593, 1690 and 256 TSCAs belong to Class A, Class B and Class C, respectively. Table 1 shows the summary of the outcome (for graphical visualization of outcome see Fig. 5 in the Appendix). Moreover, these TSCAs are τ-insensitive, i.e. if we progressively vary the temporal noise rate, the cellular dynamics remain unchanged. Figure 6 in the Appendix shows a Gallery based on Table 1 with more evidences.

However, there are 1289 cases, out of 3828 TSCAs, where the noise rate (τ) has been playing a significant role, i.e. τ-sensitive. These TSCAs show *phase transition*[1] and *class transition*[2] dynamics, for details see [14]. Figure 6 in the Appendix shows a Gallery based on these behaviours. However, the goal of the current work is to explore the pattern classification capability of TSCAs for which τ-sensitive CAs are not appropriate. Therefore, we next deal with the CAs, dynamical behaviour of which are independent of τ, i.e. τ-insensitive. For our next purpose, we identify the τ-insensitive TSCAs which converge to fixed point from any initial configuration.

2.2 Convergence

During evolution, a CA approaches to a set of configurations which form an attractor. If the set is a singleton, we call the attractor as fixed point. Whenever all the attractors are fixed points, we call the CAs as convergent.

---

[1] Some TSCAs show a discontinuity after a critical value of temporal noise rate which brutal change of behaviour is well known as phase transition.

[2] For a set of TSCAs, the class dynamics of the system changes after a critical value of τ.

Definition 1. *A TSCA(f, g)[τ] is called as convergent TSCA if the CA converges to a fixed point from any initial configuration and for any τ and n, where n is the number of cells of the TSCA.*

In other words, for a given seed, a TSCA converges to a fixed point, if both f and g may converge to a fixed point separately for the same seed. Following a large number of experiments[3], we identify the set of TSCAs that converge to fixed points. Here, the experimental study shows that 423 couple of CAs converge to fixed point starting from any initial configuration and for any τ and n, see Table 2.

However, there are some cases where the convergence feature of various TSCAs changes depending on the size n and τ. As an evidence, Fig. 3 depicts the dynamics of TSCA (30, 136) which converges to all-0 configuration after a critical value of τ (here, τ = 0.13). However, (30, 136) oscillates around a fixed non-zero density for τ = 0.08 and τ = 0.11, in Fig. 3. Earlier, we have mentioned that this type of brutal change of behaviour is well known as second-order phase transition [13]. Similarly, the couple (131, 136) converges to all-1 configuration for τ value 0.5 and 0.9, see Fig. 3. On the other hand, it shows chaotic dynamics for τ = 0.1. Here, the class dynamics of the system changes after a critical value of τ, i.e. class transition (for details, see [14]). Gallery of Fig. 6 in the Appendix shows for evidence. However, for the current study, we exclude these TSCAs.

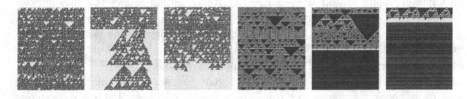

Fig. 3. Phase transition behaviour of stochastic CA (30, 136) and class transition behaviour of stochastic CA (131, 136).

Although 423 convergent TSCAs are identified to design pattern classifier, the general demand is multiple attractor TSCA.

Definition 2. *If a convergent TSCA is having more than one fixed point, the TSCA is called as Multiple Attractor TSCA.*

Previously, we have mentioned that to designing a pattern classifier, we exclude the TSCAs which

- are associated with single fixed point (see Table 2, in black); and
- are associated with large number of attractors, specifically, couples with ECA 204 (see Table 2, in underline).

---

[3] Note that, the result reported here are based on 100 initial configurations for each instance, i.e. (f, g)[τ], where the CA size is 499 (odd) and 500 (even).

Therefore, to design a pattern classifier, we need to pick a few couples from the Table 2 after excluding the above situations. Finally, we find a few of 114 couples (see Table 2, in bold) which are the candidate of the proposed pattern classifier.

Table 2. Couples of TSCAs that converge to Fixed Points. Here, TSCAs with single fixed point and large number of attractors are marked by black(traditional) and underline, respectively. The candidate pattern classifier TSCAs are marked with bold.

(2, 0)	(4, 0)	(6, 0)	(6, 4)	(8, 0)	(8, 2)	(8, 4)	(8, 6)	(10, 0)	(10, 8)	(12, 0)	(12, 8)
(14, 0)	(14, 4)	(18, 0)	(18, 8)	(22, 0)	(22, 4)	(22, 8)	(24, 0)	(24, 8)	(26, 0)	(26, 8)	(28, 0)
(28, 8)	(30, 0)	(30, 4)	(32, 0)	(32, 2)	(32, 8)	(32, 10)	(32, 18)	(32, 24)	(32, 26)	(34, 0)	(34, 8)
(36, 0)	(36, 6)	(36, 8)	(36, 32)	(38, 0)	(38, 4)	(38, 8)	(38, 32)	(40, 0)	(40, 2)	(40, 8)	(40, 10)
(40, 24)	(40, 36)	(40, 38)	(42, 0)	(42, 8)	(44, 0)	(44, 8)	(44, 32)	(46, 0)	(46, 4)	(46, 32)	(50, 0)
(50, 8)	(54, 0)	(54, 4)	(54, 8)	(54, 32)	(54, 40)	(56, 0)	(56, 8)	(58, 0)	(60, 0)	(60, 4)	(60, 8)
(60, 32)	(72, 0)	(72, 2)	(72, 4)	(72, 6)	(72, 8)	(72, 12)	(72, 24)	(72, 28)	(72, 32)	(72, 34)	(72, 36)
(72, 38)	(74, 0)	(74, 8)	(74, 32)	(74, 72)	(76, 0)	(76, 8)	(78, 0)	(78, 18)	(90, 0)	(90, 8)	(90, 32)
(94, 0)	(104, 0)	(104, 2)	(104, 8)	(104, 24)	(104, 36)	(104, 38)	(104, 44)	(104, 74)	(106, 0)	(106, 8)	(106, 72)
(108, 0)	(108, 8)	(108, 32)	(108, 40)	(110, 0)	(110, 4)	(110, 32)	(122, 0)	(122, 8)	(122, 36)	(126, 0)	(126, 4)
(126, 32)	(128, 0)	(128, 2)	(128, 4)	(128, 6)	(128, 8)	(128, 10)	(128, 12)	(128, 14)	(128, 18)	(128, 22)	(128, 24)
(128, 26)	(128, 28)	(128, 32)	(128, 34)	(128, 36)	(128, 38)	(128, 40)	(128, 42)	(128, 44)	(128, 46)	(128, 50)	(128, 54)
(128, 56)	(128, 58)	(128, 60)	(128, 72)	(128, 74)	(128, 76)	(128, 78)	(128, 94)	(128, 104)	(128, 106)	(128, 108)	(128, 110)
(130, 0)	(130, 8)	(130, 32)	(130, 40)	(130, 72)	(130, 104)	(131, 128)	(132, 0)	(132, 6)	(132, 8)	(132, 14)	(132, 38)
(132, 46)	(132, 72)	(134, 0)	(134, 4)	(134, 8)	(134, 36)	(134, 72)	(136, 0)	(136, 2)	(136, 4)	(136, 6)	(136, 8)
(136, 10)	(136, 12)	(136, 18)	(136, 22)	(136, 24)	(136, 26)	(136, 28)	(136, 32)	(136, 34)	(136, 36)	(136, 38)	(136, 40)
(136, 42)	(136, 44)	(136, 50)	(136, 54)	(136, 56)	(136, 72)	(136, 74)	(136, 76)	(136, 90)	(136, 104)	(136, 106)	(136, 108)
(138, 0)	(138, 8)	(138, 32)	(138, 40)	(140, 0)	(140, 8)	(140, 72)	(142, 0)	(142, 4)	(146, 0)	(146, 8)	(146, 32)
(146, 78)	(150, 4)	(150, 8)	(152, 0)	(152, 8)	(152, 32)	(152, 40)	(152, 72)	(152, 104)	(154, 0)	(154, 8)	
(154, 32)	(154, 40)	(156, 0)	(156, 8)	(156, 72)	(156, 126)	(156, 131)	(160, 0)	(160, 2)	(160, 8)	(160, 10)	(160, 18)
(160, 24)	(160, 26)	(160, 36)	(160, 38)	(160, 44)	(160, 54)	(160, 72)	(160, 74)	(160, 108)	(160, 131)	(162, 0)	(162, 8)
(162, 72)	(164, 0)	(164, 6)	(164, 8)	(164, 32)	(164, 40)	(164, 72)	(164, 104)	(168, 0)	(168, 2)	(168, 8)	(168, 10)
(168, 24)	(168, 36)	(168, 38)	(168, 54)	(170, 0)	(170, 8)	(172, 0)	(172, 8)	(172, 32)	(178, 0)	(178, 8)	(178, 131)
(184, 0)	(184, 8)	(200, 0)	(200, 2)	(200, 4)	(232, 0)	(200, 8)	(200, 12)	(200, 24)	(200, 28)	(200, 32)	(200, 34)
(200, 36)	(200, 38)	(204, 0)	(204, 8)	(232, 0)	(232, 2)	(232, 8)	(232, 24)	(232, 36)	(232, 38)	(232, 44)	(12, 4)
(36, 4)	**(36, 12)**	**(44, 4)**	**(44, 12)**	**(44, 36)**	**(76, 4)**	**(76, 12)**	**(76, 72)**	**(78, 76)**	**(94, 78)**	**(104, 72)**	**(108, 4)**
(108, 12)	**(108, 36)**	**(108, 44)**	**(108, 72)**	**(130, 128)**	**(132, 4)**	**(132, 12)**	**(132, 36)**	**(132, 44)**	**(132, 76)**	**(132, 108)**	**(132, 128)**
(134, 128)	**(134, 132)**	**(136, 128)**	**(136, 130)**	**(136, 132)**	**(136, 134)**	**(138, 128)**	**(138, 136)**	**(140, 4)**	**(140, 12)**	**(140, 36)**	**(140, 44)**
(140, 76)	**(140, 108)**	**(140, 128)**	**(140, 132)**	**(140, 136)**	**(142, 128)**	**(142, 132)**	**(146, 128)**	**(146, 136)**	**(150, 128)**	**(150, 136)**	**(152, 128)**
(152, 136)	**(154, 128)**	**(154, 136)**	**(156, 128)**	**(156, 136)**	**(160, 128)**	**(160, 130)**	**(160, 136)**	**(160, 138)**	**(160, 146)**	**(160, 152)**	**(160, 154)**
(162, 128)	**(162, 136)**	**(164, 4)**	**(164, 12)**	**(164, 36)**	**(164, 44)**	**(164, 108)**	**(164, 128)**	**(164, 132)**	**(164, 134)**	**(164, 136)**	**(164, 140)**
(164, 160)	**(168, 128)**	**(168, 130)**	**(168, 136)**	**(168, 138)**	**(168, 152)**	**(170, 128)**	**(170, 136)**	**(172, 4)**	**(172, 12)**	**(172, 36)**	**(172, 128)**
(172, 132)	**(172, 136)**	**(172, 140)**	**(178, 128)**	**(178, 136)**	**(184, 128)**	**(184, 136)**	**(200, 72)**	**(200, 76)**	**(200, 128)**	**(200, 130)**	**(200, 132)**
(200, 134)	**(200, 138)**	**(200, 140)**	**(200, 152)**	**(200, 156)**	**(200, 160)**	**(200, 164)**	**(232, 72)**	**(232, 108)**	**(232, 128)**	**(232, 130)**	
(232, 136)	**(232, 154)**	**(232, 164)**	**(232, 172)**	**(232, 200)**	(204, 12)	(204, 36)	(204, 72)	(204, 76)	(204, 78)	(204, 128)	(204, 132)
(204, 136)	(204, 140)	(204, 200)									

3 Multiple Attractor TSCA as Pattern Classifier

A n-cell TSCA with k fixed points can act as k-class classifier. Each class contains a set of configurations that converge to a single fixed point. Hence the fixed point can act as representative of the set. Now to design a two-class classifier, a set of fixed points, out of k fixed points, needs to represent one class whereas the rest fixed points shall represent the other class. From implementation point of view, all the fixed points along with their class information are to be stored in memory. Whenever class of an input pattern (P) is to be found out, the TSCA runs with the pattern as seed. Based on the fixed point, where the TSCA settles down, the class of P is declared.

As an example, the 4-cell convergent TSCA(108, 44)[0.1] which has five attractors may be used as a two-class pattern classifier (see Fig. 4). Assume that the fixed points 0000, 0001 and 1000 represent Class X, and the rest fixed points 0010 and 0100 represent Class Y. If a pattern, say 1101 is given, the TSCA is run with 1101 as seed. After some time, the CA reaches to a fixed point, say 1000. Since 1000 represents Class X, class of 1101 is declared as X. Hence this multiple attractor TSCA can act as two-class pattern classifier, see Fig. 4.

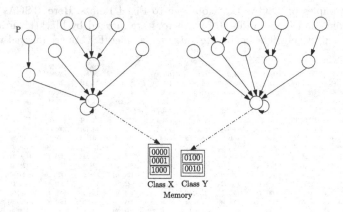

Fig. 4. The TSCA (108, 44) was classified using multiple fixed points.

For good classifiers, the patterns are to be distributed evenly throughout the attractor basins. In real-world datasets, however, the attractor basins may mix up the patterns of two classes. As a result, we evaluate the classifier's performance in terms of classification accuracy, which is defined as the ratio of properly classified patterns to total patterns. The formula for calculating efficiency is as follows,

$$\text{Efficiency} = \frac{\text{No. of properly classified patterns}}{\text{Total no. of patterns}} \times 100\%$$

However, a multiple-attractor TSCA may not be a good pattern classifier. To measure the performance and effectiveness of a TSCA, we pass it through the *training phase* and *testing phase*.

3.1   Training Phase

As shown in Table 2, there are 114 multiple fixed attractor TSCAs. These TSCAs can act as potential candidates for pattern classification. However, in order to find the most effective classifier, we train all the candidates using patterns of two disjoint datasets, say P_1 and P_2. A TSCA from the set of candidates is loaded first with patterns of P_1 and P_2, and constantly updated until the TSCA reaches to a fixed point. We keep track of all the attractors and the number of patterns which converge on them. If more patterns from pattern set P_1 converge to the attractor than the patterns from pattern set P_2, the attractor is declared to be of Class X and stored in *attractorset-X*; otherwise, the attractor is of Class Y and stored in *attractorset-Y*. At the end, we have two sets of attractors. The following formula is used to determine the efficiency of a TSCA,

$$\text{Efficiency} = \frac{\sum_{i=1}^{k} max(n_1^i, n_2^i)}{|P_1| + |P_2|}$$

Here, n_1^i and n_2^i are the maximum number of patterns converged to the ith fixed point attractor of a TSCA from dataset P_1 and P_2, respectively. $|P_1|$ and $|P_2|$ are the number of patterns of two datasets used for pattern classification. Here, k is the number of fixed points. The *training phase* produces a TSCA with highest efficiency, *attractorset-X*, and *attractorset-Y* as output. Note that, the output of this phase is used as input of the *testing phase* (see Sect. 3.2).

Table 3. Effectiveness of TSCAs During Training of Monk-1 Dataset.

TSCAs	Efficiency (in %)	Number of Attractor	TSCAs	Efficiency (in %)	Number of Attractor	TSCAs	Efficiency (in %)	Number of Attractor
(12,4)[0.1]	86.066	199	(36,4)[0.9]	68.033	67	(36,12)[0.9]	84.426	67
(44,4)[0.1]	83.607	67	(44,36)[0.1]	83.607	67	(44,12)[0.1]	84.426	67
(76,4)[0.1]	96.721	199	(76,12)[0.1]	98.361	199	(76,72)[0.1]	97.541	67
(78,76)[0.1]	65.574	23	(94,78)[0.1]	73.77	23	(104,72)[0.9]	64.754	34
(108,4)[0.1]	81.967	67	(108,36)[0.1]	85.246	67	(108,72)[0.4]	80.328	34
(108,12)[0.1]	88.525	67	(108,44)[0.1]	89.344	67	(130,128)[0.1]	50.0	2
(132,128)[0.1]	72.951	2	(132,36)[0.1]	75.41	67	(132,4)[0.1]	74.59	199
(132,12)[0.9]	87.705	199	(132,44)[0.9]	86.885	67	(132,76)[0.9]	88.525	199
(132,108)[0.9]	91.803	67	(134,128)[0.1]	50.0	2	(134,132)[0.1]	50.0	2
(136,128)[0.1]	50.0	2	(136,130)[0.1]	50.0	2	(136,132)[0.1]	50.0	2
(136,134)[0.1]	50.0	2	(138,128)[0.1]	50.0	2	(138,136)[0.1]	50.0	2
(140,128)[0.1]	88.525	2	(140,36)[0.1]	86.885	67	(140,4)[0.1]	85.246	199
(140,132)[0.1]	88.525	200	(140,136)[0.1]	86.066	2	(140,108)[0.9]	94.262	67
(140,44)[0.2]	88.525	67	(140,12)[0.1]	84.426	199	(140,76)[0.9]	94.262	199
(142,128)[0.1]	50.0	2	(142,132)[0.1]	50.0	2	(146,128)[0.1]	50.0	2
(146,136)[0.1]	50.0	2	(150,128)[0.1]	50.0	2	(150,136)[0.1]	50.0	2
(152,128)[0.1]	50.0	2	(152,136)[0.1]	50.0	2	(154,128)[0.1]	50.0	2
(154,136)[0.1]	50.0	2	(156,128)[0.1]	50.0	2	(156,136)[0.1]	50.0	2
(160,128)[0.1]	50.0	2	(160,130)[0.1]	50.0	2	(160,136)[0.1]	50.0	2
(160,138)[0.1]	50.0	2	(160,146)[0.1]	50.0	2	(160,152)[0.1]	50.0	2
(160,154)[0.1]	50.0	2	(162,128)[0.1]	50.0	2	(162,136)[0.1]	50.0	2
(164,128)[0.1]	68.033	2	(164,4)[0.1]	70.492	67	(164,36)[0.2]	70.492	67
(164,132)[0.9]	72.951	68	(164,108)[0.9]	87.705	67	(164,134)[0.7]	73.77	2
(164,160)[0.9]	73.77	2	(164,136)[0.9]	77.869	2	(164,44)[0.9]	86.066	67
(164,140)[0.8]	86.066	68	(164,12)[0.9]	85.246	67	(168,128)[0.1]	50.0	2
(168,130)[0.1]	50.0	2	(168,136)[0.1]	50.0	2	(168,138)[0.1]	50.0	2
(168,152)[0.1]	50.0	2	(170,128)[0.1]	50.0	2	(170,136)[0.1]	50.0	2
(172,128)[0.1]	81.148	2	(172,4)[0.1]	77.869	67	(172,36)[0.1]	81.967	67
(172,132)[0.1]	82.787	68	(172,136)[0.1]	83.607	2	(172,12)[0.4]	86.066	67
(172,140)[0.7]	85.246	68	(178,128)[0.1]	50.0	2	(178,136)[0.1]	50.0	2
(184,128)[0.1]	50.0	2	(184,136)[0.1]	50.0	2	(200,160)[0.1]	87.705	2
(200,162)[0.1]	86.885	2	(200,130)[0.1]	86.885	2	(200,132)[0.1]	86.885	2
(200,152)[0.1]	86.885	2	(200,128)[0.1]	87.705	2	(200,140)[0.1]	86.885	2
(200,76)[0.1]	86.066	67	(200,156)[0.1]	88.525	2	(200,72)[0.1]	86.066	67
(200,136)[0.2]	87.705	?	(200,164)[0.8]	89.344	2	(200,134)[0.4]	90.984	2
(232,130)[0.1]	81.967	2	(232,72)[0.2]	83.607	34	(232,128)[0.1]	83.607	2
(232,108)[0.1]	84.426	34	(232,164)[0.2]	85.246	2	(232,136)[0.1]	82.787	2
(232,154)[0.7]	90.984	2	(232,200)[0.1]	81.967	200	(232,172)[0.7]	88.525	2

As an example, let us consider Monk-1 dataset (11-bit data) for classification. Let us take the TSCA $(76, 72)[0.2]$ as two-class pattern classifier (similar to Fig 4), with two pattern set P_1 and P_2 loaded to the TSCA as Class X and Class Y, respectively. P_1 and P_2 contain a total of 169 patterns, out of which 2 patterns of P_2 and 4 patterns of P_1 are wrongly identified as in Class X and Class Y, respectively. Hence, 163 patterns are properly classified, which gives training efficiency as 96.4497%.

To get the best candidate TSCA, we train all the 114 TSCAs of Table 2 by Monk-1 dataset which is associated with 124 instances and 6 category features. The result of the training is noted in Table 3. We find that the TSCA$(76, 72)$ $[0.1]$ with training efficiency 97.54%, has the best efficiency. This TSCA acts as our desired classifier. In Table 3, we show (only) the best performing τ value and corresponding efficiency for each TSCA.

3.2   Testing Phase

In this phase, a new collection of patterns are used to find the efficacy of the designed classifier. The attractor sets *attractorset-X* and *attractorset-Y* with a TSCA (output of training phase) and the (new) pattern sets (P_1 and P_2) are taken as input in this phase. The TSCA is loaded with the patterns of P_1 and P_2 and updated till all the patterns converge to any fixed point attractor. The number of patterns successfully detected by the classifier is used to measure the TSCA's efficiency. For example, if an attractor is present in *attractorset-X* then count only the number of patterns from dataset P_1 converge to the attractor as correctly identified patterns, similarly, if an attractor is present in *attractorset-Y*, count only the number of patterns from dataset P_2 that converge to the attractor as correctly identified patterns. TSCAs with their training and testing efficiencies for different datasets are reported in Table 4.

Table 4. Pattern classifiers' performance over various datasets (for proposed classifier).

Datasets	TSCA Size	Training Efficiency	Margin of Error in Training	Testing Efficiency	Margin of Error in Testing	Proposed TSCAs
Monk-1	11	97.54	0.223	86.08	0.3112	$(76, 72)[0.1]$
Monk-2	11	96.45	0.2012	88.22	0.2068	$(76, 72)[0.1]$
Monk-3	11	98.36	0.123	94.21	0.2406	$(76, 72)[0.1]$
Haber man	9	80.27	0.4321	80.76	0.6730	$(132, 108)[0.4]$
Heart-statlog	16	99.26	0.541	92.59	0.7679	$(232, 154)[0.8]$
Tic-Tac-Toe	18	100	0	99.48	0.1679	$(140, 12)[0.9]$
Hepatitis	19	100	0.6089	97.3	0.7303	$(232, 172)[0.6]$
Spect Heart	22	97.33	0.4326	95.699	0.4133	$(172, 140)[0.3]$
Appendicitis	28	97.56	0.1921	95	0.7874	$(76, 72)[0.4]$

3.3   Margin of Error

As previously stated, the classifier is a *Temporally Stochastic CA*-based classifier, in which the noise rule g is applied with a probability τ and the cells are stochastically updated. This might happen in different ways for different runs, resulting in varying efficiency. As a result, these categorization differences must be recorded. To obtain these information, we determine the margin of error for both the training and testing phases. A margin of error expresses as a variation of small amount in case of change of circumstances, i.e. the maximum expected difference between the true parameter and a sample estimation of that parameter [5]. We estimate the margin of error for sample size m using the following equation [5].

$$\text{Margin of error} = Z_{n/2}\left(\frac{\sigma}{\sqrt{m}}\right)$$

Table 5. Classification accuracy compared to other well-known classifiers.

Datasets	Algorithm	Efficiency in %	Efficiency of proposed classifier with Margin of Error
Monk-1	Bayesian	99.9	86.08 ± 0.3112 (TSCA(76, 72)[0.1])
	C4.5	100	
	TCC	100	
	MTSC	98.65	
	MLP	100	
	Traditional CA	61.111	
	Asynchronous CA	81.519	
Monk-2	Bayesian	69.4	88.22 ± 0.2068 (TSCA(76, 72)[0.1])
	C4.5	66.2	
	TCC	78.16	
	MTSC	77.32	
	MLP	75.16	
	Traditional CA	67.129	
	Asynchronous CA	73.410	
Monk-3	Bayesian	92.12	94.21 ± 0.2406 (TSCA(76, 72)[0.1])
	C4.5	96.3	
	TCC	76.58	
	MTSC	97.17	
	MLP	98.10	
	Traditional CA	80.645	
	Asynchronous CA	83.749	

(*continued*)

Table 5. (*continued*)

Datasets	Algorithm	Efficiency in %	Efficiency of proposed classifier with Margin of Error
Haber-man	Traditional CA	73.499	80.76 ± 0.6730 (TSCA(132, 108)[0.4])
	Asynchronous CA	77.493	
Spect Heart	Traditional CA	91.978	95.699 ± 0.4133 (TSCA(172, 140)[0.3])
	Asynchronous CA	100	
Tic-Tac-Toe	Sparce grid	98.33	99.48 ± 0.1679 (TSCA(140, 12)[0.9])
	ASVM	70.00	
	LSVM	93.330	
	Traditional CA	93.330	
	Asynchronous CA	99.721	
Appendicitis	-	-	95± 0.7874 (TSCA(76,72)[0.4])
Heart-statlog	Bayesian	82.56	92.59±0.7679 (TSCA(232,154)[0.8])
	C4.5	80.59	
	Logit-boost DS	82.22	
Hepatitis	Bayesian	84.18	97.3 ± 0.7303 (TSCA(232,172)[0.6])
	C4.5	82.38	
	Logit-boost DS	81.58	

We have considered $m = 30$ samples for the experimentation with σ as the variance, where $\sigma = \sqrt{\frac{\sum(x_i-\bar{x})^2}{(m-1)}}$. The efficiency of the ith sample is x_i, and the mean of the sample efficiencies is $\bar{x}$. As we consider the confidence level for our sampling experiments is 95% percent [5], we set $Z_{n/2} = 1.96$. Table 4 displays the margin of error of different classifiers in training and testing phase. It is found that the margin of error is very low in both training and testing phase. Hence, during different runs, the suggested classifier's efficiency fluctuates somewhat.

3.4   Comparison

For the study of the efficiency of the proposed two-class pattern classifier, we have employed nine datasets: Monk-1, Monk-2, Monk-3, Haber-man, Heart-statlog, Tic-Tac-Toe, Spect heart, Hepatitis and Appendicitis[4]. The datasets are pre-processed suitably to fit the input features of the classifier. The classification

---

[4] http://www.ics.uci.edu/~mlearn/MLRepository.html.

accuracy of the proposed classifier is compared with different existing standard algorithms such as Bayesian, C4.5, MLP (Multilayer Perceptron), TCC, MTSC, ASVM, LSVM, Sparse grid, Traditional CA and Asynchronous CA [3,6,8,15,16].

The performance of our proposed TSCA-based classifier is compared to that of other well-known classifiers, as shown in Table 5. We observed that our proposed TSCA-based two-class pattern classifier performs much better than traditional CA-based classifier and it becomes more competitive and performs reliably better than other well known classifier algorithms.

4   Conclusion

In this paper, we have proposed a variant of CAs, termed as *Temporally Stochastic CAs* (TSCAs), in which, instead of one local rule, two rules (default rule f and noise rule g) are utilized. After analyzing their dynamics, we have identified the convergent TSCAs that have been used to design two-class pattern classifier. Here, in comparison to existing common algorithms, the proposed design of TSCA-based two-class pattern classifier offers competitive performance. Now, the natural extensions of this work on the sensitivity to temporally stochastic CAs and pattern classification include,

- Here, we have only experimentally explored the convergent TSCAs. What can be said for theoretical understanding behind the convergence?
- What can be said for classification time (i.e. convergence time) of these TSCAs?

Acknowledgements. The authors acknowledge the anonymous reviewers for their comments and suggestions, which have helped to improve the quality and readability of the paper.

Appendix

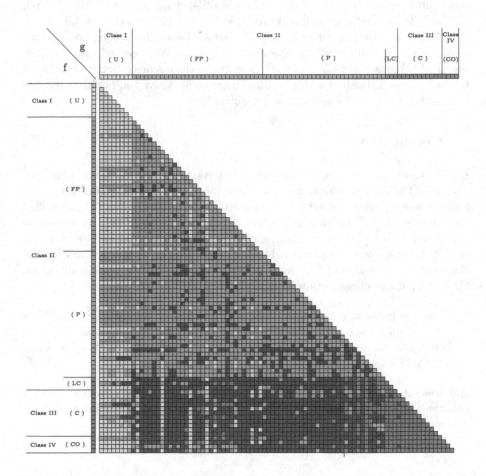

Fig. 5. Summarized behaviour of TSCAs. The 88 rules are plotted horizontally and vertically where the vertical line shows the f rules and g is represented by the horizontal line. Each box on the line (vertical and horizontal) represents a rule. The rules are numbered as per the sequence – 0, 8, 32, 40, 128, 136, 160, 168, 2, 4, 10, 12, 13, 24, 34, 36, 42, 44, 46, 56, 57, 58, 72, 76, 77, 78, 104, 130, 132, 138, 140, 152, 162, 164, 170, 172, 184, 200, 204, 232, 1, 3, 5, 6, 7, 9, 11, 14, 15, 19, 23, 25, 27, 28, 29, 33, 35, 37, 38, 43, 50, 51, 62, 74, 94, 108, 134, 142, 156, 178, 26, 73, 154, 18, 22, 30, 45, 60, 90, 105, 122, 126, 146, 150, 41, 54, 106, 110. That is, rule 0 is the first rule and rule 110 is the 88th rule. A cell (i, j) in the figure depicts the behaviour of the stochastic CA (f, g) where f and g are the rules represented by the ith box in the vertical line and jth box in the horizontal line respectively. Here, we consider the exchange symmetry between f and g. Therefore, stochastic CA (f, g) are presented, however, the exchange symmetric CA (g, f) remains blank (white). Moreover, the CA (f, g) where $f = g$, also remains blank (white). Class A, B and C are marked by yellow, orange and red respectively. The τ-sensitive dynamics phase transition and class transition are marked with blue and black respectively. (Color figure online)

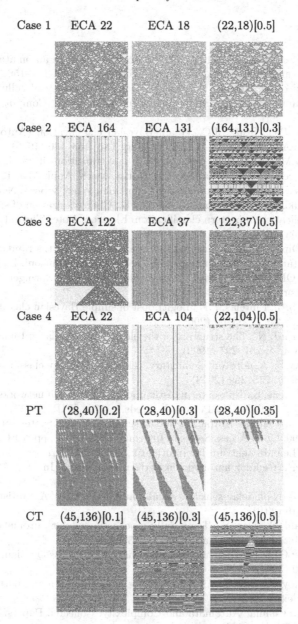

Fig. 6. (i) **Case 1:** $\mathcal{C}((f,g)) = \mathcal{C}(f) = \mathcal{C}(g) - (22,18)[0.5]$; (ii) **Case 2:** $\mathcal{C}((f,g)) \neq$ $\mathcal{C}(f)$ and $\mathcal{C}(f) = \mathcal{C}(g) - (164,131)[0.3]$; (iii) **Case 3:** $\mathcal{C}((f,g)) = \mathcal{C}(f)$ or $\mathcal{C}((f,g)) = \mathcal{C}(g)$, where $\mathcal{C}(f) \neq \mathcal{C}(g) - (122,37)[0.5]$; (iv) **Case 4:** $\mathcal{C}((f,g)) \neq \mathcal{C}(f)$ and $\mathcal{C}((f,g)) \neq$ $\mathcal{C}(g)$ and $\mathcal{C}(f) \neq \mathcal{C}(g) - (22,104)[0.5]$; (v) Phase transition (PT) behaviour of TSCAs $(28, 40)$; (vi) Class transition (CT) behaviour of TSCAs $(45, 136)$.

References

1. Arrighi, P., Schabanel, N., Theyssier, G.: Stochastic cellular automata: correlations, decidability and simulations. Fundame. Inform. **126**(2–3), 121–156 (2013)
2. Bhattacharjee, K., Naskar, N., Roy, S., Das, S.: A survey of cellular automata: types, dynamics, non-uniformity and applications. Nat. Comput. **19**, 433–461 (2020)
3. Cheeseman, P.C., Stutz, J.C., et al.: Bayesian classification (Autoclass): theory and results. Adv. Knowl. Disc. Data Mining. **180**, 153–180 (1996)
4. Cirillo, E.N.M., Nardi, F.R., Spitoni, C.: Phase transitions in random mixtures of elementary cellular automata. Phys. A Statist. Mech. Appl. **573**, 125942 (2021)
5. Cochran, W.: Sampling Techniques, 3rd edn. John Wiley & Sons, New York (1977)
6. Das, S., Mukherjee, S., Naskar, N., Sikdar, B.: Characterization of single cycle CA and its application in pattern classification. Electron. Notes Theoret. Comput. Sci. **252**, 181–203 (2009)
7. Fatès, N.: Diploid cellular automata: first experiments on the random mixtures of two elementary rules. In: Dennunzio, A., Formenti, E., Manzoni, L., Porreca, A.E. (eds.) AUTOMATA 2017. LNCS, vol. 10248, pp. 97–108. Springer, Cham (2017). https://doi.org/10.1007/978-3-319-58631-1_8
8. Kotsiantis, S.B., Pintelas, P.E.: LogitBoost of simple Bayesian classifier. Informatica (Slovenia) **29**(1), 53–60 (2005)
9. Li, W., Packard, N.: The structure of the elementary cellular automata rule space. Complex Syst. **4**, 281–297 (1990)
10. Martinez, G.J.: A note on elementary cellular automata classification. J. Cell. Autom. **8**(3–4), 233–259 (2013)
11. Paulevé, L., Sené, S.: Non-deterministic updates of Boolean networks. In: Castillo-Ramirez, A., Guillon, P., Perrot, K., (eds.), 27th IFIP WG 1.5 International Workshop on Cellular Automata and Discrete Complex Systems (AUTOMATA 2021), vol. 90. Open Access Series in Informatics (OASIcs), pp. 10:1–10:16. Schloss Dagstuhl - Leibniz-Zentrum für Informatik, Dagstuhl, Germany (2021)
12. Raghavan, R.: Cellular automata in pattern recognition. Inf. Sci. **70**(1), 145–177 (1993)
13. Roy, S.: A study on delay-sensitive cellular automata. Phys. A: Statist. Mech. Appl. **515**, 600–616 (2019)
14. Roy, S., Paul, S., Das, S.: Temporally stochastic cellular automata: classes and dynamics. Int. J. Bifurc. Chaos **32**(12), 2230029 (2022)
15. Salzberg, S.: C4.5: programs for machine learning by J Ross Quinlan. Mach. Learn. **16**, 235–240 (1994)
16. Sethi, B., Roy, S., Das, S.: Asynchronous cellular automata and pattern classification. Complexity **21**(S1), 370–386 (2016)
17. Wolfram, S.: Cellular Automata and Complexity: Collected Papers, 1st edn. CRC Press, Boca Raton (1994)

Building Correlation Immune Functions from Sets of Mutually Orthogonal Cellular Automata

Luca Mariot[1]([✉])[iD] and Luca Manzoni[2][iD]

[1] Semantics, Cybersecurity and Services Group, University of Twente,
Drienerlolaan 5, 7511GG Enschede, The Netherlands
l.mariot@utwente.nl
[2] Department of Mathematics and Geosciences, University of Trieste,
Via Valerio 12/1, Trieste, Italy
lmanzoni@units.it

Abstract. Correlation immune Boolean functions play an important role in the implementation of efficient masking countermeasures for side-channel attacks in cryptography. In this paper, we investigate a method to construct correlation immune functions through families of mutually orthogonal cellular automata (MOCA). First, we show that the orthogonal array (OA) associated to a family of MOCA can be expanded to a binary OA of strength at least 2. To prove this result, we exploit the characterization of MOCA in terms of orthogonal labelings on de Bruijn graphs. Then, we use the resulting binary OA to define the support of a second-order correlation immune function. Next, we perform some computational experiments to construct all such functions up to $n = 12$ variables, and observe that their correlation immunity order is actually greater, always at least 3. We conclude by discussing how these results open up interesting perspectives for future research, with respect to the search of new correlation-immune functions and binary orthogonal arrays.

Keywords: Boolean Functions · Cellular Automata · Correlation Immunity · Side-channel countermeasures · Orthogonal Latin Squares

1 Introduction

Boolean functions are basic combinatorial objects that map a set of fixed size bitstrings to a single output bit. Notwithstanding their simplicity, such functions find countless applications in many diverse fields of computer science and mathematics [5]. In cryptography, Boolean functions have long been used to design low-level primitives in symmetric ciphers, such as combiners and filters for linear feedback shift registers [2]. The rationale is that the resilience of these ciphers against different cryptanalytic attacks can be reduced to the cryptographic properties of the underlying Boolean functions. For example, a Boolean function used in the combiner model for Vernam stream ciphers should be at a

© IFIP International Federation for Information Processing 2023
Published by Springer Nature Switzerland AG 2023
L. Manzoni et al. (Eds.): AUTOMATA 2023, LNCS 14152, pp. 153–164, 2023.
https://doi.org/10.1007/978-3-031-42250-8_11

high Hamming distance from the set of affine functions to resist fast-correlation attacks, or equivalently it should possess a high nonlinearity [21]. At the same time, the output of the function should be statistically independent from any subset of t or fewer variables, to resist correlation attacks of order t: in other words, the Boolean functions should be correlation immune of high order t [24].

The literature related to the cryptographic applications of cellular automata (CA) features a solid body of works investigating the properties of the involved Boolean functions. For example, it has been shown that Wolfram's pseudorandom number generator (PRNG) based on a simple one-dimensional CA is unsuitable for cryptographic purposes, as the underlying local rule 30 is not first-order correlation immune and does not have a high enough nonlinearity [20]. This allows to apply respectively Meier and Staffelbach's correlation attack [22] and Koc and Apohan's inversion attack [12] to efficiently recover the initial configuration of Wolfram's PRNG. Following this research thread, a few subsequent works [6,14] focused on the search of local rules with a larger diameter and a better trade-off of nonlinearity and correlation immunity. Some of these rules with better properties have then been adopted in the design of CA-based stream ciphers such as CARPENTER and PENTAVIUM [8,13].

The correlation immunity criterion also gained relevance in recent years concerning a different type of attacks, namely *side-channel analysis* (SCA). Instead of focusing on the mathematical design of a cipher as classical cryptanalysis does, SCA targets the *implementation* of a cipher on a device. In particular, the aim of SCA is to exploit leakages on side-channel sources such as electromagnetic emanations, timings, and variations of voltages to infer the secret key used to encrypt a message on the device. One of the options to counteract these attacks is *Boolean masking*, where noise is added to the intermediate values computed by the cipher during the encryption process, changing them from one execution to the other. In this respect, correlation immune functions of high order t and low Hamming weight (i.e., with as few 1s as possible in the output of their truth tables) can be used to implement masking countermeasures, such as leakage squeezing and rotation S-box masking [3,23], which have minimal implementation overhead and optimal resistance towards SCA attacks of order t.

Contrasting with the large number of works related to the study of the cryptographic properties of CA—be it at the local rule level as mentioned above, or by considering them as S-boxes as in [17,19]—there seems to be comparatively a smaller literature dedicated to the exploration of CA as a means to construct side-channel countermeasures. To the best of our knowledge, the works by Karmarkar and Roy Chowdhury [9–11] are the only ones addressing the design of leakage squeezing countermeasures through hybrid CA. There, the authors remark that there exist several methods to design linear codes with hybrid CA by leveraging the techniques in [4], which can be readily used to implement a leakage squeezing countermeasure. However, they also argue that the linearity of such codes introduces other weaknesses, and thereby set out to study the cryptographic properties of nonlinear hybrid CA for leakage squeezing.

The goal of this paper is to investigate how cellular automata may be used to design correlation immune functions of low weight. To this end, we use a construction of mutually orthogonal CA (MOCA), i.e., a family of CA giving rise to a set of mutually orthogonal Latin squares (MOLS), recently introduced in [16]. In particular, we exploit the well-known fact that any set of MOLS is equivalent to an orthogonal array (OA) of strength 2. Then, taking any set of MOCA, we prove that the corresponding binary expansion is a binary OA of strength at least 2, leveraging on the MOCA characterization as orthogonal labelings on de Bruijn graphs. This result allows us to use the expanded binary OA of a MOCA family as the support of a Boolean function with correlation immunity order at least 2. We then perform a computational search experiment to generate all families of 3 MOCA defined by local rules of diameter $d = 4, 5$, and construct the corresponding Boolean functions. Interestingly, all generated functions turn out to have correlation immunity order at least 3, indicating that our theoretical result is not a tight lower bound. Although the Hamming weight reached by our correlation immune functions is far from optimal, we discuss how it could be improved by solving an associated optimization problem. The objective in this case is to remove a subset of rows from the binary expansion of a MOCA family while retaining the correlation immunity order of the resulting function.

The rest of this paper is organized as follows. Section 2 collects all necessary background definitions and results related to Boolean functions, cellular automata, Latin squares and orthogonal arrays used in this work. Section 3 proves the main theoretical result of the paper, i.e., that the binary expansion of a set of MOCA is the support of a Boolean function with correlation immunity order at least 2. Section 4 presents the results of the computational search experiment for families of $k = 3$ MOCA, giving rise to Boolean functions of up to $n = 12$ variables. Finally, Sect. 5 recaps the main contributions of this paper, and discusses some directions for future research.

2 Preliminary Definitions

In this section, we recall all relevant definitions to describe our results in the remainder of the paper. We start with basic concepts and results of Boolean functions, and how correlation immune functions can be characterized by orthogonal arrays. Then, we give a formal definition of the CA model used in our work, and describe the CA-based construction of mutually orthogonal Latin squares of [16].

2.1 Boolean Functions and Orthogonal Arrays

As a general reference, we follow Carlet's recent book on Boolean functions [2].

Let $\mathbb{F}_2 = \{0, 1\}$ be the finite field with two elements, with sum and multiplication defined respectively as the XOR (denoted by $\oplus$) and logical AND (denoted by concatenation). For any $n \in \mathbb{N}$, the set $\mathbb{F}_2^n$ of all n-bit bitstrings is endowed with the structure of a vector space, with vector sum defined as bitwise XOR, and multiplication by a scalar $a \in \mathbb{F}_2$ being the field multiplication of a with each coordinate of a vector $x \in \mathbb{F}_2^n$. Given two vectors $x, y \in \mathbb{F}_2^n$, their Hamming distance $d_H(x, y)$ is the number of coordinates where x and y disagree, while their scalar product is defined as $x \cdot y = \bigoplus_{i=1}^{n} x_i y_i$. The support of a vector $x \in \mathbb{F}_2^n$ is the set $supp(x) = \{i : x_i \neq 0\}$, and its Hamming weight $w_H(x)$ is the cardinality of $supp(x)$. Equivalently, $w_H(x)$ corresponds to the Hamming distance $d_H(x, \underline{0})$ between x and the null vector $\underline{0} \in \mathbb{F}_2^n$. In practice, the Hamming weight is the number of nonzero coordinates in x.

For all $n \in \mathbb{N}$, a *Boolean function* of n variables is a mapping $f : \mathbb{F}_2^n \to \mathbb{F}_2$. The most straightforward way to represent f is by means of its truth table. Suppose that a total order is fixed on the vectors of $\mathbb{F}_2^n$ (e.g., the lexicographic order). Then, the truth table of f is the vector $\Omega_f \in \mathbb{F}_2^{2^n}$ defined as:

$$\Omega_f = (f(0, \ldots, 0), f(0, \ldots, 1), \ldots, f(1, \ldots, 1)) \ . \tag{1}$$

In other words, the truth table is the 2^n-bit vector that specifies for each input vector $x \in \mathbb{F}_2^n$ in lexicographic order the corresponding output value $f(x)$. Similarly to what we defined above for binary vectors, the support of f is the set $supp(f) = \{x \in \mathbb{F}_2^n : f(x) \neq 0\}$, while its Hamming weight is $w_H(f) = |supp(f)|$. Equivalently, support and weight of f are defined respectively as the set of nonzero coordinates and the size of such set in the truth table Ω_f.

Another method to represent a Boolean function usually adopted in cryptography is the *Walsh transform*. Given $f : \mathbb{F}_2^n \to \mathbb{F}_2$, the Walsh transform of f is the function $W_f : \mathbb{F}_2^n \to \mathbb{Z}$ defined for all $a \in \mathbb{F}_2^n$ as:

$$W_f(a) = \sum_{x \in \mathbb{F}_2^n} (-1)^{f(x) \oplus a \cdot x} \ . \tag{2}$$

Intuitively, $W_f(a)$ measures the correlation between f and the linear function defined by the scalar product $a \cdot x$. The Walsh transform is useful to assess several cryptographic properties of f, among which correlation immunity is of special interest for this paper. A Boolean function $f : \mathbb{F}_2^n \to \mathbb{F}_2$ is correlation immune of order $1 \leq t \leq n$ if any subset of $1 \leq k \leq t$ input variables is statistically independent from the output of f. This property has an equivalent characterization through the Walsh transform (originally due to Xiao and Massey [27]): f is t-th order correlation immune if and only if $W_f(a) = 0$ for all coefficients $a \in \mathbb{F}_2^n$ of Hamming weight k, with $1 \leq k \leq t$.

Correlation immunity plays an important role in the context of correlation attacks on stream ciphers based on the combiner model [24]. More recently, this criterion also gained relevance for designing masking countermeasures to withstand side-channel analysis. In this case, the goal is to find a t-th order correlation immune function to resist SCA attacks of order t. At the same time, it is desirable that this function has the lowest Hamming weight possible, to have an efficient implementation of the masking countermeasure.

Beside the Walsh transform, correlation immune functions have also a nice combinatorial characterization in terms of orthogonal arrays. Formally, an orthogonal array of N runs, k factors, s levels and strength t (denoted as an $OA(N, k, s, t)$) is a $N \times k$ array with entries from a set S with s elements such that, for any $N \times t$ subarray, each t-uple of S^t occurs exactly $\lambda = N/s^t$ times [7]. The value λ is also called the index of the OA, and is completely determined by the other parameters. The link between binary OA (i.e., with $s = 2$ levels) and correlation immune functions is given by the following result proved in [1]:

Lemma 1. *A Boolean function* $f : \mathbb{F}_2^n \rightarrow \mathbb{F}_2$ *is correlation immune of order t if and only if its support* $supp(f) = \{x \in \mathbb{F}_2^n : f(x) \neq 0\}$ *is an* $OA(N, n, 2, t)$.

In other words, one can reduce the design of n-variable, t-th order correlation immune Boolean functions for SCA masking countermeasures to the search of binary OA of n factors and strength t. The requirement of minimizing the Hamming weight of the function corresponds to the minimization of the number of runs N in the OA. Once such an OA has been found, one can define the corresponding correlation immune function f by taking the runs of the OA as the vectors in the support of f.

2.2 Cellular Automata and Latin Squares

In this work, we use cellular automata (CA) as a particular kind of vectorial Boolean functions, which we formally define below:

Definition 1. *Let* $n, d \in \mathbb{N}$ *with* $d \leq n$, *and let* $f : \mathbb{F}_2^d \rightarrow \mathbb{F}_2$ *be a d-variable Boolean function. A cellular automaton of length n, diameter d and local rule f is a mapping* $F : \mathbb{F}_2^n \rightarrow \mathbb{F}_2^{n-d+1}$ *defined for all* $x \in \mathbb{F}_2^n$ *as:*

$$F(x_1, \ldots, x_n) = (f(x_1, \ldots, x_d), f(x_2, \ldots, x_{d+1}), \ldots, f(x_{n-d+1}, \ldots, x_n)) . \quad (3)$$

Intuitively, each output coordinate $i \in \{1, \ldots, n - d + 1\}$ of the CA F is determined by evaluating f on the local neighborhood $(x_i, \ldots, x_{i+d-1})$. Remark that the output is smaller than the input: indeed, we can apply f as long as there are enough neighboring coordinates to the right of the current output cell i. Therefore, we do not enforce any boundary conditions on the CA state, as it is commonly done in the CA literature. This means that the CA cannot be iterated for multiple time steps, but this issue does not concern us since we are interested only in the single-step application of F. This model is also called no-boundary CA in related works [16, 19].

We now introduce the basic concepts related to Latin squares to recall the main results of [16]. For all $n \in \mathbb{N}$, let us denote by $[n] = \{1, \ldots, n\}$ the set of the first n natural numbers. A Latin square of order n is a $n \times n$ matrix L such that each row and each column of L is a permutation of $[n]$. Equivalently, this means that each number from 1 to n occurs exactly once in each row and in each column of L. Then, two Latin squares L_1, L_2 of order n are called orthogonal if their superposition yields all pairs in the Cartesian product $[n] \times [n]$. Formally, for any distinct pairs of coordinates $(i_1, j_1), (i_2, j_2) \in [n] \times [n]$, one has:

$$(L_1(i_1, j_1), L_2(i_1, j_1)) \neq (L_1(i_2, j_2), L_2(i_2, j_2)) . \quad (4)$$

A set of k Latin squares $L_1, \ldots, L_k$ of order n that are pairwise orthogonal is also called a set of k-MOLS (mutually orthogonal Latin squares). The construction of MOLS is a rich research line in the combinatorial designs literature, and finds several applications in cryptography, coding theory and statistics [25]. Interestingly, k-MOLS of order n are also equivalent to orthogonal arrays with $N = n^2$ runs, k factors, n levels and strength 2. Indeed, one can construct an $OA(N, k, n, 2)$ from a set of k-MOLS by "linearizing" each Latin square as a column of the OA: for each $i \in [k]$, the i-th column of the OA corresponds to the Latin square L_i in the MOLS set, with its entries listed in lexicographic order.

The authors of [16] proposed a method to construct sets of k-MOLS from cellular automata, by focusing on the subclass of bipermutive rules. Formally, a local rule $f : \mathbb{F}_2^d \to \mathbb{F}_2$ is called bipermutive if it is defined as $f(x_1, \ldots, x_d) = x_1 \oplus \varphi(x_2, \ldots, x_{d-1}) \oplus x_d$ for all $x \in \mathbb{F}_2^d$, where $\varphi : \mathbb{F}_2^{d-2} \to \mathbb{F}_2$ is any function of the $d - 2$ central variables. Then, one can construct a Latin square L_F of order $n = 2^{d-1}$ from a CA $F : \mathbb{F}_2^{2(d-1)} \to \mathbb{F}_2^{d-1}$ as follows:

1. The left half of the CA input $(x_1, \ldots, x_{d-1})$ is used to index the rows of L_F.
2. The right half $(x_d, \ldots, x_{2(d-1)})$ is used to index the columns of L_F.
3. The output $F(x_1, \ldots, x_{2(d-1)})$ of the CA is used as the entry indexed respectively by the coordinates $(x_1, \ldots, x_{d-1})$ and $(x_d, \ldots, x_{2(d-1)})$.

Clearly, the procedure above assumes that a bijective mapping $\phi : \mathbb{F}_2^{d-1} \to [n]$ is used to convert the binary vectors of $\mathbb{F}_2^{d-1}$ in numbers from 1 to 2^{d-1}, and vice versa. The authors of [16] focused on the construction of MOLS from bipermutive CA by further focusing on the class of linear rules. Here, however, we will consider the general setting of MOLS defined by generic bipermutive CA. In particular, we define two bipermutive CA $F_1, F_2 : \mathbb{F}_2^{2(d-1)} \to \mathbb{F}_2^{d-1}$ to be orthogonal (or equivalently they are OCA) if the corresponding Latin squares are orthogonal. Accordingly, a family of k pairwise orthogonal bipermutive CA $F_1, \ldots, F_k$ will be called a set of k-MOCA (mutually orthogonal cellular automata).

3   Construction of Correlation Immune Functions

We now prove our main result, namely that a set of k-MOCA can be used to define a binary OA of strength at least 2. This will allow us, in turn, to construct correlation immune functions of order at least 2. To this end, let us first review the concept of coupled de Bruijn graph introduced in [18], which will be useful in our proof.

Recall that a de Bruijn graph of order b over a set S of m symbols is defined as $G_{m,b} = (V, E)$, where $V = S^b$, while two vertices $u, v \in V$ are connected by a directed edge if and only if they overlap respectively on the rightmost and leftmost $b - 1$ coordinates. Assume now that $S = \mathbb{F}_2$, and let $b = d - 1$. A local rule $f : \mathbb{F}_2^d \to \mathbb{F}_2$ of diameter d can be represented as a labeling function $l_f : E \to \mathbb{F}_2$ on the edges of $G_{2,b}$. In particular, for each pair $(u, v) \in E$, we set $l(u, v) = f(u \odot v)$, where $u \odot v \in \mathbb{F}_2^d$ represents the fusion of u and v as defined in [26]. In other words, $u \odot v$ is the d-variable vector formed by adding the last coordinate of v to u. Then, it can be seen that the output of a CA equipped with rule f corresponds to a path on the edges of the associated de Bruijn graph, following the overlapping vertices that form a particular input. Remark that if

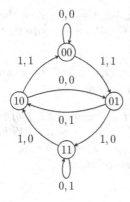

$(v_1, v_2) \rightarrow (u_1, u_2)$	l_f	l_g
$00 \rightarrow 00$	0	0
$10 \rightarrow 00$	1	1
$01 \rightarrow 10$	0	1
$11 \rightarrow 10$	1	0
$00 \rightarrow 01$	1	1
$10 \rightarrow 01$	0	0
$01 \rightarrow 11$	1	0
$11 \rightarrow 11$	0	1

Fig. 1. Example of orthogonal labelings for the de Bruijn graph $G_{2,2}$ induced by the CA local rules 90 and 150 of diameter $d = 3$.

f is bipermutive, then the labels of the outgoing (respectively, ingoing) edges of any vertex $v \in V$ form a permutation of $\mathbb{F}_2$. This implies that one can traverse the edges in both directions, and that the CA is surjective.

Suppose now that we have two labelings $l_f, l_g : E \rightarrow \mathbb{F}_2$ defined by bipermutive rules $f, g : \mathbb{F}_2^d \rightarrow \mathbb{F}_2$. We call the corresponding graph as the coupled de Bruijn graph associated to f and g, since each label is now a pair of bits $(f(u \odot v), g(u \odot v))$ for each edge $(u, v) \in E$. We call two bipermutive labelings l_f, l_g orthogonal if for each pair of vectors $(x, y) \in \mathbb{F}_2^b$ there exists exactly one path on the edges of the coupled de Bruijn graph that is labelled by (x, y). It is not difficult to see that this is an equivalent characterization of orthogonal CA. We formally state this fact below, since it will become useful later in our proof:

Lemma 2. *Let $d \in \mathbb{N}$ with $b = d - 1$, and $f, g : \mathbb{F}_2^d \rightarrow \mathbb{F}_2$ be two bipermutive rules of diameter d. Then, the CA $F, G : \mathbb{F}_2^{2b} \rightarrow \mathbb{F}_2^b$ respectively equipped with rule f and g are orthogonal if and only if the labelings on the coupled de Bruijn graph of f and g are orthogonal.*

To fix ideas, let $d = 3$, and assume that the two bipermutive local rules are $f(x_1, x_2, x_3) = x_1 \oplus x_3$ and $g(x_1, x_2, x_3) = x_1 \oplus x_2 \oplus x_3$ (respectively rules 90 and 150 in Wolfram's notation). The two rules induce orthogonal CA with Latin squares of order $2^2 = 4$, and the corresponding coupled de Bruijn graph is depicted in Fig. 1. One can see that the two labelings l_f, l_g defined in the table are indeed bipermutive and orthogonal. In particular, for each of the 16 pairs $(x, y) \in (\mathbb{F}_2^2)^2$ there is exactly one path of length 2 in $G_{2,2}$ labeled by (x, y).

Let $F_1, F_2, \ldots, F_k : \mathbb{F}_2^{2b} \rightarrow \mathbb{F}_2^b$ be a set of k-MOCA respectively defined by local rules $f_1, \ldots, f_k : \mathbb{F}_2^d \rightarrow \mathbb{F}_2$ of diameter d, with $b = d - 1$. We define the $N \times n$ array A where $N = 2^{2b}$ and $n = kb$ as follows: for each $(x, y) \in \mathbb{F}_2^{2b}$, the row of A indexed by (x, y) is equal to:

$$A(x, y) = (F_1(x, y), F_2(x, y), \ldots, F_k(x, y)) \ . \tag{5}$$

In other words, A is formed by simply juxtaposing the output of the k MOCA for each possible combination of input $(x, y) \in \mathbb{F}_2^{2b}$. We now prove that this array is an OA of strength 2.

Lemma 3. *The array A defined in Eq. (5) is an $OA(N, n, 2, 2)$, where the number of runs is $N = 2^{2b}$ and the number of factors is $n = kb$.*

Proof. We need to show that in any subset of $t = 2$ columns i, j of A each pair of bits $(x_i, x_j) \in \mathbb{F}_2^2$ occurs exactly $\lambda = N/2^t = 2^{2b-2}$ times. Without loss of generality, we can assume that $k = 2$, since $F_1, \ldots F_k$ is a family of k-MOCA. Hence, we have two main cases to check for two columns $i \neq j$:

1. i, j belong to the output of the same CA F_l.
2. i, j belong to the output of two different CA F_l, F_m (which are orthogonal).

    Let us start from the first case, i.e., i and j are chosen among the columns of the same CA F_l. Let $(\tilde{x}_i, \tilde{x}_j) \in \mathbb{F}_2^2$ be the value of the two bits of which we want to compute the multiplicity of occurrence in columns i and j. Since the two CA F_l and F_m are orthogonal, it means that by fixing the output of F_m to a specific vector $(y_1, \ldots, y_b) \in \mathbb{F}_2^b$, each possible vector $(x_1, \ldots, x_b) \in \mathbb{F}_2^b$ occurs exactly once as an output of F_l. Suppose now that we fix the i-th and j-th coordinates respectively to $\tilde{x}_i$ and $\tilde{x}_j$ in the output of F_l. Since we have 2^{b-2} free coordinates, it follows that the pair $(\tilde{x}_i, \tilde{x}_j)$ occurs 2^{b-2} times if we keep the output of F_m fixed to $(y_1, \ldots, y_b)$. If we consider the occurrences of $(\tilde{x}_i, \tilde{x}_j)$ in F_l across all possible outputs of F_m we need to multiply 2^{b-2} by 2^b, i.e., the number of possible ways to fix the output of F_m. Therefore the total number of occurrences is $2^{b-2} \cdot 2^b = 2^{2b-2}$.

    Suppose now that i and j are columns respectively of F_l and F_m. If all output coordinates of F_l and F_m are fixed respectively to x and $y \in \mathbb{F}_2^b$, then there exists a single row of A labeled by x and y, since F_l and F_m are orthogonal, and by Lemma 2 there is a unique path on the coupled de Bruijn graph labelled by (x, y). We proceed by induction on the number of free coordinates in (x, y) to show that if we only have two of them fixed, i.e., $\tilde{x}_i$ and $\tilde{y}_j$, then there are exactly 2^{2b-2} paths on the de Bruijn graph that feature $\tilde{x}_i$ and $\tilde{y}_j$ in those coordinates. As a base case, suppose that we have only one free coordinate in the pair of paths, i.e., all other $2b - 1$ are fixed. Then, since each of the two labelings is bipermutive, it follows that there are exactly 2 paths labelled by the $2b - 1$ fixed coordinates. For the induction step, suppose that there are $1 \leq p < 2b$ free coordinates, and thus 2^p paths labelled by the remaining $2b - p$ fixed coordinates by induction hypothesis. If we free an additional coordinate, we need to multiply the number of paths with p free coordinates by 2, since each of them can be completed in 2 different ways in the additional free coordinate, due to the bipermutivity of the two rules. Hence, the number of partially labelled paths with $p+1$ free coordinates is 2^{p+1}. If we take the particular case where only 2 coordinates i and j are fixed respectively to $\tilde{x}_i$ and $\tilde{y}_j$ (or equivalently, $2b - 2$ are free), it follows that there are 2^{2b-2} paths partially labeled by $\tilde{x}_i$ and $\tilde{y}_j$. □

Remark 1. One of the anonymous reviewers correctly remarked that there is a more compact proof for Lemma 3: for the first case, it suffices to observe that the coordinate functions f_i are all balanced (because of bipermutivity). For the second case, each pair of b-tuples $(x_1, \ldots, x_b), (y_1, \ldots, y_b)$ occurs exactly once in each pair of column for two different CA F_l, F_m, because of their orthogonality. Hence, in each pair i, j in these tuples the same pair of bits occurs the same number times, since the remaining positions are set freely. We decided however to keep the proof above since it further demonstrates a property of the coupled de Bruijn graph associated to a pair of orthogonal CA: namely, that it is strongly balanced in the sense that any partially labelled path on it occurs the same number of times.

Putting together Lemma 1 and 3, we have thus obtained the following result to construct a second-order correlation immune function from a set of k-MOCA:

Theorem 1. *Let* $F_1, \ldots, F_k : \mathbb{F}_2^{2b} \to \mathbb{F}_2^b$ *be a set of k-MOCA of diameter $d = b + 1$, and let $n = kb$. Then, the n-variable function $f : \mathbb{F}_2^n \to \mathbb{F}_2$ whose support is defined by the array A in Eq. (5) is correlation immune of order at least 2. In particular, the Hamming weight of f is $N = 2^{2b}$.*

Remark that the case where $k = 2$ trivially gives the constant function $f(x) = 1$ for all $x \in \mathbb{F}_2^n$. As a matter of fact, the number of input variables is $n = kb = 2b$, which means that the truth table of f is composed of 2^{2b} values. At the same time, the number of runs of the OA corresponding to $k = 2$ MOCA is also $N = 2^{2b}$. Therefore, the support of f coincides with its whole truth table. For this reason, in what follows we will address mainly the case where $k = 3$.

4   Computational Search Results

To investigate the construction described in the previous section, we performed an exhaustive search of all k-MOCA for $k = 3$ and $d = 4, 5$. In particular, we discarded $d = 3$ since there are no families of 3-MOCA in that case. On the other hand, going for higher values of k and d makes the search space too huge to be exhaustively visited in a limited time. Following Theorem 1, this means that we addressed the construction of correlation immune functions of $n = 9, 12$ variables.

We first generated all pairs of OCA (i.e., 2-MOCA) of diameters $d = 4, 5$ by using the combinatorial algorithm described in [15]. Then, we incrementally constructed the families of 3-MOCA by exhaustively visiting each of the $2^{2^{d-2}}$ bipermutive rules of diameter d, and checking that the corresponding Latin squares were orthogonal with each of those in the previously generated lists of OCA. Next, we defined the corresponding Boolean functions of $n = 3b$ variables using Theorem 1, and computed their Walsh transform to verify their order of correlation immunity. Table 1 reports the main results of this computational search experiment. In particular, for each considered diameter (d) the table gives the number of 3-MOCA generated (#3-MOCA), the number of variables (n), the Hamming weight (w_H), the correlation immunity order (CI) and the number of functions achieving that order $(\#CI)$, and the best known lower bound on the Hamming weight for the corresponding order of correlation immunity $(\text{Min}(w_H))$, taken from [2].

Table 1. Classification of correlation immune functions generated by 3-MOCA of diameter $d \in \{4, 5\}$.

d	#3-MOCA	n	w_H	CI	$\#CI$	$\text{Min}w_H$
4	2	9	64	3	2	20
5	36	12	256	3	27	24
5	36	12	256	4	9	24

From the table, one can see that all generated functions actually have a correlation immunity order higher than 2. Indeed, both functions of $n = 9$ variables generated from the 3-MOCA of diameter $d = 4$ have correlation immunity order 3, as well as the majority of functions of $n = 12$ functions obtained from 3-MOCA of diameter $d = 5$. Further, a few functions of $n = 12$ variables obtained from this latter case are even 4-th order correlation immune. This empirical observation suggests that the correlation immunity order proved in Theorem 1 may not be a tight lower bound. Further experiments on larger diameters should be performed to see if this hypothesis holds, or if there exist functions constructed through our methods that are effectively second-order correlation immune. Additionally, one can remark that the Hamming weight of the functions generated through our method are far from the known best lower bounds, reported in the last column of Table 1. Indeed, for $n = 9$ variables we obtain functions of weight 64, while the best lower bound is 20. For $n = 12$ variables the gap is even greater, since the weight of our functions is 256, while the lower bound is 24.

5   Conclusions

In this work, we proposed a method to construct correlation immune Boolean functions from sets of mutually orthogonal cellular automata. Our main theoretical result shows that the binary array formed by juxtaposing the output tables of a set of k MOCA is an orthogonal array of strength 2. Hence, on account of Lemma 1 such an array can be used as the support of a Boolean function with correlation immunity order at least 2. Our exhaustive search experiments on the sets of 3-MOCA defined by rules of diameters $d = 4, 5$ show an interesting fact, namely that the resulting Boolean functions always have a higher order of correlation immunity, namely at least 3.

There are several directions along which this work can be extended in future research. The most natural open question remains whether our Theorem 1 is really a tight lower bound on the correlation immunity of the Boolean functions constructed through k-MOCA. If further experiments show that the lowest correlation immunity order is always at least 3, then it would be interesting to try refining Lemma 3, and prove that the binary OA obtained from a set of k-MOCA has always at least strength 3.

A second direction concerns the non-optimal weights of the correlation immune functions generated by our method. Indeed, one possible approach to improve on this aspect would be to adopt the so-called expurgation procedure used in the field of error-correcting codes. In the context of orthogonal arrays, this basically amounts to the removal of a subset of rows, such that the resulting array is still an OA of the same strength (but clearly with a smaller index λ). The choice of the rows to be removed can be conceived as a combinatorial optimization problem, which could be addressed with different optimization algorithms.

Acknowledgements. The authors wish to thank one of the anonymous reviewers who suggested a more compact proof for Lemma 3.

References

1. Camion, P., Carlet, C., Charpin, P., Sendrier, N.: On correlation-immune functions. In: Feigenbaum, J. (ed.) CRYPTO 1991. LNCS, vol. 576, pp. 86–100. Springer, Heidelberg (1992). https://doi.org/10.1007/3-540-46766-1_6
2. Carlet, C.: Boolean Functions for Cryptography and Coding Theory. Cambridge University Press, Cambridge (2021)
3. Carlet, C., Danger, J.-L., Guilley, S., Maghrebi, H.: Leakage squeezing of order two. In: Galbraith, S., Nandi, M. (eds.) INDOCRYPT 2012. LNCS, vol. 7668, pp. 120–139. Springer, Heidelberg (2012). https://doi.org/10.1007/978-3-642-34931-7_8
4. Chaudhuri, P.P., Chowdhury, D.R., Nandi, S., Chattopadhyay, S.: Additive Cellular Automata: Theory and Applications, Volume 1, vol. 43. Wiley, Hoboken (1997)
5. Crama, Y., Hammer, P.L.: Boolean Functions - Theory, Algorithms, and Applications, Encyclopedia of Mathematics and Its Applications, vol. 142. Cambridge University Press, Cambridge (2011)
6. Formenti, E., Imai, K., Martin, B., Yunès, J.-B.: Advances on random sequence generation by uniform cellular automata. In: Calude, C.S., Freivalds, R., Kazuo, I. (eds.) Computing with New Resources. LNCS, vol. 8808, pp. 56–70. Springer, Cham (2014). https://doi.org/10.1007/978-3-319-13350-8_5
7. Hedayat, A.S., Sloane, N.J.A., Stufken, J.: Orthogonal Arrays: Theory and Applications. Springer, New York (1999). https://doi.org/10.1007/978-1-4612-1478-6
8. John, A., Nandu, B.C., Ajesh, A., Jose, J.: PENTAVIUM: potent Trivium-like stream cipher using higher radii cellular automata. In: Gwizdalla, T.M., Manzoni, L., Sirakoulis, G.C., Bandini, S., Podlaski, K. (eds.) Cellular Automata, ACRI 2020. LNCS, vol. 12599, pp. 90–100. Springer, Cham (2021). https://doi.org/10.1007/978-3-030-69480-7_10
9. Karmakar, S., Chowdhury, D.R.: Countermeasures of side channel attacks on symmetric key ciphers using cellular automata. In: Sirakoulis, G.C., Bandini, S. (eds.) ACRI 2012. LNCS, vol. 7495, pp. 623–632. Springer, Heidelberg (2012). https://doi.org/10.1007/978-3-642-33350-7_64

10. Karmakar, S., Chowdhury, D.R.: Leakage squeezing using cellular automata and its application to scan attack. J. Cell. Autom. **9**(5–6), 417–436 (2014)
11. Karmakar, S., Chowdhury, D.R.: Scan-based side channel attack on stream ciphers and its prevention. J. Cryptogr. Eng. **8**(4), 327–340 (2018)
12. Koc, C.K., Apohan, A.: Inversion of cellular automata iterations. IEE Proc. Comput. Digit. Tech. **144**(5), 279–284 (1997)
13. Lakra, R., John, A., Jose, J.: CARPenter: a cellular automata based resilient pentavalent stream cipher. In: Mauri, G., El Yacoubi, S., Dennunzio, A., Nishinari, K., Manzoni, L. (eds.) ACRI 2018. LNCS, vol. 11115, pp. 352–363. Springer, Cham (2018). https://doi.org/10.1007/978-3-319-99813-8_32
14. Leporati, A., Mariot, L.: Cryptographic properties of bipermutive cellular automata rules. J. Cell. Autom. **9**(5–6), 437–475 (2014)
15. Mariot, L., Formenti, E., Leporati, A.: Enumerating orthogonal Latin squares generated by bipermutive cellular automata. In: Dennunzio, A., Formenti, E., Manzoni, L., Porreca, A.E. (eds.) AUTOMATA 2017. LNCS, vol. 10248, pp. 151–164. Springer, Cham (2017). https://doi.org/10.1007/978-3-319-58631-1_12
16. Mariot, L., Gadouleau, M., Formenti, E., Leporati, A.: Mutually orthogonal Latin squares based on cellular automata. Des. Codes Cryptogr. **88**(2), 391–411 (2020)
17. Mariot, L., Leporati, A.: A cryptographic and coding-theoretic perspective on the global rules of cellular automata. Nat. Comput. **17**(3), 487–498 (2018)
18. Mariot, L., Leporati, A.: Inversion of mutually orthogonal cellular automata. In: Mauri, G., El Yacoubi, S., Dennunzio, A., Nishinari, K., Manzoni, L. (eds.) ACRI 2018. LNCS, vol. 11115, pp. 364–376. Springer, Cham (2018). https://doi.org/10.1007/978-3-319-99813-8_33
19. Mariot, L., Picek, S., Leporati, A., Jakobovic, D.: Cellular automata based S-boxes. Cryptogr. Commun. **11**(1), 41–62 (2019). https://doi.org/10.1007/s12095-018-0311-8
20. Martin, B.: A Walsh exploration of elementary CA rules. J. Cell. Autom. **3**(2), 145–156 (2008)
21. Meier, W., Staffelbach, O.: Fast correlation attacks on stream ciphers. In: Barstow, D., et al. (eds.) EUROCRYPT 1988. LNCS, vol. 330, pp. 301–314. Springer, Heidelberg (1988). https://doi.org/10.1007/3-540-45961-8_28
22. Meier, W., Staffelbach, O.: Analysis of pseudo random sequences generated by cellular automata. In: Davies, D.W. (ed.) EUROCRYPT 1991. LNCS, vol. 547, pp. 186–199. Springer, Heidelberg (1991). https://doi.org/10.1007/3-540-46416-6_17
23. Nassar, M., Souissi, Y., Guilley, S., Danger, J.: RSM: a small and fast countermeasure for AES, secure against 1st and 2nd-order zero-offset SCAs. In: Rosenstiel, W., Thiele, L. (eds.) 2012 Design, Automation & Test in Europe Conference & Exhibition, DATE 2012, Dresden, Germany, 12–16 March 2012, pp. 1173–1178. IEEE (2012)
24. Siegenthaler, T.: Decrypting a class of stream ciphers using ciphertext only. IEEE Trans. Comput. **34**(1), 81–85 (1985)
25. Stinson, D.R.: Combinatorial Designs - Constructions and Analysis. Springer, New York (2004). https://doi.org/10.1007/b97564
26. Sutner, K.: De Bruijn graphs and linear cellular automata. Complex Syst. **5**(1), 19–30 (1991)
27. Xiao, G., Massey, J.L.: A spectral characterization of correlation-immune combining functions. IEEE Trans. Inf. Theor. **34**(3), 569–571 (1988)

Author Index

© IFIP International Federation for Information Processing 2023
Published by Springer Nature Switzerland AG 2023
L. Manzoni et al. (Eds.): AUTOMATA 2023, LNCS 14152, p. 165, 2023.
https://doi.org/10.1007/978-3-031-42250-8

Printed in the United States
by Baker & Taylor Publisher Services